D0083177

ECUADOR

WESTVIEW PROFILES · NATIONS OF CONTEMPORARY LATIN AMERICA
Ronald Schneider, Series Editor

†Available in hardcover and paperback.

ABOUT THE BOOK AND AUTHOR

A country often neglected in discussions of Latin America, Ecuador offers intriguing insights into the interwoven patterns of continuity and change characteristic of the region. In this introduction to Ecuador, Dr. Schodt begins with a discussion of culture and geography—especially critical for understanding this country, where the physical partitioning by the Andes has had profound economic and political consequences and where cultural and linguistic differences further divide the population. The author then considers Ecuador's early history, emphasizing the importance of patterns imposed by regionalism and structured by the nation's colonial heritage. This leads to a discussion of the cacao and banana booms—and of the consequences of these periods of economic bonanza for domestic politics—that focuses on the expansion of the electorate and the emergence of two competing populist movements.

In the final chapters, Dr. Schodt examines the political and economic implications of the petroleum boom, emphasizing the growing role of the state in the Ecuadorian economy. This analysis of the petroleum period concludes with a discussion of Ecuador's prospects for the future, taking account of the conjuncture of the dramatic increase in Ecuador's external indebtedness that took place in the late 1970s and early 1980s, the election in 1984 of a government committed to reversing the growth of state intervention in the economy, and the sharp decline in 1986 in the world price of petroleum.

David W. Schodt is associate professor of economics at St. Olaf College, Northfield, Minnesota. A former Peace Corps volunteer who served in Ecuador from 1969 to 1972, he has maintained an interest in the country and is the author of a number of articles on the Ecuadorian economy.

ECUADOR

An Andean Enigma

David W. Schodt

Westview Press / Boulder and London

Westview Profiles/Nations of Contemporary Latin America

All photographs by the author, except "Drying cacao in a Guayaquil street," originally published in C. Reginald Enock, *Ecuador* (T. Fisher Unwin, 1914), and "Texaco oil rig in Lago Agrio in 1970," reprinted by permission of Texaco, Inc.

Cover photos (clockwise): Indian schoolchildren near Ibarra; Texaco oil rig in Lago Agrio in 1970; Government palace in Quito; The Church of San Francisco in Quito

Published in 1987 in the United States of America by Westview Press, Inc.; Frederick A. Praeger, Publisher; 5500 Central Avenue, Boulder, Colorado 80301

Library of Congress Cataloging-in-Publication Data
Schodt, David W. (David William)
  Ecuador : an Andean enigma.
  (Westview profiles. Nations of contemporary Latin
America)
  Bibliography: p.
  Includes index.
  1. Ecuador—Politics and government—1944–
2. Military government—Ecuador—History—20th century.
3. Ecuador—Economic conditions—1972–
I. Title. II. Series.
F3738.S34 1987   986.6′074   86-33999
ISBN 0-8133-0230-7

Printed and bound in the United States of America

The paper used in this publication meets the requirements of the American National Standard for Permanence of Paper for Printed Library Materials Z39.48-1984.

10   9   8   7   6   5   4   3   2   1

For Elizabeth and Sara

Contents

Tables and Illustrations

Foreword

Ninth in population of Latin American countries, Ecuador has received relatively little attention from U.S. social scientists, most of whom, if interested in the Andean region, have tended to be attracted to the larger countries such as Bolivia, Colombia, and Peru. And those few studies of Ecuador that have been written—of which George Blanksten's now dated book, *Ecuador: Constitutions and Caudillos* (1951), was the earliest contribution—have generally focused on political events, such as the country's seemingly chronic political instability and the fascinating phenomenon of President José María Velasco Ibarra's five terms.

Ecuador has certainly been ripe for a new approach by someone not only capable of synthesizing the limited amount of scholarship available on this country, from both U.S. and Ecuadorian writers, but also able to provide a coherent analysis of the sometimes bewildering patterns of Ecuadorian political and economic development. This is precisely what David Schodt has done. More than just a carefully crafted economic history of this Andean nation, the present volume contains an interpretive account of the ways in which political events, although they appear at times to be fairly autonomous, have more commonly reflected the underlying economic changes associated with Ecuador's boom-and-bust history as an exporter of primary products. In short, the book lets us know not only what Ecuador is today but also how it came to be and what transformations may be expected in the future.

Sympathetic, yet far from uncritical, the author presents a coherent interpretation of Ecuador, one in which clarity is achieved without oversimplification. The final result provides not only a wealth of information but also a careful analysis of the political and economic changes that have occurred in this little-studied Andean country. The book is of equal value to readers focusing on Ecuador itself, to those seeking to build an appreciation of the broader Andean region, and to those attempting to redefine propositions concerning that diverse group of countries geographically defined as Latin America. Hence this book is an especially welcome addition to the Westview series, Nations of Contemporary Latin America.

Ronald M. Schneider

Preface

This book is the product of an involvement with Ecuador that spans a fifteen-year period. I first visited the country in 1969, just prior to the petroleum boom, and stayed for two and a half years. During that time I had the opportunity to travel throughout much of Ecuador and to live in two different regions, first in the highland city of Ibarra and subsequently in the low-lying Amazonian region to the east of the Andes Mountains. My initial impressions of this country, which has remained an enigma to most people beyond its borders, were manifold; in particular, I was overwhelmed by the beauty of its geographically diverse regions, discouraged by a persistent poverty that seemed little affected by economic growth, impressed by its people, and quite bewildered by a politics in which frequent change appeared to be largely detached from any observable reality. I returned to Ecuador in 1978 (the first of many subsequent visits) to witness the numerous changes that had occurred during seven years of rapid, petroleum-induced, economic growth.

This work is an attempt to understand some of the apparent continuities and contradictions characterizing Ecuador's political and economic changes. The petroleum boom is only the most recent of three periods of export-led growth, having been preceded at the turn of the century by the cacao boom and during the 1950s by the banana boom. Each period brought its own changes, yet one can discern patterns of continuity throughout all three, particularly with regard to the unfolding of political events. The present study examines the interplay between economic and political change, relying on three interrelated themes to structure this effort: first, regionalism, the political consequence of the geographical forces that have made this country such a visual delight for the visitor; second, the recurrent cycles of boom-and-bust export-led economic growth; and third, the state, whose historical role has been one of mediating between regional demands and the wealth created by the export sector.

I would like to express my appreciation to the number of individuals who have assisted in various ways with this project. Howard Handelman, John Martz, John Tutino, and Elizabeth Ciner read either parts or all of various drafts of the manuscript and provided many helpful suggestions and criticisms. Patricio León and Salvador Marconi of the Ecuadorian Central Bank were exceedingly generous with their time, patiently answering my many questions about the structure of the Ecuadorian economy. Moritz Thomsen, though he is undoubtedly unaware of it, provided inspiration for how one might write about Ecuador, setting a literary standard toward which this book can only aspire. The staff of the Ecuadorian Fulbright Commission, of which Gonzalo Cartagenova and María Mogollón deserve particular mention, has assisted me on numerous occasions. Finally, I am indebted to the editors at Westview Press for their courteous and professional assistance.

David W. Schodt

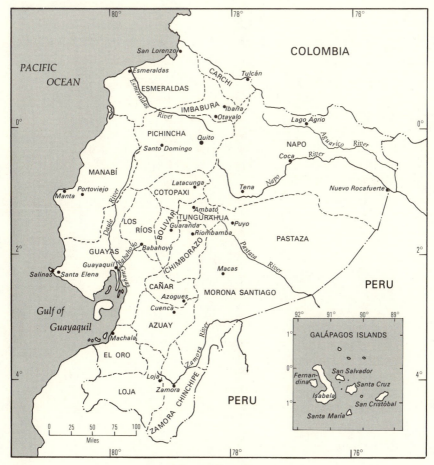

Map of Ecuador

1

Introduction

A country often overlooked in discussions of Latin America, Ecuador has a rich and colorful history, the study of which offers intriguing insights into the interwoven patterns of continuity and change characterizing the region. Small in size, Ecuador is noted for its exceptionally varied topography and is historically identified with its exports of cacao and bananas. Indeed, both its diverse geography and its export economy have contributed as much as its notable political figures to the shaping of Ecuador's destiny. Of course, individuals have influenced the course of history. Such leaders as Gabriel García Moreno, Eloy Alfaro, Galo Plaza, and José María Velasco Ibarra pointed the country in new directions. But the patterns of Ecuadorian politics were established by a geography that defined the nation in terms of competing regions and by an export-dependent economy notoriously subject to the vagaries of world markets.

In the late 1960s, the discovery of petroleum and its subsequent rise to prominence as Ecuador's leading export initiated a period of rapid economic and social change in a country late to modernize by Latin American standards. These changes seemed to herald altered patterns of political behavior as per capita incomes rose, industrialization accelerated, urbanization quickened, and a middle class emerged. Improvements in communication hastened national integration. The state, historically never a dominant actor in the economy, expanded its role dramatically as petroleum income swelled public revenues. Governments came into power led by individuals with a singular commitment to social and economic reforms. Yet despite these very dramatic changes, Ecuador's politics continues to be haunted by traditional patterns of behavior, seemingly little altered by the economic progress experienced during the petroleum boom.

REGION, PEOPLE, AND ECONOMY

Visitors to Ecuador will find a fascinating diversity of geography and peoples. Visually it is a stunning land, where snow-capped

1

TABLE 1.1
Social indicators

Indicator	1970	1980
Gross domestic product/capita (1984 dollars)	749.0	1300.0
Illiteracy rate (percentage of adult population)	26.8	21
Life expectancy at birth	55.9	61.2
Infant mortality (deaths per 1,000)	107.0	82.0
Population without drinking water	71.6	56.5

SOURCE: The gross domestic product figures are from Interamerican Development Bank, *Economic and Social Progress in Latin America*, 1986, p. 394; life expectancy and infant mortality rates are from World Bank, *Ecuador: An Agenda for Recovery and Sustained Growth*, 1984, p. 99; and the illiteracy rates and population without drinking water figures are from Rob Vos, "Access to Basic Services and Public Expenditure Incidence, Ecuador 1970-1980" (Quito: PREALC, 1982), p. 103.

volcanoes compete with lush tropical rain forests and thatched Andean huts for attention. Small landholdings dot the mountainsides, giving a picturesque appearance to the highland landscape that has been described as a "rumpled patchwork quilt." Yet the same features that attract the visitor pose formidable obstacles to the country's economic and political development. The physical grandeur of the country also masks the stubborn problems of poverty and inequality that persist in spite of the dramatic economic changes accompanying the petroleum boom.

With a land area of approximately 281,341 square kilometers (108,623 square miles), Ecuador is the second smallest republic in South America, roughly equal in size to the state of Colorado. Situated astride the equator, from which it derives its name, the country is located on the northwestern coast of South America, bounded on the north by Colombia and on the south and east by Peru. In the most recent census, taken in 1982, Ecuador's population was estimated at 8,050,630. Just slightly more than 50 percent of the population lives in rural areas. The rate of population growth, among the highest in Latin America, is estimated to be between 2.6 and 3.4 percent per year (see Table 1.1 for additional social indicators).[1]

Although there are no reliable estimates of the ethnic composition of the populace, Ecuador's Indian population is generally acknowledged to be proportionately one of the largest in South America. Most rough estimates suggest that approximately 40 percent of the population is

Indian, 40 percent is mestizo, 10 to 15 percent is white (typically claiming descent from the Spanish colonizers), and 5 to 10 percent is black.[2] Unlike certain other South American countries, Ecuador has attracted very few immigrants from outside the region.

The official language of the country is Spanish, although a large proportion of the Indian population speaks a version of Quechua, the lingua franca of the former Inca empire, or other minor languages such as Shuar or Chibchan. Ecuador has no state religion, but more than 90 percent of the population is at least nominally Catholic. The Ecuadorian Catholic Church is one of the most conservative in Latin America.

The class structure of contemporary Ecuadorian society remains strongly influenced by a colonial heritage in which a small Spanish elite ruled over a large Indian underclass. Slow economic growth and delayed modernization greatly limited opportunities for social mobility, as did Ecuador's relative isolation from outside influence. The small group of whites occupies the upper levels of the social hierarchy and dominates the sources of economic and political power—historically through ownership of land and control of the export and financial sectors, though increasingly through holdings in commerce and industry as well. It is this group that traditionally has defined national Ecuadorian culture exclusively in terms of the country's Hispanic heritage.[3]

The middle class, historically small in numbers, is largely made up of mestizos and less well-off whites, who occupy positions in the bureaucracy, the military, or in the professions and smaller businesses. Caught in a society defining itself in terms of only two classes, economically dependent on the upper class, and anxious to distance itself from the lower class, the middle class has traditionally identified with upper-class values and traditions. As a result it has provided little in the way of an independent contribution to the defining of Ecuadorian cultural values. It was not until the petroleum boom caused a surge in economic growth that the size of the middle class and its political, cultural, and economic influence expanded significantly.

Indians, blacks, and poor mestizos, still by far the largest social group, occupy the bottom rung of the social hierarchy. The rural lower class consists of day laborers, small landowners, and independent artisans; their urban counterparts are manual laborers, construction workers, domestics, petty merchants, and street vendors. Many are also either unemployed or underemployed (without adequate work). Although the lower class is rich in artisan and folk traditions, its contributions to Ecuadorian culture and national identity have only

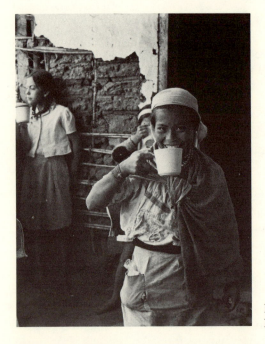

Indian schoolchildren in the Ecuadorian sierra

begun to be recognized in recent years. Admittedly, since the 1920s there has been a strong current of social protest in both Ecuadorian art and literature, as exemplified by the social realism of artists such as Eduardo Kingman and by novels such as *Huasipungo* (1934), Jorge Icaza's powerful condemnation of the hacienda system. But the audience for these expressions of protest has always been small, in that it is restricted to the literate upper class, and their effect on Ecuadorian society has been very limited. Not until the 1970s, with the development of a stronger sense of self-identity on the part of some members of the middle class as well as the increased numbers of foreign visitors interested in local traditions and cultures, did a broadening of interest begin to appear in Ecuadorian culture beyond that traditionally defined by the white elite. Certainly the unprecedented step taken by former President Jaime Roldós in 1979, when he delivered part of his inaugural address in Quechua, is one indication of this shift.

Any efforts to define Ecuador in terms of encompassing national characteristics, however, run the risk of being undermined by the country's profound regional differences. Despite the country's small size, most generalizations about it quickly succumb to the differences imposed by climate and topography. Partitioned from north to south by the twin ranges of the towering Andes Mountains, the mainland is divided into three geographically distinct regions: the high, temperate inter-Andean valley known as the sierra, located at elevations ranging between 1,500 and 3,000 meters (5,000 and 10,000 feet); the coast, a low-lying largely tropical zone spanning the area between the Pacific Ocean and the western cordillera of the Andes; and the oriente, or amazon lowlands, a tropical rain forest lying to the east of the Andes at between 250 and 900 meters (800 and 3,000 feet) in altitude.

A fourth region, comprising the Galápagos Islands, is a small archipelago lying some 1,000 kilometers (620 miles) off the coast. Isolated from the mainland, sparcely populated (less than 1 percent of the total), and without commercially exploitable resources, the islands have played only a marginal role in Ecuador's political and economic development. Nevertheless, the Galápagos Islands possess a colorful history of their own, attracting the interest of international visitors since their discovery by Europeans sometime in the late sixteenth century. A refuge for pirates during the seventeenth century, the islands became a supply port in the eighteenth and nineteenth centuries for smugglers and whalers, who found the meat from the native giant tortoise (the "Galápagos," from which the islands derive their name) a welcome relief from their otherwise monotonous diet of salt pork and biscuits. In 1835, Charles Darwin's visit to the islands, his observations there, and his subsequent writings on the origin of species drew the attention of the scientific community to what was once described by Herman Melville as "five and twenty heaps of cinders." As a rich repository of unique and varied species of flora and fauna, in fact, the Galápagos Islands continue to fascinate scientists and, in recent years, have drawn ever-increasing numbers of tourists from all parts of the world.[4]

Stretching a distance of some 600 kilometers (375 miles) from the northern border with Colombia to Peru in the south, and occupying 26 percent of the land area, the sierra is in reality a series of some twelve narrow, interconnected basins, bounded on the east and west by the high ranges of the Andes and on the north and south by lower transverse ridges. Most settlement prior to 1900 was located in these high intermontane basins, where staple crops such as barley, corn, potatoes, wheat, and various fruits and vegetables could be cultivated with relative ease. At the beginning of the nineteenth century, 90 percent of Ecuador's population lived in the sierra. By 1982, migration and faster rates of population growth in other regions, principally the coast, had reduced the sierra's share of the population to 47 percent.

Nearly all of Ecuador's traditional Indian population is located in rural areas of the sierra (see Table 1.2 for a breakdown of population

TABLE 1.2
Population by province, 1950 and 1982

Province	1950		1982	
	Population	Percent	Population	Percent
SIERRA	1,856,445	58.0	3,790,583	47.1
Azuay	250,975	7.8	443,044	5.5
Bolivar	109,305	3.4	141,566	1.8
Cañar	97,681	3.0	174,674	2.2
Carchi	76,595	2.4	125,452	1.6
Cotopaxi	165,602	5.2	279,765	3.5
Chimborazo	218,130	6.8	320,268	4.0
Imbabura	146,893	4.6	245,745	3.1
Loja	216,802	6.8	358,952	4.5
Pinchincha	386,520	12.1	1,376,831	17.1
Tungurahua	187,942	5.9	324,286	4.0
COAST	1,298,495	40.1	3,947,975	49.0
El Oro	89,306	2.9	337,818	4.2
Esmeraldas	75,407	4.1	247,311	3.1
Guayas	582,144	18.2	2,047,001	25.4
Los Ríos	150,260	4.7	457,065	5.8
Manabi	401,378	12.5	858,780	10.7
ORIENTE	46,471	1.5	263,797	3.3
Morona Santiago	21,046[a]	0.7	70,217	0.9
Napo	25,425[b]	0.8	115,110	1.4
Pastaza			31,779	0.4
Zamora Chinchipe			46,691	0.6
GALAPAGOS	1,346	---[c]	6,119	---[c]
TOTAL ECUADOR	3,202,757	100.0[d]	8,050,630	100.0[d]

[a]Includes the population of Zamora Chinchipe.
[b]Includes the population of Pastaza.
[c]Less than 0.1 percent of the total population.
[d]Totals and subtotals may not sum to 100 due to rounding.

SOURCE: Adapted from Banco Central del Ecuador, *Boletín Anuario*, No. 7 (1984), pp. 186-187.

figures by province). Although centuries of subjugation by common oppressors have erased many of the former differences among Indian groups, a few such groups have enjoyed a degree of economic independence, thereby retaining a strong sense of ethnic pride and preserving unique cultural traditions. Most distinctive are the Otavalan Indians, who have earned a wide reputation for the high quality of their woolen weavings. Easily recognized by their traditional dress of white cotton shirt and pants, dark blue poncho, and dark fedora, Otavalan men travel widely to sell their products, some even as far as North America and Europe. Other Indian groups retaining a distinct

Market day in the sierra

cultural identity are the Salasacans, from the area near Ambato, who have a long history as independent farmers, and the Saraguros, from near Loja in the far south, who have had considerable success raising cattle.[5]

Early cities such as Quito (the capital, founded in 1534), Cuenca (1557), and Loja (1548) were established in the intermontane basins. Because their contact with the outside world was limited, the sierra cities developed as bastions of conservative Spanish culture. Nowhere is the country's colonial heritage more visible and pronounced than in these cities. As the former administrative capital of the Audiencia of Quito, Quito in particular became one of the principal artistic centers in the Spanish colonies. Today, even though modern office buildings and apartments increasingly crowd the city skyline, Quito retains some of the finest examples of colonial art and architecture in Latin America.

Geographic barriers to communication and commerce also fostered a profound sense of regional identity that did not succumb easily to the efforts of Ecuador's rulers to meld the disparate regions into a single nation. Isolated from the coast by the western cordillera of the Andes and from each other by rugged terrain, the highland

View of modern Quito

cities evolved as the hubs of largely self-sufficient regions in which the hacienda was the dominant form of rural social and economic organization. Spanish subjugation of the Indian population through the hacienda system bequeathed to the present day an agrarian structure in which landownership remains highly concentrated in the hands of an elite minority. Although other forms of wealth accumulation, such as investments in commerce, industry, or urban real estate, have tended to replace the hacienda, much of the contemporary sierra elite can still trace its lineage to the early landowning *hacendados*.

Commerce within the sierra was restricted, hindered by the relative absence of roads and the lack of differentiation among products produced in different areas of the highland region. Traditionally, most of a specific hacienda's production, beyond that required for local needs, supplied consumers in one of the nearby sierra cities. Communication among these cities was difficult. As late as 1920, the 223-kilometer (140-mile) journey from Quito north to Tulcán, near the Colombian border, took five days.[6]

The lack of roads also impeded trade between the sierra and the coast. In 1908, the completion of a rail line between Quito and Guayaquil provided some stimulus to commerce. Trade between the sierra and the coast increased further during the cacao boom, but

TABLE 1.3
Structure of the Ecuadorian economy, 1950 and 1985
(percentage shares of gross domestic product)

Sector	Year	
	1950	1985[a]
Agriculture	31.1[b]	13.6
Manufacturing	17.1	18.8
Services	26.2	17.5
Wholesale and retail trade	14.1	15.6
Transportation	5.1	8.6
Construction	1.4	5.4
Petroleum and mining	1.0	17.0
Other	4.0	3.5

[a]Figures for 1985 are provisional.
[b]Percentage shares are calculated from current sucres.

SOURCE: Calculated from Banco Central del Ecuador, *Cuentas Nacionales*, Nos. 7 and 8 (Quito, 1985 and 1986).

the high costs of production and transportation put sierra products at a competitive disadvantage relative to imported foods. Not until the advent of motor transport and the expansion of the coastal market induced by the banana boom of the 1950s did trade with the coast increase significantly. Nor was foreign trade particularly important to the sierra economy, with the exception of brief periods during the seventeenth and early twentieth centuries when textile exports flourished. Only during the former period were sierra exports, destined primarily for Peruvian markets, an important share of total Ecuadorian exports. In the latter period, textile exports, then destined for Colombian markets, never exceeded 11 percent of total exports.[7] In the late 1970s, a sierra-based manufacturing industry began to develop, oriented toward production for export markets within the Andean Common Market. But this industry, too, never accounted for more than a very minor share of Ecuador's total exports. (See Table 1.3 for a breakdown of the Ecuadorian economy.)

The coast, a fertile alluvial plain ranging in width from 30 kilometers (20 miles) in the south to 180 kilometers (110 miles) at the latitude of Guayaquil, accounts for 25 percent of Ecuadorian territory and approximately 50 percent of its population. Sparsely inhabited during the immediate preconquest period, the region grew rapidly in population as labor demands arising from the expansion of agricultural exports drew Indian and mestizo migrants from the sierra. The former, once they had abandoned their traditional language, culture, and costume, were rapidly assimilated into the broad mestizo lower class. The *montuvios,* as the coastal peasants are known, differ from their sierra counterparts. The challenge of migration has drawn the more adventurous and slightly better-off sierra Indians and mestizos to the coast. More likely to own land and more acculturated into Spanish society, the montuvios have earned a reputation for independence. Only the Colorado and Cayapa Indian groups—the indigenous inhabitants of the northern coastal region—remain relatively unassimilated, each retaining its own language and customs. The two groups, however, account for only a small fraction of the coastal population; together they number no more than 4,000.[8] Most of Ecuador's small black population is also located in the coastal region, principally in the northern province of Esmeraldas.

Long the country's most dynamic economic region, the coast has benefited from excellent growing conditions for tropical products, an extensive network of rivers navigable by canoe and raft, easy maritime transport along the coast, and natural harbors (of which Guayaquil is one of the finest on the west coast of South America), all providing access to foreign markets. Produced along the coast are nearly all of the country's nonpetroleum exports, among which the most important are cacao, bananas, coffee, and shrimp. Most of Ecuador's industry is also located on the coast, principally in its largest city, Guayaquil.

The economic imbalance between the sierra and the coast has been a source of intense rivalry between the two regions. Guayaquil residents, for example, are fond of complaining (not without some justification) that Quito merely spends the national wealth that Guayaquil creates.

Guayaquil was established in 1538, shortly after Quito's founding. Although the city was initially subservient to Quito, the rapid growth in its economic importance and population allowed it to assert its independence at an early date. A major shipbuilding center early on, Guayaquil had become the country's preeminent financial and commercial center by the late 1800s. Even during the seventeenth century, nearly all of the sierra's textile exports to Peru passed through Guayaquil. Most imports also entered the country through this city. In the nineteenth and early twentieth centuries, cacao became Ecuador's leading export, thus establishing agricultural exports as the basis for the country's subsequent economic development and further stimulating the growth of Guayaquil and the coast. In the 1950s, the banana boom provided further impetus to the growth of the coastal economy. Other cities such as Esmeraldas, Portoviejo, Manta, and Machala also grew as the coastal economy expanded, and larger numbers of migrants were drawn from the sierra.

Waterfront street in Guayaquil

Guayaquil today is a noisy, bustling, commercial city, much in contrast to its more sedate rival in the sierra. Although there are pockets of striking colonial architecture, Guayaquil has none of the charm of Quito; nor does it have that city's unparalleled natural setting. The coastal port, however, is the economic heart of the country and, with a population of more than 1 million, its most populous city. In addition, both Guayaquil's wealth, an important resource for presidential candidates, and the electoral weight of its population have given the port city an increasingly important role in national politics.

The oriente accounts for 46 percent of the land area and 3 percent of the population. Covered with dense rain forest and isolated from the rest of the country by the eastern cordillera of the Andes, this region prior to the 1970s was populated only by a small number of colonists and scattered Indian groups such as the Shuar, Cofán, Waorani, and lowland Quechua. The economic importance of the oriente was minimal. Most of the Indian groups were hunter-gatherers or subsistence farmers. As the region held no known resources of commercial value, there were no economic incentives to develop it. As late as the early 1960s, no roads penetrated further into the oriente than the foothills of the eastern cordillera. This situation changed in

1967, however, with the discovery of petroleum in the northeastern corner of the region. Roads were pushed deep into the oriente, and migration from the coast and the sierra brought additional colonists. But unlike the effects on the coast that resulted from the earlier cacao and banana booms, economic development of the oriente was not directly stimulated by the petroleum boom. Revenues from petroleum exports flowed into the government treasuries in Quito, not into the oriente, whose importance to the national economy remained marginal.

THE POLITICAL LANDSCAPE

The modern state of Ecuador was formally established as a presidential democracy in 1830, when the country announced its independence from Gran Colombia. A unitary state, the nation today is divided administratively into 20 provinces, of which 10 are in the sierra, 5 are on the coast, 4 are in the oriente, and 1 covers the Galápagos Islands. Provinces are further subdivided into cantons (126), and into rural (720) and urban (227) parishes.

Ecuadorian politics is in some ways as bewildering as its topography. Political instability has been a characteristic feature. One government has followed another as if on some sort of political merry-go-round, driven by recurrent economic crises and constantly shifting political alliances. Until recently, the average president had served fewer than three years of what is constitutionally a four-year term. Constitutions have not so much defined the dimensions of political contest as they have ratified extraconstitutional procedure. Since independence, Ecuador has had seventeen constitutions; the most recent was adopted in 1978. Yet until recently, life for the vast majority of Ecuadorian citizens was remarkably untouched by these numerous political transitions. Ecuadorian politics has traditionally been largely an elite contest, with political participation limited to a small fraction of the population until the 1970s.

Historically, both the geographical fragmentation of the country and the heavy dependence of the economy on the export of a small number of primary products have had profound implications for the manner in which Ecuadorian politics has evolved. Regional rivalries dominated the nation's early history. Geographical isolation ensured that the Ecuadorians' first loyalty was to the region; national concerns held little importance. For nearly a hundred years after independence, national governments were obliged to resort to military force to put down regional rebellions. Regional demands for public spending also inflated government budgets. Increasingly, the political legitimacy of Ecuadorian governments became a function of their ability to finance

TABLE 1.4
Ecuador's principal exports, 1847-1985
(in percentages of total value of exports)

Year	Exports						
	Cacao[a]	Bananas	Coffee	Petroleum	Fish[b]	Rice	Other[c]
1847	57.4	---[d]	0.1	---	---	---	42.5
1857	64.0	---	0.8	---	---	0.8	34.7
1879	53.5	---	0.9	---	---	---	45.6
1890	67.3	---	5.9	---	---	---	26.8
1900	70.7	---	5.4	---	---	---	23.9
1910	57.8	0.2	5.4	---	---	---	36.6
1920	71.3	0.2	1.8	---	---	---	26.7
1930	29.0	---	9.4	21.4	---	4.6	35.6
1940	17.5	3.8	9.8	14.8	---	8.7	45.4
1950	29.1	12.8	27.6	1.8	0.1	10.7	17.9
1960	13.3	60.8	18.4	---	2.4	2.5	2.6
1970	11.0	46.8	25.1	0.4	2.6	---	14.1
1980	8.4	9.4	5.2	62.0	5.2	---	9.8
1985[e]	7.5	6.6	6.4	67.1	9.1	---	3.2

[a]Cacao includes both raw cacao and semi-elaborates.
[b]Fish includes fish, shrimp, and fish products.
[c]The composition of this category varies from year to year but includes exports such as sugar, tagua,
panama hats, balsa, and industrial products.
[d]Less than 0.05 percent.
[e]Preliminary figures.

SOURCE: Export percentages for 1847-1960 were calculated from Linda Alexander Rodríguez, *The Search for Public Policy: Regional Politics and Government Finances in Ecuador, 1830-1940* (Berkeley: University of California Press, 1985), pp. 178-183. Export percentages for 1980 and 1985 were calculated from Banco Central del Ecuador, *Memoria 1985* (Quito, 1986), Cuadro LXV, pp. 264-265.

regional public-works projects. The growth of the coastal export economy provided a new source of revenue for governments, which turned increasingly to the taxation of foreign trade to finance their expenditures. The political importance of the state grew as it became the primary mechanism for redistributing export wealth. But the combination of large spending demands and growing reliance on coastal exports to finance these demands both augmented the domestic political influence of coastal economic elites and made the national government increasingly vulnerable to fluctuations in the international market for Ecuador's products. An important contributor to Ecuador's seemingly endemic political instability, export fluctuations have led the country through a roller-coaster history of alternating periods of prosperity and depression, as first cacao, then bananas, and finally petroleum propelled the economy (see Table 1.4).

Geography and export-led economic growth structured Ecuadorian politics in other ways as well. Political organizations tended to be fragmented along regional lines. Weak economic linkages between the export sector and other areas of the Ecuadorian economy impeded the degree to which the entire country shared in the periods of export prosperity. The outward-looking orientation of Ecuador's economic elites reduced their interest in redistributive public policies, such as land reform, which might have expanded the domestic market and reduced the level of rural poverty. The relatively slow growth of urbanization and industrialization prior to the 1970s retarded the development of mass-based political organizations. The petroleum boom and its accompanying social changes, such as the emergence of a middle class, brought an increase in political participation. New political parties emerged as responsible alternatives to the personalistic movements that had dominated electoral politics since the demise of Liberal and Conservative party hegemony in the 1930s. But even these new parties found it difficult to overcome the obstacles created by geography and economy, in that they developed without strong ties to popular organizations and were unable to secure the support of elites.

Certainly petroleum brought a dramatic economic change to Ecuador, a change exceeding that associated with any previous export boom. Incomes rose, industrialization accelerated, the domestic market expanded, and new roads knit the regions together more tightly than ever before. Petroleum also shifted the regional balance of power from the coast toward the sierra, strengthened the power of the state, and increased its independence from domestic economic elites. The conjunction of Ecuador's new wealth (and the economic changes it engendered) with the rise to power of reform-minded governments raised expectations for change in a society that had heretofore proved quite resistant to such reformist endeavors. Yet the political difficulties encountered by these governments, and by the subsequent, more conservative government, suggest that Ecuadorian political institutions may not have matured to the degree that its economy has, and that domestic politics remains profoundly influenced by the performance of the country's export markets.

In subsequent chapters we shall explore these issues. Chapter 2 establishes the early historical context, with an emphasis on the importance of the patterns imposed by regionalism and structured by Ecuador's colonial heritage. Discussed in Chapter 3 are the cacao and banana booms, as well as the implications of these periods of economic bonanza for domestic politics. Chapter 4 continues the discussion of the interplay between economics and politics, focusing on the expansion of the electorate and the emergence of populist political movements. Chapters 5 through 7 consider the economic and political implications of the petroleum boom, with the state at the center of the analysis. Chapter 8 concludes with an examination of the possibilities for the future of this little-known country, all the while emphasizing the ways in which traditional patterns may shape future change.

NOTES

1. Most Ecuadorian sources use this estimate. See, for example, Banco Central del Ecuador, *Boletín Anuario*, No. 7 (1984), p. 185. The World Bank, however, currently estimates the rate of population growth at 2.6 percent. See World Bank, *World Development Report, 1985* (New York: Oxford University Press, 1985), Table 19, p. 211.

2. Thomas E. Weil et al., *Area Handbook for Ecuador* (Washington, D.C.: Government Printing Office, 1973), p. 65.

3. Juan Cueva Jaramillo, "Etnocentrismo en la cultura ecuatoriana en 150 años de vida Republicana," in Luis Mora Ortega, ed., *Arte y Cultura, Ecuador: 1830–1980* (Quito: Corporación Editora Nacional, 1980), pp. 45–68.

4. See John Hickman, *The Enchanted Islands: The Galapagos Discovered* (Dover, N.H.: Tanager Books, 1985), for a discussion of early visitors to the Galápagos Islands.

5. Ibid., pp. 68–69.

6. Dawn Ann Wiles, "Land Transportation Within Ecuador 1822–1954," Ph.D. dissertation (Ann Arbor: University Microfilms International, 1971), pp. 110–124.

7. Anne Collin Delavaud, ed., *Atlas del Ecuador* (Paris: Les Editions J. A., 1982), p. 44.

8. Linda Alexander Rodríguez, *The Search for Public Policy: Regional Politics and Government Finances in Ecuador, 1830–1940* (Berkeley: University of California Press, 1985), Table 3, p. 22.

2

Spanish Conquest and the Making of the Republic

Historical patterns inherited from the country's precolonial and colonial past have continued to exert a strong influence over Ecuador's political and economic development. The grafting of Spanish rule onto the conquered Inca society established a colonial system with a large Indian underclass and a small Hispanic elite whose power and privilege became consolidated in the highland hacienda. Formidable geographical obstacles divided the country into isolated regions with divergent economic interests. Even with independence, Ecuadorians tended to identify first with the region and only second, if at all, with the nation. Frequent outbreaks of civil war marked the postindependence period as national governments struggled to impose a central authority. Economic changes exacerbated regional conflict as the growth of the coastal export economy increasingly eroded the traditional social and economic dominance of the highlands.

THE CONQUEST

Contemporary Ecuador covers an area roughly contiguous with the northern section of the former Inca empire. During the latter half of the fifteenth century, the Incas had gradually extended their dominion northward from Cuzco, the capital of the empire. By about the end of the century, Huayna Cápac had led his forces as far north as the present northern Ecuadorian border, imposing Inca authority over the indigenous tribes of the region and establishing Quito as a major administrative and military outpost.

The Inca civilization was remarkable in many respects, none of which was more so than their extraordinary organizational genius. It was their military prowess that allowed them to extend an empire over a territory of some 980,000 square kilometers (380,000 square miles), and through administrative skill they sustained a society that flourished in spite of large distances and severe natural obstacles. The Incas themselves were a small group of royalty presiding over a large subjugated population. Authoritarian and hierarchical, Inca society "combined absolute despotism with a respect for the social and political forms of the subject peoples. The Inca ruled as an absolute monarch, but his will reached the common man through the local chiefs [curacas], whose authority and privileges were maintained, if not reinforced."[1] To facilitate administration of the diverse tribes under the dominion of their empire, the Incas imposed the common languge of Quechua on their subjects. An extensive network of roads and bridges facilitated the movement of goods and armies over exceedingly rugged terrain. Terracing and irrigation made possible the cultivation of the narrow Andean valleys.

Land under the Incas was divided into three parts: one reserved for the Incas; a second for the Sun, the principal diety; and a third that was allocated as communal property to the Indian communities, or ayllus, which formed the basic organizational units of the empire. Each community owed tribute, which was paid in labor on the lands belonging to the Incas and to the Sun. Although a large part of the production resulting from labor tribute went to support the Incas and their administration, there is good evidence that a portion was stored in graneries from which it could be drawn to feed the population in the event of poor harvests.[2] Periodically, Indians were also obliged to supply labor for special projects through an institution known as the mita. No communities or individuals, however, were taxed on the production of their own fields.[3]

Inca dominance over the northern region of their empire was relatively short-lived, however, as no more than forty years passed between Huayna Cápac's establishment of Quito and the Spanish arrival there in 1534. Led by Bartolomé Ruiz, the Spaniards first reached the Ecuadorian coast at Esmeraldas on an exploratory voyage in 1526. Favorable reports from this expedition led to Francisco Pizarro's departure from Panama in 1531 in search of the fabled riches of "Tahuantinsuyo." Pizarro's small force of 180 soldiers and 26 horses retraced Bartolomé Ruiz's sea voyage to Esmeraldas and from there sailed further down the Ecuadorian coast, drawn by accounts of the vast riches of a large civilization to the south.[4]

In 1532, Pizarro's forces landed at Túmbez on what is now the northern Peruvian coast, to be joined shortly by Hernando de Soto and an estimated additional 100 soldiers. From Túmbez the expedition set out eastward toward the mountains, arriving at the Inca city of Cajamarca in November of the same year. It was here that Atahualpa, son of Huayna Cápac and recent victor in a bloody civil war against his brother Huáscar, was seized and mercilessly put to death by the Spaniards. Given the overwhelming numerical superiority of the Indians, it took the Spaniards a remarkably short period to extend their control south to the city of Cuzco. Weakened by internal division, the central region of the Inca empire was brought under Spanish domination in less than a year, although significant rebellions continued to erupt for a period of years thereafter.[5]

With the conquest of the central region consolidated, the Spaniards turned toward the north. Spurred by rumors of a wealth to be found in Quito rivaling that of Cuzco, Sabastián de Benalcázar, one of Pizarro's lieutenants, marched northward at the head of a band of 200 men. Entering what is now southern Ecuador, Benalcázar forged an alliance with the Cañari tribe. Rebellious under the recently established Inca rule and bitter over their brutal defeat by Atahualpa in one of the first battles of the civil war, the Cañaris were eager to avenge themselves against their conquerors.[6] Thus aided, the Spaniards were able to fight their way along the inter-Andean valley to Quito, overcoming the fierce resistance offered by the Inca master tactician, Rumiñahui. To no avail, Rumiñahui had conducted what must rank as one of the earliest scorched-earth campaigns in defense of his territory. In 1834, the Villa de San Francisco de Quito was established on the ruins of the northern Inca capital, and by 1535 the Spaniards had established their domination of the northern regions of the Inca empire.

In practice, however, Spanish control was most complete over those regions in which the Incas had previously subjugated the indigenous populations, principally those located within the inter-Andean valley. It was here that the major Spanish settlements, such as that at Quito, were established. Control over the coastal plain to the west of the Andes ranges, and over the Amazonian highlands to the east, where the Incas had been less successful at subjugating the indigenous populations, was never as firmly established. With the important exception of the port city of Guayaquil, first founded by Sebástian de Belalcázar in 1535, the coast remained largely unsettled by Spaniards until late into the colonial period. The lure of gold and the hope of finding a navigable outlet to the Atlantic drew the Spaniards' attention to the jungled oriente. But their failure to find either gold or a commercial route to the Atlantic—in addition to attacks by hostile Indians and a generally unhealthy climate—limited Spanish settlement of the region to a few isolated missionary outposts.

Bust of Rumiñahui with contemporary Otavalan Indians

THE COLONIAL ERA

The Spaniards extended to Quito the institutions of administration they had introduced in Mexico and Peru. A central function of these institutions was the control of land and Indian labor. The Crown rewarded loyal subjects, typically the originally conquerors, with the grant of an *encomienda*—that is, with the right to collect tribute and labor services from the Indian population in a prescribed area, theoretically in exchange for tending to their spiritual and material welfare. The Quito city council (*cabildo*), established in 1547 with jurisdiction over a vast area stretching from Cuenca in the south to Pasto in the north, was responsible not only for the normal functions involved in administering a city (such as garbage collection) but also for the distribution of land. In 1563, the northern region was elevated to the status of Audiencia, part of the Viceroyalty of Peru. As in other parts of the Spanish Americas, the Audiencia was the highest tribunal of justice as well as a general administrative board for the region. By the end of the sixteenth century, reforms introduced by

Viceroy Francisco de Toledo had greatly extended the Audiencia's authority to directly regulate Indian tribute and labor service.

The encomienda system was a Spanish institution grafted onto the traditional Inca social structure. In broad terms, the *encomendero*'s right to tribute simply replaced that claimed by the Inca. The Inca community, or ayllu, was retained largely intact, and the encomendero typically negotiated the tribute payment with the curacas. By the middle of the sixteenth century, however, the system had come under criticism from a number of different groups. The Spanish Crown had long debated the merits of abolishing the encomienda system and making the Indians subject to its direct control, fearing the otherwise growing local autonomy of the encomendero elite. At the same time, both Spanish officials and local elites recognized the need to mobilize a large and stable Indian work force for the booming Peruvian mines. Other groups, among them some of the more progressive priests, saw reform of the encomienda as a way of protecting the Indian population from the increasing abuses of the encomenderos.[7]

In the 1540s, the Crown had decreed an end to the encomendero's right to labor service, mandating that tribute be collected only in money or goods and that the rate be fixed by the Audiencia.[8] Toledo's reforms in the 1570s continued the erosion of the encomendero's power, stipulating the establishment of a new class of appointed officials, the *corregidores de indios*. These officials, nominally responsible for the welfare of the Indian population within their jurisdictions, were given the authority to regulate and organize Indian labor. Corregidores administered a system of forced labor, the colonial mita, in which a fixed percentage of the Indian population was assigned to work on a rotating basis for periods of time up to one year. The *mitayos*, as these workers were called, received a wage, but one that rarely permitted the accumulation of any capital; typically, then, the mitayos were left indebted at the end of their service.[9]

Although Toledo's reforms increased Crown tributes and resolved the colonists' labor problems, there is little evidence that the plight of the Indians was substantially improved. By the beginning of the seventeenth century, most of the corregidores had succumbed to the same temptations for corruption as had their predecessors, the encomenderos.

The encomienda, never as important an institution in colonial Quito as it had been in Peru and Mexico, was rapidly displaced by the reformed tribute and the mita for control of the Indian population.[10] Administered by the Crown, these new institutions rapidly became the mainstays of the Quito economy. One of the first acts of the new Audiencia was to impose the Crown's decree that tribute would not be paid in the form of labor services, with the stipulation that one-half of any tribute obligation was to be paid in gold and the other half in goods, at rates fixed by the authorities.[11] Tributes were a major source of Crown income. From the mid-1600s on, tribute collections were the Crown's largest single income producer in colonial Quito, supplying between 30 and 50 percent of total revenues.[12] The mita played a similarly important role, becoming the principal means for supplying labor to farms and ranches throughout the colonial period. Up to one-fifth of the Indian population, a higher proportion than elsewhere in the Viceroyalty, was subject to mita demands at any given time.

Essentially three hierarchical social groups defined colonial society within the Audiencia.[13] The upper class comprised the peninsular Spanish, who monopolized the higher offices in the civil and ecclesiastical bureaucracies, having received these positions by royal appointment; the Spanish-born and creole elites, whose wealth was in land or commerce and who had typically purchased positions on the city council; and a distinctly less privileged strata of inferior magistrates, clerks, and regular clergy, either peninsular Spanish or creole. A second social group comprised those of mixed race (the mestizos and others) who occupied service and craft positions and frequently acted as overseers of Indians in the textile workshops and on Spanish-owned estates. Although equal in law to the first group, the members of this second group were widely regarded as socially inferior, the victims of extreme social prejudice. The third social group, at the bottom of the social hierarchy, was occupied by Indians and black slaves, the latter significant in numbers only on the coast.

Neither Indian labor nor land, the principal sources of wealth, was scarce during the colony's first half-century. Spaniards had "flocked to Quito from Peru because Indians were easily obtainable," and the city council commonly supplied new arrivals with new land.[14] Unlike the situation in Peru, where the need for mine workers put heavy pressure on the Indian labor force, mining was not particularly important to colonial Quito. Never as richly endowed with precious metals as its neighbor to the south, Quito's production of gold and silver had declined to economically unimportant levels even before the end of the sixteenth century.[15] In the absence of mining, demands for Indian labor in the early years of the colony were limited principally to agricultural and personal service. Not until the late seventeenth century, when the booming textile industry began to require growing numbers of workers, did Indian labor become scarce—a scarcity that turned acute with the spread of deadly epidemics at the end of the century.

Colonial section of Quito

The abundance of land is less readily explained. One reason may have been that the Spaniards were able to acquire large amounts of Indian land at a very early date. Given the lack of mineral resources and export industries, land undoubtedly took on added value. Apparently even the encomenderos, who received tribute from their Indian charges, could not live well on this income.[16] As the cities grew, the profitability of commercial agriculture increased. A city ordinance approved by the Audiencia in the first years of the colony gave the cabildo the right to distribute lands that belonged to Indian towns. In 1589, so much land had been distributed that the president of the Audiencia, Manuel de Barros, put a halt to the custom of supplying newly arrived Spaniards. Whatever the reason, by the late sixteenth century large numbers of Indians were either landless or without sufficient land to support themselves and their families. One consequence of this early landlessness was the rapid growth of a population of Indian wage laborers, particularly in the textile mills, who were bound to their employers through a system of debt peonage known as *concertaje*.[17]

The growth of a textile industry in the sierra during the seventeenth century altered the shape of the colonial society and economy. Indians in the highlands had a well-developed tradition of textile weaving that predated the conquest. The Spaniards introduced wool-producing merino sheep, which multiplied so rapidly in the fertile

Andean basins that by 1620 as many as 600,000 were grazing in the Latacunga and Riobamba areas.[18] The large population of Indians, many of whom were already landless, as well as the lack of competing labor demands from mining guaranteed a cheap and plentiful supply of labor. And not least, a large demand for cheap Quito textiles from the flourishing mining communities in Peru ensured a high degree of profitability for the textile mills, in spite of very high transportation costs.[19]

Textile mills, or *obrajes* as they were known, spread throughout the north-central region of the sierra. In 1595, 6 obrajes were operating in Quito. Toward the end of the seventeenth century more than 200 obrajes were in operation, employing in excess of 28,000 Indians and earning Quito the designation of "the sweatshop of Spanish South America." Both Spaniards and creoles earned modest fortunes from the textile trade. Nor were the obrajes only a private source of wealth. Encourged by the Crown, textiles also contributed substantially to the royal treasuries through sales-tax payments. The Church ran its own obrajes and received a significant portion of the tithe from the industry.[20]

Quito's textile boom and the sierra's emergence as an international trading center, however, was short-lived. During the seventeenth century, the annual value of textile exports is estimated to have been 1.5 million pesos; by the eighteenth they had dropped to an annual value of some 600,000 pesos.[21] A number of factors appear to have contributed to its virtual demise by the middle of the eighteenth century. Although information on colonial demographics is notoriously poor, it is almost certain that a series of epidemics in the 1690s killed off one-third of the Indian population. Increased competition from European and Chinese textiles (particularly as the commercial route around Cape Horne came into use), declining demand from the Peruvian mining districts whose riches were being exhausted, and a growth of trade protection within the Americas all figured into the declining profitability of the Quito textile industry.[22] By 1720 only about sixty obrajes remained in operation, and commercial agricultural production, primarily destined for the sierra market, once again became the highland's principal economic activity.[23]

With the collapse of the textile boom and the retreat to commercial agriculture, both landownership and control over a now relatively more abundant Indian labor force took on a renewed importance, accelerating the growth of the landed estate. By the nineteenth century, control over land and labor, institutionally separated by the Spanish administration through the encomienda and the corregidores de indios, was gradually becoming consolidated in the large estate known as the *hacienda*. The hacienda was characterized by a resident labor force of *huasipungueros*, who received usufruct rights to a plot of land (*huasipungo*) in exchange for their work on the estate.[24] With independence and the end of Spanish administrative control, the landowning sierra creoles became the dominant economic and social elite, their base of power firmly established in the hacienda.

The growth of the sierra textile trade also benefited the city of Guayaquil, through which most of the region's exports passed en route to Lima and Santiago. The coastal economy during the colonial period differed markedly from that of the highlands primarily because labor was scarce, despite the abundance of land. Small in numbers prior to the conquest, the indigenous populations on the coast had not been effectively subjugated by the Incas and thus resisted Spanish domination. Population losses from battles with the colonists and, more important, the devastating effects of disease during the mid-sixteenth century left few workers for the Spanish. With a limited tributary population, coastal encomiendas were not particularly profitable. Between 1540 and 1605 the number of encomiendas in Guayaquil fell from thirty to thirteen, and their average income fell by 50 percent.[25]

Guayaquil colonists turned to other sources of income. Both shipbuilding and the export of cacao became profitable alternatives. By the 1580s, Guayaquil had become the principal shipyard for the Pacific coast. Black slave labor, imported from Panama and Lima, augmented a local work force of wage laborers. Having benefited from an abundant supply of excellent hardwoods for ship construction and a protected harborage, the port supplied both warships and merchant vessels. Guayaquil merchants also acquired their own fleet of ships to transport textiles, wood, and cacao to markets along the Pacific coast.

By the eighteenth century, cacao exports had assumed a dominant position in the coastal economy. Their rise and fall determined the prosperity of this region and, with the decline of the highland textile industry, also that of the sierra. Dwarfed in importance by rising cacao earnings, shipbuilding apparently persisted until the nineteenth century, when it declined to an insignificant level because of its failure to make the transition to steamship technology.[26] Although retrospective estimates are hampered by what we know to have been the extensive smuggling caused by Crown restrictions on Guayaquil cacao exports, there is no doubt that production expanded rapidly. One scholar has estimated that "from the beginning of the seventeenth century until 1821, cacao production experienced a six-fold increase . . . [and] by the end of the Colonial period, cacao sales out of

Guayaquil represented from two-thirds to three-fourths of all exports from the Audiencia of Quito."[27] With rising exports of cacao, customs duties began to displace the Indian tribute as the principal source of Crown revenue from the colony. In 1807, the Indian tribute produced 248,951 pesos, or 45 percent of total government income; customs duties supplied only 81,663 pesos, or 15 percent of the total. By 1830, the growing importance of the coastal economy was reflected in a reversal in the importance of these two sources of government income. The Indian tribute still provided a significant 201,379 pesos, or 37 percent of government income, but customs duties had risen to 311,500 pesos, or 57 percent of the total.[28]

Cacao production expanded into the abundant land north of Guayaquil. Facilitated by an extensive system of navigable rivers, production costs were low relative to those in the major competing regions around Caracas, in contemporary Venezuela.[29] The principal deterrent to the expansion of cacao production in the colonial period was the shortage of labor. In the mid-eighteenth century, the cacao zone was virtually unpopulated. As slave labor was too expensive to use for cacao production, labor had to be attracted from adjoining regions, primarily from the sierra. To accomplish this end, a system of wage labor, without the semifeudal arrangements of the highlands, was introduced on the coast at a very early date. Large numbers of workers were induced to work on the cacao plantations, and from 1765 to 1805 the coastal population grew at a rate of 2.6 percent per annum.[30] An important consequence of this early introduction of wage labor was that "Guayaquil's economy passed from encomienda to plantation without an intervening phase of hacienda, as occurred in most of South America."[31]

INDEPENDENCE

Resentment among the creole elites toward the Spanish authorities grew during the eighteenth century, and by the start of the nineteenth century isolated demands for independence from groups within colonial Quito were beginning to be heard. The decline in power of the Spanish monarchy and the increased resentment over tribute payments and economic restrictions on trade were two factors contributing to the rising spirit of rebellion. But it would be difficult to argue that support for independence was ever widespread. Most of the population had little understanding of the issues and perceived little forthcoming benefit from independence; the elites, who had far more at stake, were profoundly divided along regional lines. There was no sense of national unity, and the disparate economic bases of the various regions provided little incentive for cooperation.

The economically depressed north-central region, in which Quito is located, saw the least benefit from continued allegiance to Spain. With the textile industry in a shambles, opportunities for upward mobility for the creole elite within a society dominated by the Spanish bureaucracy were few, and tribute payments to the Crown were seen as an unwanted drain on the limited wealth of an already impoverished region. Independence promised increased opportunities for redistributing coastal wealth to creole elites in the sierra.

In 1785, efforts by the Crown to collect back taxes spurred demands for independence from Quito. Then, on August 10, 1809, a junta of Quito elites carried out a successful, though short-lived, coup against the Spanish authorities. But the absence of widespread support in the capital and opposition to this independence movement from other cities in the Audiencia, particularly Guayaquil, led to its overthrow and to the massacre of its leaders before a year had passed. Guayaquil's lack of support for the Quito coup resulted from two factors. In 1789, the Crown's removal of the much-protested restrictions on the export of cacao from this city ushered in a period of renewed economic prosperity on the coast, in sharp contrast to the depressed northern sierra economy.[32] More pragmatically, Guayaquil feared reprisals from the Royal fleet in Lima, a fear justified by Peru's invasion of the city in 1809 following the Quito coup.

Whatever demands for independence may have been expressed in Guayaquil after 1809, they were muted by fears of the Spanish Pacific fleet. But by 1820, the ability of the Spanish to carry out a reprisal against the city had been virtually eliminated. Simon Bolívar had taken most of Colombia by then, and José de San Martín had just landed a republican force of 4,000 men in southern Peru.[33] Guayaquil declared its independence from Spain on October 9, 1820, and war materiel in support of the republican forces under Bolívar's lieutenant, Antonio José de Sucre, moved through the port. Sucre marched from the coastal city toward Quito, where he joined forces with those of the Venezuelan Juan José Flores in the decisive battle for that city's independence on May 24, 1822. Five days later, Quito swore allegiance to Gran Colombia; Guayaquil, divided by demands for its own independence, an allegiance with Peru, and an allegiance with Gran Colombia, followed suit after a slightly longer period.

Gran Colombia, the uneasy union of what was to become Ecuador, Colombia, and Venezuela, survived a turbulent eight years. In 1830 Venezuela announced its independence from Gran Colombia and similar declarations from Quito and Guayaquil rapidly followed.

Guayaquil elites, in particular, had grown increasingly resentful of a 30 percent tax levied on cacao exports to finance Bolívar's Peru campaign. On May 13, 1830, the independent republic of Ecuador was proclaimed, and five months later a constituent assembly named Juan José Flores the first president. Flores served as president for three terms (1830–1834, 1839–1843, and 1843–1845). Evidence of his accomplishments while in office is limited, in part because Ecuadorian historians have expressed less than great affection for this foreign-born president; nevertheless, his success in maintaining a modest amount of order in the unruly new republic must be considered significant.

Flores faced heavy opposition even during his first term. His autocratic rule, his limited aptitude for administration, and his tax reforms, particularly his efforts to shore up sagging government revenues by extending the Indian tribute to the entire adult male population, brought increasing criticism.[34] Growing nationalist sentiment in Ecuador, led by the publication El Quiteño Libre, provided a specific outlet for opposition to this ruler. Elements of regional conflict were also present. Although Venezuelan by birth, Flores had married into the Quito aristocracy. Guayaquil objected not only to his nationality but also to his perceived loyalty to the sierra and his preferential treatment of this region. In 1834, at the end of Flores's first term, civil war broke out between Quito and Guayaquil over which region would control the next government. Flores's control of the military and his shrewd installation of Guayaquileño Vicente Rocafuerte as president during the period 1834–1839 quelled this uprising.

Regionalism plagued all of the early Ecuadorian presidents. All struggled to hold the fledgling nation together against the centrifugal tendencies associated with disparate regions only formally subject to national authority. With independence, even the limited legitimacy enjoyed by the Spanish authorities had evaporated, and Ecuador's first presidents had to contend with a loose federation of regions having little economic incentive to cooperate with a national government and even less sense of national identity. Formidable geographical barriers to internal communication and trade imposed severe constraints on national integration. Loja and Cuenca, for example, had closer ties to Peru through proximity and trade than to the national government in Quito; Guayaquil, its exports the principal source of national government revenue, chafed at underwriting an increasing share of the Quito government's budget, from which it perceived little return.

Ecuador's first constitution explicitly recognized the regional character of the new republic, formally establishing Ecuador as a confederation of the three departments of Quito, Guayaquil, and Cuenca. This arrangement barely survived five years. A new constitution, adopted in 1835 to legitimize Flores's installation of Vicente Rocafuerte as president and his own assumption of the position of commander in chief of the armed forces, abolished the confederative arrangement. This disenchantment with federalism, however, occurred not because of any newly awakened spirit of national identity but, rather, because individual provinces within the departments had resented their lack of representation. The 1835 constitution replaced departments with provinces as the basic subnational units of government, thus formally increasing the degree of political decentralization. In practice, however, the authoritarian rule of Flores and subsequent presidents offered little opportunity for the exercise of local autonomy beyond what geography and tradition had already conferred on the provinces.

In 1839 Flores returned to the presidency. But by this time the opposition to him—already aroused by rising nationalist objections to continued government by a foreigner, by antimilitarism, and by his increasingly authoritarian rule—was brought to the boiling point with the adoption of the constitution of 1843, referred to as the "Charter of Slavery," which extended Flores's term and formally assigned to him what were essentially dictatorial powers. This constitution also restricted the privileges of the Catholic Church and cost Flores the support of the clergy. A coastal rebellion in 1845 ousted Flores, throwing the country once again into civil war and ushering in a period of economic recession and political unrest from which Ecuador would not emerge for fifteen years.

GABRIEL GARCIA MORENO AND THE TRIUMPH OF CONSERVATISM (1860–1875)

The years following Flores's departure saw the already weak ties binding the fledgling nation stretched to the point of rupture. National government lost whatever claims to legitimacy it had earlier possessed, and the country trembled on the brink of anarchy. In 1859, designated the "terrible year" by Ecuadorian historians, the country split into four regions under the weak leadership of President Francisco Robles. Loja, anxious to be free of the domination of Cuenca, declared itself a federal district and elected its own president, Manuel Carrión Pinzon. Guayaquil, under the control of General Guillermo Franco, signed a treaty annexing itself to Peru. Cuenca first declared itself autonomous and shortly thereafter entered into an alliance with Guayaquil. Quito formed a three-man provisional government under the leadership of civilian Gabriel García Moreno to oppose the forces of President Robles.

The tremendous disorder into which the country had been thrown finally settled into an armed struggle between García Moreno's forces, under the direction of former president Juan José Flores, and those headed by the Guayaquil leader Guillermo Franco. On September 26, 1980, García Moreno and Flores overcame Franco's troops and marched triumphantly into Guayaquil. Several months later, in 1861, following what had become the common practice of using a new constitution to ratify extraconstitutional change, a constituent assembly, composed primarily of delegates from the victorious highlands, promulgated a new constitution and elected García Moreno president of the republic.

A Guayaquileño educated in Quito and Europe, and married into the Quito aristocracy, García Moreno rapidly established a reputation as Ecuador's preeminent conservative politician. Though earlier a sharp critic of former president Flores's authoritarianism, García Moreno—like his liberal predecessor, Vicente Rocafuerte, who once wrote that to rule in Ecuador "makes enlightened despotism necessary"—soon turned to authoritarian methods.[35] His strong personal religious beliefs convinced him that only with the discipline of the Catholic Church could Ecuador modernize. Thus he was led to create a regime that has been described as "the most theocratic in all the independent history of Latin America."[36]

Pragmatic concerns also motivated García Moreno's alliance with the Church. As a civilian president, he needed to establish a base of political support outside the armed forces. It would be false to suggest, however, that the military under García Moreno played only a minor role in politics. García Moreno came to power in 1860 and again in 1869 with the assistance of the armed forces, and he relied on their continued support to remain in power. But his alliance with the Church allowed him a degree of political independence he would not otherwise have been permitted.

García Moreno brought to Ecuador a fifteen-year period of relative stability, enjoying considerable support from the landowning upper class, which accepted his authoritarianism as a necessary price for his policies of economic modernization.[37] He began the Quito-Guayaquil railroad, initiated a program of road building and infrastructural development (under which Guayaquil was the first region to benefit), greatly expanded educational facilities (including the establishment of a technical institute), and issued Ecuador's first national currency. But the issue of church-state relations drew the battle lines between the liberals and the conservatives, and between the coast and the sierra. The 1861 constitution, written under García Moreno's guidance, had established Catholicism as the state-sanctioned religion. In 1862, García Moreno signed a concordat with the Vatican that surrendered the state's traditional control over the Church, thus greatly increasing its role in civil affairs. Education became virtually the exclusive preserve of the Church, and large numbers of foreign priests, particularly Jesuits, were brought to Ecuador to fill teaching positions. A subsequent constitution, promulgated in 1869 at the beginning of García Moreno's second term, further increased the influence of the Church in secular matters, infuriating both liberal and regional interests. Stipulating that Catholicism was a prerequisite for citizenship, it also antagonized certain individuals who had previously enjoyed considerable freedom in their practice of Catholicism and who, in their own view, were now "being told they must conform to narrow and inflexible norms established largely by foreigners but enforced by a martinet in the national presidency."[38] Regional interests, notably those in Guayaquil, already chafing under the extreme degree of governmental centralization that characterized García Moreno's presidency, denounced the codification of this de facto practice in the new constitution.[39] Opposition to the president grew increasingly bitter, and on August 6, 1875, as he prepared for a third term, García Moreno was assassinated.

One consequence of García Moreno's twenty-five year domination of Ecuadorian politics was the radical polarization of political debate. García Moreno came to define Ecuadorian conservatism, whereas the reaction to him defined liberalism. The principal issue dividing these groups was the relationship between church and state. Certainly regional differences existed and these reinforced the theological division—conservatives identified with the interests of the sierra, and liberals identified with those of the coast—but they were minor in comparison. Formal political parties, organized during the late nineteenth century, grew out of these early divisions. The Radical Liberal party was founded in 1878, the Conservative party in 1883, and the Progresista party in 1888. Organized as a middle ground by Cuenca conservatives opposed to García Moreno's intolerance and authoritarianism, the Progresistas were influential only for the brief period from 1888 to 1895. The conservatives and liberals, in contrast, maintained an electoral hegemony that lasted well into the 1930s.

THE ACTIVE STATE

Gabriel García Moreno is widely credited with having been the architect of the modern Ecuadorian state, but the growth in state responsibilities that took place during his presidencies owed more to traditional factors such as militarism, regionalism, and the structure of the economy than to ideology or the efforts of this individual.[40] Previous Ecuadorian presidents, such as Flores and Rocafuerte, had also desired to use the state as an agent for economic and social modernization. But their ability to realize these hopes was severely constrained by the combined effects of low public revenues and the large expenditures necessary to maintain the loyalty of the military and to finance the costs of frequent civil wars. Between 1830 and 1860, military expenditures averaged around 50 percent of the budget; between 1860 and 1875, they dropped to an average of just under 30 percent.[41] The problem with public revenues was simply that the low level of economic development in Ecuador, together with a powerful reluctance on the part of the country's elites to submit to taxation, limited the activities that could be taxed. During the colonial period, the Indian tribute and the tithe (in this case, a tax on agricultural production) constituted the principal sources of public revenue. By the time of independence, cacao exports had become the most dynamic sector of the economy and customs duties had become the most important source of public revenue. With the abolition of both the Indian tribute in 1857 and the tithe in 1889, public revenues became even more dependent on the export sector. The state of the public treasury was directly linked to the state of the export market, in this case that for cacao. Vicente Rocafuerte, who perhaps more than other early presidents is credited with having advocated an active state, lamented the depleted public treasury as "exhausted by war, the lack of exports, and the underdeveloped state of agriculture."[42]

García Moreno's ability to expand the scope of state activity was directly related to the rapid expansion of the export sector in the latter half of the nineteenth century. But the increase in customs duties alone could not finance the growing demands, particularly those of the coastal economic elites, for increased state expenditures on education and infrastructural development. Surely García Moreno's reputation resulted in part from his shrewd ability to manipulate the traditional constraints on state expenditure policy. His alliance with the Church not only provided him with some degree of autonomy with respect to military demands; it also increased the government's share in the tithe. Amendments to the Concordat of 1862, adopted in 1867, raised the government's share from one-third to one-half, and in 1872 it was increased to two-thirds. García Moreno's establishment of a banking system, clearly an important step toward modernizing the economy, also greatly facilitated his use of internal debt to finance his policies. The private banking system was the only source of government loans inasmuch as Ecuador's very poor record with the international financial community had made external financing impossible. At the same time, however, increased recourse to internal debt contributed to strengthening the power of the coastal elites over the Quito government, as most of the country's wealth was concentrated in Guayaquil's financial community.

NOTES

1. Alfred Métraux, *The History of the Incas* (New York: Schocken Books, 1969), p. 93.

2. See John Hemming, *The Conquest of the Incas* (New York: Harcourt Brace Jovanovich, 1970), pp. 345–373. Hemming notes, for example, that "much of the tribute extracted during Inca times was stored for the welfare of the people, particularly during times of crisis" (p. 357).

3. Métraux, *History*, p. 94.

4. Oscar Efren Reyes, *Breve Historia General del Ecuador* (Quito: Duodécima Edicion, n.d.), pp. 142–209.

5. See Hemming, *The Conquest*, pp. 189–346.

6. Ibid., pp. 153–154.

7. Steve J. Stern, *Peru's Indian Peoples and the Challenge of Spanish Conquest: Huamanga to 1640* (Madison: University of Wisconsin Press, 1982), p. 48.

8. John Leddy Phelan, *The Kingdom of Quito in the Seventeenth Century* (Madison: University of Wisconsin Press, 1967), p. 59. Although the corregidor collected the tribute, encomenderos received a share after state and church expenses were paid.

9. Stern, *Peru's Indian Peoples*, pp. 85–89.

10. Nicholas P. Cushner, *Farm and Factory: The Jesuits and the Development of Agrarian Capitalism in Colonial Quito, 1600–1767* (Albany: State University of New York Press, 1982), p. 22.

11. Phelan, *The Kingdom*, p. 59.

12. Cushner, *Farm and Factory*, p. 32.

13. Phelan, *The Kingdom*, pp. 234–239.

14. Cushner, *Farm and Factory*, p. 39.

15. Phelan, *The Kingdom*, p. 66.

16. Ibid., p. 60.

17. Cushner, *Farm and Factory*, pp. 34–40.

18. Phelan, *The Kingdom*, p. 67.

19. John Super, "Partnership and Profit in the Early Andean Trade: The Experiences of Quito Merchants, 1580–1610," *Journal of Latin American Studies*, 2, 2 (1979):273–279.

20. Cushner, *Farm and Factory*, p. 90; and Phelan, *The Kingdom*, pp. 69–70.

21. Michael L. Conniff, "Guayaquil Through Independence: Urban Development in a Colonial System," *The Americas*, 33 (January 1977):385–410.

22. Dora León Borja and Adám Szászdi Nagy, "El Comercio del Cacao de Guayaquil," *Revista de Historia de América*, 57/58, (1964):26–27.

23. Osvaldo Hurtado, *Political Power in Ecuador* (Boulder, Colo.: Westview Press, 1985), p. 31.

24. See James Lockhardt, "Encomienda and Hacienda: The Evolution of the Great Estate in the Spanish Indies," *Hispanic American Historical Review*, 49, 3 (August 1969):411–429.

25. Conniff, "Guayaquil Through Independence," p. 387.

26. Hurtado, *Political Power*, pp. 28, 70.

27. Ibid., p. 31.

28. Linda Alexander Rodríguez, *The Search for Public Policy: Regional Politics and Government Finances in Ecuador, 1830–1940* (Berkeley: University of California Press, 1985), Table 4, p. 60.

29. León Borja and Szászdi Nagy, "El Comercio del Cacao de Guayaquil," p. 49.

30. Michael T. Hammerly, *Historia social y económica de la antigua provincia de Guayaquil, 1763–1842* (Guayaquil: Archivo Histórico del Guayas 1973), ch. 4; cited in Conniff, "Guayaquil Through Independence," p. 400.

31. Conniff, "Guayaquil Through Independence," p. 388.

32. León Borja and Szászdi Nagy, "El Comercio del Cacao de Guayaquil," p. 39.

33. Conniff, "Guayaquil Through Independence," p. 408.

34. Mark Van Aken, "The Lingering Death of the Indian Tribute in Ecuador," *Hispanic American Historical Review*, 61, 3 (1981):445.

35. Roberto Andrade, *Historia del Ecuador* (Guayaquil: Reed and Reed, 1937), Vol. 7, pp. 2528–2529, cited in Frederick B. Pike, *The United States and the Andean Republics* (Cambridge: Harvard University Press, 1977), p. 108.

36. John D. Martz, *Ecuador: Conflicting Political Culture and the Quest for Progress* (Boston: Allyn and Bacon, 1972), p. 63.

37. Peter H. Smith, "The Image of a Dictator: Gabriel García Moreno," *Hispanic American Historical Review*, 45, 1 (February 1965):3.

38. Pike, *The United States*, pp. 113–114.

39. Martz, *Ecuador*, p. 64.

40. Alexander Rodríguez, *The Search*, p. 53. The remainder of this section draws from Rodríguez, pp. 53–87.

41. Ibid., p. 223–227.

42. Ibid., p. 75.

3

Exports and Politics: From Cacao to Bananas

Political and economic change are intertwined in all countries, although the precise nature of their relationship is often difficult to identify. A prosperous economy makes political choices easier: Economic growth means that some groups in society can gain without others having to lose. And as governments (particularly those in existence since the Keynesian revolution of the 1930s) have begun to be held accountable for economic prosperity, their popularity has been enhanced by strong economies.

The linkages between economic performance and political stability are somewhat more transparent in Latin America than in the more industrialized countries of the world.[1] Countries without highly diversified economies, particularly those in which the foreign-trade sector is large and a single primary product commands the major share of total exports, are highly susceptible to fluctuations in the world market. In such economies it is common for the governments to depend heavily on customs duties for revenue. Thus, fluctuations in the world market are rapidly translated into an increase or decrease in the governments' ability to sustain an accustomed level of expenditure. At the same time, the legitimacy of many of the governments in Latin America is established more by their ability to provide concrete benefits to competing interest groups than by their adherence to constitutional procedures. When export earnings are depressed, a government's legitimacy may rapidly erode, thus setting the stage for a nonconstitutional change of power.

Ecuador is a country in which the linkages between economic fluctuations and political stability are particularly well defined. Since the late 1800s, the export sector has been the leading sector of the economy, and a single export—first cacao, then bananas, and now petroleum—has accounted for the lion's share of export earnings.

Governments, not surprisingly, have depended heavily on customs duties for revenues, and their ability to spend has risen and fallen with fluctuations in the world market for Ecuador's principal export. Demands for government expenditures, however, have traditionally been high. Patronage demands in an economy with limited opportunities for employment outside the public sector have resulted in a significant drain on public budgets. Military spending and public-works programs have also consumed public revenues, as Ecuadorian governments have struggled to impose their authority and win support in a nation where regional, not national, interests have predominated.

The ability to satisfy competing demands for public expenditures is by no means the only source of political legitimacy and stability, but for Ecuador it has been an important one. Ecuador's endemic political instability has been closely related to the behavior of its exports. Few ousted presidents, for example, were victims of power struggles alone.[2] Liberal governments used cacao revenues to contain the divergent regional interests while embarking on a program of economic modernization. With the tradition of an active state firmly established by the liberals, Ecuadorians came to expect a certain level of government expenditure, regardless of who was in power. When cacao revenues fell after 1920, liberal governments lost an important source of legitimacy, and the country fell into a period of acute political instability. The growth of banana exports in the late 1940s made possible a renewed period of political stability, which was subsequently undermined by the stagnation of this export.

THE CACAO BOOM

Ecuador might not have been richly endowed with precious metal resources, but cacao was surely a golden export for the country during the late nineteenth and early twentieth centuries. The *pepa de oro*, or golden seed, provided Ecuador with what for the time were fabulous earnings. Rapidly expanding world demand for cacao and ideal growing conditions on the coast had established Ecuador as the world's leading producer by the turn of the century. In 1904, Ecuador exported 28,216 metric tons (27,770 tons), an amount equal to between one-half and one-third of total world production. By 1914, Ecuador's exports of cacao had reached a high of 47,210 metric tons (46,466 tons). Cacao was not Ecuador's only export, but until the late 1920s it was clearly the most important one. From 1885 to 1922, cacao represented between 65 and 70 percent of the value of all exports. Coffee, tagua nuts, "panama" hats, rubber, and gold were also exported, but none of these products ever amounted to more than 15 percent of the value of total exports during the cacao boom.[3]

Ecuador's golden age of prosperity was but an ephemeral one, as by the 1920s a combination of heightened international competition and local devastation of the cacao plantations by disease had brought an abrupt end to the cacao boom. By the 1930s, cacao exports had fallen to between one-third and one-quarter of the level of exports during the earlier part of the century.

Cacao originated in the Americas and was originally consumed as a beverage, particularly in Mexico where the Aztecs were accustomed to preparing a frothy mixture of cacao, water, spices, chile, and corn. By the colonial period, cacao had come to be regarded as a dietary staple by all Mexican social classes. As reported by the procurator of the cabildo of Mexico in 1782, "It is an incontestable truth that in this Kingdom cacao is a basic necessity, so much so it has no substitute."[4]

First introduced to Europe in 1528 by the Spanish as a bitter beverage drunk by the Mexico upper class, cacao had limited appeal. It was not long, however, before the Europeans had learned to combine cacao with sugar, cinnamon, and vanilla—like the lower-class Mexicans before them, who had done so for economic reasons. Drunk in this form, cacao was consumed in increasing amounts by the Europeans. But it was the European development of chocolate products that initiated an explosive growth in popular consumption. In 1828 the Dutch learned to combine cacao with additional cacao butter and sugar to make a chocolate candy; then, in 1860 the Swiss developed the first milk chocolate; and in the 1880s the soda fountain and chocolate bar became items of mass culture and consumption in the United States. From 1870 to 1897, world per capita consumption of coffee increased by 25 percent, tea by 100 percent, and cacao by a staggering 800 percent.[5] Driven by accelerating demand, world cacao exports doubled from 1895 to 1905, only to double again between 1905 and 1915. Given the world's infatuation with chocolate, cacao production became a highly lucrative enterprise. Costs of production were relatively low, world prices were high, and the threat of either natural or synthetic substitutes was remote.

Ecuador's coastal plain, with its relatively rich soil and hot, humid growing conditions, was ideally suited to the cultivation of cacao. Indeed, an indigenous variety of cacao, known as *arriba* for its location up-river or "above" Guayaquil, was already growing in large areas on the coast at the time of the Spanish conquest. Until nearly the end of the nineteenth century, arriba cacao constituted the bulk of Ecuador's cacao exports. It was a rugged, high-yielding

Drying cacao in a Guayaquil
street (circa 1910)

variety of cacao that commanded a premium in European markets
for its strong and bitter flavor.[6]

As world demand for Ecuadorian cacao increased, the existing
plantings of cacao were expanded, primarily along the riverbanks,
which provided the best growing conditions and facilitated the transport of cacao to markets. Much of the coastal plain drained into
rivers that were tributaries of the Guayas River, on which the port
city of Guayaquil is located. River transport kept down the cost of
transporting cacao to market, but it also meant that few roads were
developed as a result of the cacao boom. As late as 1890, no roads
connected Guayaquil with any other city in the country. Despite
increased planting of arriba cacao, by 1880 world demand for cacao
was growing at a faster rate than Ecuadorian production. Further
production increases required the introduction of less hardy, less
desirable, non-native varieties of cacao, particularly from Venezuela
and Trinidad, which could be grown in higher and drier areas of the
coastal plain where the arriba could not be produced. With these
additional plantings, Ecuadorian cacao production continued to increase, although the overall decrease in quality contributed to the
erosion of Ecuador's competitive position in world markets.

Plantation agriculture formed the basis for cacao production.
According to one estimate, approximately 80 percent of the cacao

delivered to Guayaquil and Bahía de Caráquez, another port, was grown on large plantations.[7] After 1889, it was not uncommon to find estates with 28,000 hectares (70,000 acres) and more than 2 million trees. The plantation system of production dominated for two reasons. One concerns the historical fact that large land grants by the municipality of Guayaquil to early colonists resulted in the concentration of land holdings. Probably no more than twenty families dominated cacao production.[8] The second reason derives from the relatively large capital requirements associated with cacao production. Because approximately eight years are required to bring cacao plantings into full production, small producers without access to large amounts of capital had no way of rapidly expanding production, even if they had been able to acquire additional land. At the same time, the capital requirements of cacao production were not so large as to require producers to seek foreign sources of capital. Unlike guano production in Peru or copper production in Chile, cacao production in Ecuador was predominantly an Ecuadorian enterprise, with profits accruing to Ecuadorians rather than foreigners.[9]

The employment of labor on the cacao plantations of the coast offers a sharp contrast to the labor practices on the estates of the sierra. Coastal workers were not as easily subjected to control by landowners as were their counterparts in the sierra. The indigenous populations of the coast were never as numerous as those of the sierra, and, for the most part, they had never been incorporated into the Inca empire. In addition, the feudal patterns of the highlands were not easily replicated on the coast. Slave labor, though important to the Guayaquil shipyards, had never been employed on a large scale in Ecuador. Disease, particularly yellow fever and malaria, also retarded the growth rate of the coastal population. The net effect of these factors was that cacao production, even though its labor requirements were not great, was characterized by a persistent labor shortage throughout the period of expansion.

The absence of a feudal tradition and the relative scarcity of coastal labor led to the establishment of a system of wage labor in cacao production. As a consequence, wages on the coast were considerably higher than those in the sierra. Lois Crawford Roberts estimates that coastal workers earned a daily wage of one sucre; workers in the sierra, in contrast, earned less than half this amount.[10] In these circumstances it was not surprising that the coast, in spite of disease and a radically different climate, was perceived as a mecca by sierra workers.

There is some debate about the size of the migration that actually took place.[11] Most reports suggest that the numbers were large in absolute terms, though limited with respect to the demand for labor from the cacao plantations—an observation reinforced by the persistent shortage of coastal labor. Certainly the long and difficult journey, as well as the system of concertaje (debt peonage) binding workers to their employers in the sierra, restricted the numbers of people who actually made the move. Indeed, a good argument can be made that the concertaje system persisted as long as it did precisely because *serrano* (highland) landowners feared a large-scale migration of their labor force. Although coastal plantation owners also employed concertaje to bind their workers, by the early 1900s most had become convinced that a wage-earning, free labor force was cheaper in the long run.[12] Their efforts to abolish the concertaje system became an additional issue of contention between coastal and sierra landlords.

Whether primarily due to migrants from the sierra or to natural increases from medical advances against diseases such as yellow fever, the coastal population did expand at a relatively rapid rate during the cacao boom. Between 1889 and 1926, the share of Ecuador's population living on the coast rose from 19 percent to 38 percent.[13] Particularly after the collapse of the cacao boom in the 1920s, Guayaquil's population increased at an even faster rate. Large numbers of workers were simply dismissed from failing plantations, the loss of employment leaving most of these wage laborers with little means of subsistence. Some proportion sought land in more remote areas of the coast and some became small rice producers in the Guayas basin, but many moved to Guayaquil in search of employment. The city, which had already grown under the stimulus of the cacao boom, underwent further expansion with the arrival of unemployed cacao workers. Between 1890 and 1930, Guayaquil's population increased by 160 percent, from 45,000 to roughly 116,000 inhabitants.[14]

The period of prosperity brought to Ecuador by the pepa de oro did not last long. World demand continued to rise, though not at the astonishingly rapid rates of earlier decades. But stockpiles accumulated during World War I, and rising world production, particularly that from Brazil and British West Africa, began to depress prices. In 1920, the price of cacao in the New York market was 50 cents; one year later it had fallen to 19 cents.[15] Not only did world prices fall, but disease began to ravage Ecuadorian cacao plantations. Beginning in 1916, the imported Venezuelan variety of cacao tree was attacked by an indigenous fungus known as *monilia*. In 1922, witches' broom, another fungal disease, attacked the native arriba variety of cacao, spreading rapidly across the coastal plantations. No cost-effective means of combating these diseases existed. By 1931, the value of cacao exports as a percentage of total exports had fallen to 22 percent from a high of 77 percent in 1914.[16] By the late 1930s, Ecuadorian cacao production had declined to a meager 2 percent of total world production.[17]

The cacao boom brought unprecedented wealth to Ecuador. Because ownership and control of cacao production largely resided in Ecuadorian hands, not foreign ones, the income from cacao exports accrued to nationals. Yet, despite the large increases in Ecuadorian earnings, the long-term effects of cacao on the Ecuadorian economy and society were not in proportion to these earnings. In large part, this is explained by the nature of cacao production in Ecuador. Because cacao was grown on the coastal plain, where it was easiest to ship the seeds to market by river, there was little economic incentive for private capital to finance the construction of a system of roads. Liberal governments did embark on a program of railroad building, but these lines connected internal markets in which the value of products transported could not offset the very high costs of construction through mountainous terrain. The principal infrastructural improvements directly associated with cacao were those undertaken to modernize port facilities in Guayaquil.

Neither domestic industry nor agriculture received much impetus from cacao. Direct linkages between cacao production and other sectors of the economy were weak; some part of the cacao wealth flowed directly out of the country to support an expatriate community of plantation owners and their families in Paris. The financial sector was the major beneficiary of the cacao boom. The general increase in income and the larger proportion of coastal workers in the money economy provided only a limited stimulus to domestic production. A small number of basic consumer goods began to be produced locally, but the domestic market remained too highly restricted for these industries to become a significant part of the economy. The purchasing power of most of the population remained small, and the desire of the elites for imported rather than locally produced goods, even when the latter were available, was great. The increased demand for basic foodstuffs did stimulate agricultural production in the sierra. But sierra production did not increase sufficiently, nor could it be delivered at a low enough cost to the coast to prevent an increasing dependence on imported basic foodstuffs. Except for textiles, expenditures on imported foodstuffs constituted the largest single share of total import expenditures during the boom years.[18]

Although the cacao boom and its subsequent collapse produced little direct structural change, it did stimulate important demographic and political changes. The population of the coast grew as did that of its major city, Guayaguil. This was a population less subject to traditional forms of control, such as that of the landowner and the church, than its counterparts in the sierra. The nature of cacao production did not create an urban working class, but it did give rise to a class of urban marginal workers, primarily in Guayaquil, who were far more volatile politically than either the urban or the rural workers in the sierra. For example, in November 1922, Ecuador's first mass urban protest erupted in Guayaquil. Initially a protest by railroad workers over declining standards of living due to the cacao crash, it precipitated a series of strikes by other groups of coastal workers and quickly led to broad political demands that went beyond the initial narrow focus on working conditions and wages. Political elites were forced to seek new formulas for the accommodation of demands from this new group of political participants.

The cacao boom also financed the successful liberal revolution of 1895, ending the lengthy period of conservative domination. Wealthy coastal growers and exporters provided the funds needed to raise an army and to install Eloy Alfaro, an experienced soldier and businessman, as its commander.[19] Once in office, Alfaro and other liberal politicians enjoyed large public revenues, raised principally from taxes on the growing volume of imports stimulated by cacao wealth. Government revenues financed an ambitious program of infrastructural development in which roads, bridges, and railroads were built, urban services were enhanced, and electric lighting was introduced. Accordingly, although the production and export of cacao required little accompanying infrastructural development, the wealth so generated allowed the public sector to undertake such projects, thus also reinforcing a growing public sentiment in favor of an active state. Unfortunately, even though this was a time of visible progress, the competing demands of the regions and the military conspired to dilute the effects of government spending. Government efforts to satisfy regional demands for public works, for example, resulted in much duplication of underfinanced and often unfinished projects.

LIBERAL POLITICS

Eloy Alfaro, the shining light of Ecuadorian liberalism, was born on July 25, 1842, in the town of Montecristi in the coastal province of Manabí, to an Ecuadorian mother and a Spanish father. According to most accounts, he became an ardent opponent of the conservatives at an early age.[20] At twenty-two he led a group of revolutionary *montoneros* (guerrilla fighters) in a series of attacks against the government forces of the conservative president García Moreno. Roundly defeated in 1865 he fled to Panama, where he married, dedicated himself to promoting the growing trade in panama hats, and amassed a fortune. Later returning to Ecuador, Alfaro led the montonero faction of the Liberal party in armed opposition to the central government. Named civil and military chief of Manabí and Esmeraldas provinces in 1882, he continued to lead the radical liberal opposition forces until they were defeated by the forces of the progresista Plácido Caamaño in 1884; after that, Alfaro again fled the country for Central America.[21]

By 1892, political developments in Ecuador were considerably more favorable for a liberal victory. The middle ground between liberalism and conservatism that the progresistas had sought to hold was no longer tenable. Long under attack from the conservatives and the Church for its perceived anticlericalism, the Progresista movement lost its liberal support when the government of Luis Cordero, attempting to pacify the clergy, declared that in the event of a conflict between church and state, the former would always take precedence.[22] The conservatives took advantage of liberal disaffection with Cordero's government to organize a National Directorate made up of representatives of both parties to oppose the president. Their opposition, coupled with the implication of the government in an international scandal involving the use of the Ecuadorian flag to cloak the secret sale of a Chilean warship to Japan, forced Cordero's resignation in 1894 and led to the rapid demise of the Progresista party. Vice-President Lucio Salazar, an extreme conservative, assumed the presidency on April 15, 1895.[23] What looked like a reassertion of conservative hegemony, however, proved to be no more than the last effort by an enfeebled Conservative party to recapture the presidency. Liberal montonero groups on the coast intensified their opposition and were joined by warring factions of the Conservative party in the sierra, as armed insurrections erupted across the country in Manabí, Latacunga, Ambato, El Oro, Los Ríos, Guayaquil, and Quito in a pattern reminiscent of earlier periods.[24] Wealthy cacao interests on the coast, which had not looked unfavorably on the progresistas (who by and large had served them well), had no interest in the return to power by the conservatives and saw in the growing anarchy an opportunity for the consolidation of Liberal party hegemony.[25] They threw their support, and money, to Eloy Alfaro, who returned from Nicaragua in 1895 to lead the coastal montoneros to victory over the government forces. Alfaro, like earlier leaders who had assumed power through armed struggle, convened a constituent assembly that wrote a new constitution and elected him president for the period 1897–1901.

Alfaro's victory established a thirty-year period of liberal domination of Ecuadorian politics, but it was by no means an unchallenged domination. Opposition from armed montoneros during any given presidential term, and the problem of succession in a political system where parties were weak and *personalismo* played such an important role, created large demands on scarce government resources—demands both political and financial. At the same time, liberal commitments to secular education and public-works projects placed additional demands on government resources. Even though the large public revenues available during the cacao boom played a pivotal role in maintaining liberal domination, "the liberals ruling Ecuador had to contend with the same forces that had shaped the nation's politics since independence—regionalism, militarism, authoritarianism and personalism."[26]

Eloy Alfaro came to power as a military leader at the head of a revolutionary army, as had so many of his predecessors. As the standard bearer for liberalism, he formally espoused the separation of church and state, the expansion of personal freedoms, and economic development led by a program of public works. These concerns were reflected in the liberal constitution of 1897, a relatively moderate document in the context of the bitter resentment many liberals held toward the authoritarian and theocratic rule of García Moreno. Personal freedoms were enhanced, yet this period was basically a continuation of trends established under earlier progresista governments. And in practice, Alfaro tended toward highly personalistic and authoritarian rule. The sharpest break with past constitutions occurred in its treatment of the church-state question. Yet even here, the document was rather cautious, declaring religious freedom and establishing secular education, yet explicitly confirming Catholicism as the state religion. Notwithstanding this concession, groups of conservative montoneros, with the moral if not financial backing of the Catholic Church, continued to engage Alfaro's forces in armed skirmishes throughout his first term. Conservatives even endeavored to launch an invasion from Colombia, where a proclerical regime was in power; but this effort was defeated when Colombia and Ecuador signed a peace agreement in 1900.[27] The constant military conflict consumed a large share of government resources. In 1900, military expenditures amounted to slightly more than 40 percent of the budget, an amount that, on a per capita basis, was approximately three times that of U.S. military expenditures in the same year.[28]

Apart from his importance in establishing liberal hegemony, Alfaro is recognized for his completion of the Guayaquil-to-Quito railroad, a project begun under García Moreno. Passionately convinced of the importance of railroads to economic progress in Ecuador, Alfaro contracted with the American Archer Harman to authorize the formation of the Guayaquil and Quito Railway Company in 1897. The contract was the object of intense domestic criticism, primarily directed against the terms under which the government had floated bonds to finance the project. With the completion of the railroad in 1908, however, public criticism turned to praise, even though the railroad "did not unlock national treasures as in the two sister republics [Peru and Bolivia] for Ecuador's highland interior lacked mineral resources."[29] Indeed, the inability of the railroad to earn a profit resulted in its sale to the Ecuadorian government in 1924.[30] Notwithstanding this experience, railroads continued to be viewed as a key to economic progress throughout the liberal period. Nor were Ecuadorian liberals alone in this perception, as a fever of railroad construction was sweeping through Latin America. In 1840, no railroad track existed in Latin America; by 1930, just under 95,000 kilometers (59,000 miles) had been laid.[31]

By the end of Alfaro's first term in 1901, although armed opposition from the conservatives continued, the liberals were sufficiently in control that the principal problem of succession had become one of agreeing on which liberal candidate would be installed as president. Alfaro's choice, the successful candidate, was Leonidas Plaza, a very capable military leader who had fought with Alfaro against the conservatives and who had occupied important civilian posts following the liberal victory. Alfaro chose Plaza because the latter was acceptable to the military and, most important, because Alfaro believed he could control Plaza more effectively than he could the other military candidate, Manuel Antonio Franco, an extreme anticlerical. At the last minute, however, Alfaro realized that he would not be able to control Plaza either (the latter had begun to demonstrate his own independence from Alfaro), and he withdrew his support. The rift between the two men contributed to growing divisions among the liberals. From 1901 to 1916 the liberal governments were preoccupied with containing armed insurrections from within their own parties, and the conservatives gradually abandoned armed struggle for electoral politics and a degree of accommodation with the ruling liberals.

Plaza governed from 1901 to 1905, a period characterized by his commitment to progressive policies. A strong military leader, he nevertheless came to believe, unlike Alfaro, that "personalism and authoritarianism hindered Ecuador's modernization" and sought to strengthen political institutions and to expand civil liberties, particularly freedom of the press.[32] At the end of his first term, Plaza supervised the installation of a civilian president, Lizardo García, a Guayaquil merchant and banker who had become a vocal opponent of Alfaro. As García commented on one occasion, "if there is truly a schism in Ecuadorian politics, it is between alfarismo and the nation's honorable men."[33] Not surprisingly, the selection of García was bitterly opposed by Alfaro, who once again assumed power at the head of an insurrectionary army.

In 1906 Alfaro again convened a constituent assembly that produced a new constitution—"the most advanced ever in terms of the number and degree of protection of basic guarantees, and the first to proscribe the intervention of the church in secular affairs"—and elected him to a second term (1907–1911).[34] But Alfaro was under heavy attack from both liberals and conservatives. In spite of his recourse to large public revenues, "owing largely to the continuing bitterness of the doctrinal issue and his own disregard of constitutional procedures, Alfaro had not been able to legitimize his two administrations on the basis of material accomplishments."[35] Large demands for military expenditures also undoubtedly limited his ability to use public-works expenditures to win public favor.

Although increasingly discredited, Alfaro served out his term and managed to install Emilio Estrada, a leading coastal businessman, as the next president. But by this time the liberals were split into several irreconcilable camps. With Estrada's untimely death in 1911, only months after his inauguration, the country erupted into a bloody civil war that lasted five years. Various factions were drawn into the fighting, but the principal battles were waged between rebel forces led by Eloy Alfaro and the government's forces led by Leonidas Plaza and his second in command, General Julio Andrade. Alfaro's forces were defeated in bitter fighting that, during January 1912 alone, left more than 3,000 men dead.[36] Imprisoned by the government's forces, Alfaro and other rebel leaders were attacked by angry mobs, dragged from their cells, and brutally murdered.[37] Without Alfaro, the struggle for the presidency was reduced to one between the liberals Plaza and Andrade. The latter was killed by an unknown assassin, and Plaza assumed the presidency for his second term (1912–1916).

Plaza's second term was characterized by a continuation of the progressive policies that had marked his first term, in spite of constant civil war among the liberal factions. He embarked on an extraordinarily ambitious campaign of railroad construction, partly out of conviction and partly as a pragmatic response to competing regional demands. By 1922 no fewer than twenty-one railroads were specified in the national budget; very few of these were ever completed, however.[38] Public-works and military expenses drained the public treasury at a time when cacao revenues were beginning to fall. Rising public deficits forced Plaza and subsequent liberal governments to turn increasingly to the Guayaquil banks for loans, a practice begun under García Moreno and institutionalized by Eloy Alfaro. Public opinion began to turn against Plaza, with the sierra in particular chafing under what it perceived as long years of coastal domination and the growing control of coastal banks over national affairs. Yet Plaza managed to engineer an orderly process of succession in which three civilian presidents succeeded one another in the period 1916–1925.

THE LIBERAL STATE

Liberal governments confirmed the tradition of the active state. As with their predecessors, the ability of liberals to implement their programs was shaped by the same forces that had shaped Ecuadorian politics since independence: regionalism, militarism, and the growing dependence of the state on a volatile export sector for revenue. Unlike their predecessors, liberal governments came into power on the heels of the cacao boom. They did more than earlier governments—the period was a time of visible progress—but, aside from the religious issue, the pattern of politics did not change significantly.

The liberals came into power in a revolution financed in large part by cacao revenues. Subsequently, liberal governments used revenues derived from the cacao boom to finance an ambitious program of public-works expenditures that, like earlier governments, they perceived to be a cornerstone for economic progress. In spite of unprecedentedly large public-sector revenues, however, the liberal governments faced both larger demands for expenditures and more limited control over revenues than had been the case for earlier governments. While cacao exports continued to rise, the liberals were able to satisfy competing demands and maintain the legitimacy of their governments. But with the economic crisis caused by the decline in cacao exports, the liberal governments were forced to turn increasingly to Guayaquil banks for loans to finance their governments. The legitimacy of these governments was eroded both by their inability to continue to meet expenditure demands and by the widespread perception that control of the nation's destiny had in effect passed from elected officials to these banks.

Ecuadorian liberals subscribed to a far more active role for the state than would have been suggested by the principles of classical liberalism, as did their counterparts elsewhere in Latin America. As one Ecuadorian liberal commented, "I will make a confession that until now I have not dared to make. . . . We still require the tutelage of the wise man . . . the sword in one hand, the torch of civilization in the other."[39] Osvaldo Hurtado noted that "the Liberals, once they achieved power, were transformed into defenders of strong central authority."[40] Indeed, to a very considerable extent, the circumstances confronting any government in this period demanded a strong central authority.

Liberal governments, like their predecessors, were obliged to allocate a large share of the public budget to military expenditures, both to maintain the loyalty of that institution and to pay for the costs of nearly incessant civil strife. From 1895 to 1920, military expenditures consumed an average of 27 percent of the budget, rising as high as 43 percent in some years.[41] The secularization of the state also increased expenditure demands as government replaced the Church as a provider of public works, public welfare, and investment capital.[42] Debt service, particularly during the later years of the liberal period, accounted for a large share of the budget, occasionally as much as 40 percent. Growing public acceptance of an active state also placed increasing demands on the budget. Particularly in Quito, where the local economy remained relatively stagnant, government became an increasingly important source of employment. At the same time, the need to satisfy regional demands in order to sustain support for the national government led to the adoption of far more projects than were rationally desirable or could be accommodated within the budget. Not surprisingly, even given the large revenues enjoyed by liberal governments, a "legacy of liberal governments remained one of uncompleted public works." In 1905, for example, only 55 of 346 authorized public-works projects were under construction; the remainder were abandoned or never begun.[43]

One consequence of large government revenues and large demands for public expenditures was the early emergence of a large public sector in Ecuador. By 1913, in comparison with other Latin American countries with approximately similar foreign trade earnings per capita, public expenditures in Ecuador on a per capita basis were largest. As Dana Munro, foreign trade adviser to the U.S. State Department, wrote in 1920, "There appears to be no good reason why Ecuador should spend so much more than her neighbors. . . . The government appears to assign much larger sums of money to purely local propositions than is usual even in other Latin American countries."[44]

The rapid decentralization of the public sector that occurred in reaction to García Moreno's highly centralized presidencies frustrated efforts by liberals to rationalize and control public expenditures. Public-sector decentralization during the progressive period had been particularly forceful. It was undertaken partly as an effort to prevent abuses of authority by autocratic executives such as García Moreno, partly as a way to ensure some fiscal stability in a country torn by civil war, and partly as a regional effort to appropriate spending authority from the executive. The two principal vehicles for public-sector decentralization were the creation of autonomous public agencies and the earmarking of public revenues for particular projects. In 1900, for example, the national government collected 8,137,161 sucres; but of these, 4,837,692, or 60 percent, were not subject to budgetary control. In 1905, 84 autonomous juntas, "each with its separate organization and bureaucracy, administered the decentralized projects." The minister of the treasury complained in 1922 that "patriotism consists in subordinating national interests of the Republic to the selfish aspirations of the regions for an illusory material progress."[45] In spite of repeated efforts by the liberals to regain control of the budget, in 1924 more than 80 percent of public revenues were decentralized.[46]

Liberal governments were financed largely through customs duties and private bank loans. During the period 1895–1925, customs duties supplied between 53 and 91 percent of public revenues raised from sources other than borrowing. Ecuadorian elites demonstrated a profound resistance to other types of taxes, and given the virtual absence of a middle class, as well as the large proportion of the population living on the fringes of the market economy, there were few alternative sources of revenue. The liberals experimented briefly with ways of taxing alcohol production, as had earlier governments; but rather than raising significant additional revenues, they succeeded only in further antagonizing large sectors of the sierra elite for whom alcohol was an important source of income.

Not surprisingly, the fortunes of the liberal governments were intimately linked to the performance of cacao exports. As long as export earnings remained high, liberal governments could accommodate competing demands for expenditures from the military and the regions, maintaining their legitimacy through essentially "pork-barrel" politics. Even when export earnings were high, however, bank loans customarily financed part of the total government expenditures. The extreme fiscal decentralization and the consequent loss of budgetary control, combined with frequent unanticipated military demands, made budget deficits a chronic problem. Ecuador's poor reputation in international credit markets, a result of frequent repudiation of its foreign debt, restricted the possibilities for foreign borrowing. As a consequence, liberal governments did what all Ecuadorian governments had done since García Moreno: They turned repeatedly to domestic banks for loans. Between 1869 and 1925, bank loans had financed part of government expenditures in all but six of those years.[47]

The collapse of the cacao boom in 1920 trapped liberal governments between falling revenues from customs duties and a public grown accustomed to a high level of expenditures. Efforts to increase revenues by developing alternative taxes or by reforming the existing inefficient system of tax administration found no political support, and liberal governments turned to the Guayaquil banks on an unprecedented scale. Internal public debt doubled between 1920 and 1925.[48] Most of the private bank debt was concentrated in a single bank, the Banco Comercial y Agrícola, which consequently gained large political influence.

Bank loans ensured that government revenues did not fall, but as a result of accelerating inflation and devaluation of the sucre, government expenditures fell sharply in real terms.[49] Hence the strategy of "pork-barrel" politics became increasingly ineffective as liberal governments desperately multiplied the number of public-works projects but found they could not fund most of them. With the discrediting of the liberal governments came widespread support for the young military officers who took power in a bloodless coup on July 9, 1925.

MILITARY INTERVENTION AND ECONOMIC STAGNATION

The coup of July 9, 1925, marked the emergence of the Ecuadorian military as an institutional political actor. Although the military had had a long history of political involvement prior to this date, it had served largely as the vehicle by which the personal political ambitions of its leaders were realized. Indeed, with the exception of García Moreno, every major political leader in the period 1830–1916 was a military officer. It was military force that created the republic and military force that maintained this republic during the immediate postindependence period. Ecuador was a country with little sense of national identity, a country in which local and regional interests predominated. National governments were continually faced with civil war, constantly obliged to rely on force rather than legitimacy to establish their claims to authority. Consequently, civilian and military spheres of influence were not well differentiated, and there was little sense of an institutional identity within the military. The years from 1830 to 1925 marked an age of personal, not institutional, military power. The military *caudillos* (autocratic leaders) "were political and military figures at the same time, and there is little evidence of military self-awareness or self-identification."[50]

After 1916 the nature of military involvement in politics changed as the age of the military caudillo drew to an end and the military began to view itself in institutional terms. At the same time, the military became increasingly subordinated to civilian control. Eloy Alfaro and his successor, Leonidas Plaza, initiated efforts to professionalize the military. Under liberal governments, the Escuela Militar for training officers was established in Quito in 1901, military laws were codified, battlefield promotions were prohibited, and soldiers were banned from political parties or clubs.[51] Although the ensuing military struggles between Alfaro and Plaza limited the immediate effectiveness of such reforms, their establishment nevertheless marked the beginning of a growing institutionalization of the military. In particular, the establishment of the Escuela Militar, from which an increasing proportion of officers were drawn, began to change the traditional pattern of military recruitment. No longer were officers drawn primarily from the upper class; instead, the middle class became the principal source for recruitment for the Ecuadorian officer corps.[52] Though more professional, the Ecuadorian officer corps ceased to regard itself as socially equal to the country's politicians, most of whom came from the upper and upper-middle classes. In addition, except for a brief period under Leonidas Plaza when officers from the coast loyal to him were promoted, the officer corps was drawn overwhelmingly from the sierra. For example, more than 90 percent of the 1918 class at the Escuela Militar came from the sierra.[53]

Their sierra origins made the younger military officers receptive to charges that liberal governments had mortgaged the nation to the coastal banking elites. Their backgrounds in the economically vulnerable middle class made them sympathetic to arguments that government bore some responsibility for the social and economic dislocation that followed the collapse of the cacao boom. Both of these concerns were exploited by two sierra publications: the socialist newspaper, *La Antorcha*, and another newspaper primarily concerned with military reform and read principally by the military, *El Abanderado*. In late 1924, these papers cooperated to launch "a campaign to convince the young officers that only they could save the country from the impending crisis."[54]

By this time, support for a coup was fairly widespread, extending even to such coastal elites as the importers, who were angry at the government's devaluation policies. The coup of July 9, 1925, began in Guayaquil with the arrest of the manager of the Banco Comercial y Agrícola, Francisco Urbina Jado (widely regarded as the man to whom national government had sold its soul), but quickly shifted to Quito. However idealistic the young officers may have been about promoting national concerns over regional interests, power was rapidly transferred to older officers and sierra politicians, who used the coup to shift power from the coast back to the highlands.

As an expression of its ambivalent attitude toward military rule and its subordination to civilian politicians, the military first appointed two successive civilian-dominated juntas and then, in March 1926, installed Isidro Ayora, rector of the Central University and minister of social welfare, as provisional president. According to one Ecuadorian historian, Ayora agreed to accept the position on the condition that the military would not intervene—a provision that, in effect, guaranteed him dictatorial powers.[55] He had served as provisional president for three years when he convened a constituent assembly that, in the time-honored Ecuadorian tradition, drafted the country's thirteenth constitution and elected him president.

Significant reforms were legislated during the period from 1925 to 1931, following the 1925 coup. Not surprisingly, however, many of these efforts quickly fell victim to traditional patterns of Ecuadorian politics. Financial reform occupied first place on the junta's agenda. Without any doubt, change in this area was urgently needed. Indeed, the Guayaquil financial community had been pressing unsuccessfully for reforms since the 1920s. The measures adopted under the junta were significant and long overdue. However, contrary to the measures that the Guayaquil bankers had advocated, the changes were used in such a way as to break the financial hegemony of the coastal banks and to shift the locus of financial power to Quito.[56] For example, in 1927 a central bank, with a headquarters in Quito and a branch in Guayaquil, was created and capitalized with the gold reserves of a now much-enfeebled private banking system. The private banks received only partial payment for their gold reserves, a move that ensured the destruction of the Banco Comercial y Agrícola. Other financial legislation included the creation of the office of superintendent of banks, a return to the gold standard, and a restructuring of the tax system. These reforms increased the financial power of Quito relative to Guayaquil, thus also greatly expanding government revenues and increasing the degree of centralization in their collection.

Not surprisingly, the period following the July revolution was one of intense regional conflict. The collapse of the cacao boom had weakened the power of the coastal elites and facilitated the rise to power of sierra interests. Enjoying the increase in public revenues made possible by the tax reforms, post-1925 governments did what Ecuadorian governments had always done to contain regional conflict: They embarked on a large program of public-works projects. Public-works expenditures, only 9.5 percent of national government expenditures in 1923, had risen to 22 percent by 1929.[57] Guayaquil, the seat of resistance against the government, received a large share of these expenditures as Isidro Ayora sought to maintain the loyalty of the region.[58] Still, the coast complained bitterly that progress in the highlands was being made possible only through the impoverishment of the coastal economy, the source of most public revenue. Postcoup governments also greatly expanded the national bureaucracy in an effort to provide jobs for the Quito professional class. As Ecuadorian historian Oscar Efren Reyes has noted, "Jobs were created without function, or with subdivided functions . . . [and] salaries for the upper bureaucracy were tripled or quadrupled."[59]

Postcoup governments also sought, or were obliged, to accommodate regional interests in other ways. The 1929 constitution granted congress, the principal exponent of regional interests, such power over the executive that no president could effectively govern. Any member of congress could call for a vote of no confidence against any government minister and, if successful, force that minister's resignation.[60] In addition, a senate was created that provided for both regional and functional representation, with the latter including members from both the coast and the sierra for each major interest group. For example, agricultural interests had two senators, one from the coast and one from the sierra.

Social reforms also figured into the agenda of the governments during the 1925–1931 period. The military officers who carried out the coup, though moved to action primarily by their desire to limit the power of coastal banking interests over the national government, were also concerned with implementing policies designed to enlarge the state's responsibility for disadvantaged groups in Ecuadorian society. Nor was the military alone in this concern. Lower- and middle-class groups actively demanded attention, and labor unrest reached unprecedented levels. Indeed, the 1922 strike, which virtually paralyzed Guayaquil, and a campesino uprising around the highland city of Ambato a year later (both of which were brutally repressed by government forces) confronted the country's elites with the need for new political solutions. In 1923, the Liberal party adopted a platform it described as "socialist," calling for progressive labor legislation, affordable housing, profit sharing, rural medical facilities, social security, and land reform.[61] Two years later, the conservatives met to issue a strikingly similar platform. Many of these social concerns were written into law following the 1925 coup and established as constitutional rights in the 1929 constitution. But the immediate practical significance of this legislation was limited. In a pattern similar to that experienced with financial reform, these social reforms, while important and well intentioned, more successfully served to consolidate elite power at a time of social unrest than to provide widespread benefits to the lower class or to significantly increase their political participation.

THE INTERREGNUM

Initial enthusiasm for the policy changes introduced by the 1925 coup and institutionalized under Isidro Ayora fell victim to growing economic dislocation by the end of the decade. Never recovered from the collapse of the cacao boom, the Ecuadorian economy was dealt another blow by the collapse of world markets during the Great Depression. The expansion of government revenues following reform of the tax system was increasingly perceived to be at the expense not only of the coast but also of an increasingly impoverished nation. The urban lower class was particularly discontent as one of the tax reforms had raised taxes on imported items destined for general consumption, such as cotton textiles, lard, and wheat flour.[62] As long as government revenues remained high, public-works programs and expanded employment opportunities could counteract this discontent. But as exports fell and government revenues correspondingly declined, it became increasingly difficult to buy off discontent. In an effort to maintain expenditures, the government turned to the new central bank for loans. The resulting expansion of the money supply during this period set off "one of the worst inflations experienced by any American nation," and the cost of living rose sharply.[63] Popular and regional discontent forced Isidro Ayora's resignation in 1931, ushering in a seventeen-year period of acute political instability.

Ecuador's troubles were compounded in 1941, when Peruvian troops marched into Ecuador, seizing an area of the oriente approximately equal to one-half of what Ecuador then claimed as national territory and depriving the nation of a port on the Amazon River. Dispute over the territory in question resulted largely from uncertainty as to the limits of the colonial territorial divisions. Ecuador claimed boundaries established by an 1830 treaty between Gran Colombia and Peru; the latter subscribed to an 1802 agreement between the Spanish crown and the Viceroyalty of Peru.[64] In 1942, after a swift victory by superior Peruvian forces over the outnumbered and ill-equipped Ecuadorian army, the two countries signed the Protocol of Rio de Janeiro, ratifying Peru's claim to the contested territory.

The decision dealt a devastating blow to the morale of the Ecuadorians, for whom the Amazon held a special place in the national consciousness. Ever since Francisco de Orellana's epic journey from

Quito to the Amazon River in 1541, the Ecuadorians had looked east with expectations for fulfillment of the region's promise; during the 1930s, Shell Petroleum Company's explorations in the oriente had fueled the Ecuadorians' dreams of Amazonian riches. In this context, it is hardly surprising that the loss of the contested Amazon territory contributed importantly to the overthrow of President Arroyo del Río in 1944 and that demands for its restitution became a perennial theme of Ecuadorian political debate.[65]

Presidents who came into power during the turbulent period following Isidro Ayora's resignation attempted to deal with the economic crisis as best they could but were severely constrained in their efforts by low government revenues and the power of an increasingly obstructionist congress. Government policy took two directions. First, further social legislation was introduced in an effort to reduce social tension. Second, the government also experimented with various economic policies, such as exchange controls and protectionist measures, intended to reduce Ecuador's dependence on imports and to stimulate domestic production.

This policy of protected industrialization, known as import-substitution industrialization, was widely adopted by Latin American countries during the period of economic isolation experienced in the 1930s and 1940s. Its implementation in Ecuador, however, did little to stimulate domestic production, and the import restrictions cut sharply into government revenues. Ecuador was far less industrialized prior to the 1930s than countries such as Argentina or Chile, where import-substitution industrialization policies were more successful. The cacao boom had provided little stimulus to domestic industrialization. Some early production of food and beverages had been developed on the coast by importers, and some highland landowners had invested in modern textile mills. But these industries were secondary sources of income for their owners and supplied a highly restricted domestic market that was further contracted during the 1930s and 1940s.[66] Thus, it is not surprising that efforts to promote domestic industrialization in Ecuador during that period had little effect. Instead, the country turned to a search for an export crop to replace the golden cacao seed. It found its "El Dorado" in bananas, and this green gold financed an unrivaled period of economic expansion.

THE BANANA BOOM

Prior to 1934, banana exports from Ecuador were insignificant both as a share of total exports and as a share of world production.

Between 1910 and 1933, the value of banana exports, most of which were destined for markets in Chile and Peru, never exceeded 1 percent of the value of total exports. In 1933 the United Fruit Company, with its eye on the U.S. market, acquired an old cacao plantation, Tenguel, formerly one of the largest producers but virtually abandoned following the collapse of the cacao boom, and began to produce and market Ecuadorian bananas. Banana exports rose briefly during the depression years, though never to very significant levels; they then fell as the overseas market collapsed with the outbreak of World War II. Beginning in 1947, however, supply constraints in the traditional banana-producing areas caused by disease and natural disasters, as well as large increases in demand, particularly from the European countries, combined to create a powerful stimulus for the expansion of Ecuadorian production. From the end of World War II to 1955, the volume of banana exports from the traditional producing countries in Central America and the Caribbean remained relatively constant while total world import demand grew by 35 percent. Given the relative constancy of imports by the United States, the largest consuming country, most of the increase in world demand came from the European market, where, over the same period, imports increased by 195 percent. Ecuadorian banana exports rose from 68,944 metric tons (67,858 tons) in 1947 to 612,615 metric tons (602,968 tons) in 1955—a staggering 800 percent that filled the gap between rising European consumption and flat Central American production.[67]

Ecuador was ideally suited to replace Central America and the Caribbean as a major supplier of bananas. Idle land on the coast previously dedicated to cacao production was rapidly converted to bananas, and government-sponsored programs of colonization opened up new areas of the coast to banana production. The soil and climate were excellent, and the coastal zone was relatively free of the infestations—Sigatoka Leaf Spot and Panama disease—that had devastated the Central American and Caribbean region plantations in the late 1930s and early 1950s, respectively. In addition, the country's equatorial location protected the banana plants from the tropical storms that frequently laid waste to plantations in Central America and the Caribbean.[68] During the early years of the banana boom, while most plantings occupied former cacao lands, the same system of river transportation that had brought cacao to market could be used for bananas. Initially constrained by the absence of roads, the expansion of production into previously uncultivated areas was facilitated by a government-sponsored road-construction program. The only significant disadvantage faced by Ecuadorian producers—namely, their relatively higher costs of transportation to markets in the United

States and Europe—was more than offset by higher production costs on the Central American and Caribbean plantations. In 1958, for example, the cost per pound of harvested bananas in Ecuador was 70 percent less than that in Central America.[69]

Ecuador appeared to have struck it rich again with an export that, replacing the failed promise of the *pepa de oro*, financed a renewed period of economic prosperity and underwrote an unprecedented fifteen-year period of political stability. In only five years, Ecuador was transformed from an insignificant exporter of bananas into the world's largest supplier (a position it maintained until 1983, when severe flooding caused by a temporary shift in the El Niño ocean current temporarily disrupted production). By 1960, Ecuadorian banana exports accounted for nearly 30 percent of the value of total world exports, and their importance to the domestic economy began to rival that of cacao.[70] Bananas rapidly displaced other exports, providing more than 60 percent of total Ecuadorian export earnings during the early 1960s. In the ten-year period from 1947 to 1957, gross domestic product in constant sucres grew at an average annual rate of 5.3 percent.[71] During the same period, government income also increased as customs duties again rose to account for around 50 percent of national government income.[72]

Although both cacao and bananas stimulated periods of rapid economic growth, there were important differences between the two products in the way the booming export sector was linked to other areas of the economy. Unlike cacao, banana production in Ecuador was not plantation based. Although Ecuador had its large producers, such as the United Fruit operation at Tenguel, these were not on the grand scale of the cacao plantations, nor did they ever account for such a large share of total exports. United Fruit's acreage in bananas, for example, represented less than 2.5 percent of the country's total banana acreage; its exports from company-owned land did not exceed 5 percent of Ecuador's total banana exports.[73] Producers with holdings in excess of 500 hectares (1,200 acres) accounted for 1 percent of the farms and 15 percent of the land in banana production.[74] These large producers controlled about 20 percent of the country's exportable production.[75] Small- to medium-sized farms predominated, particularly in the newly colonized areas around Santo Domingo where large areas of virgin jungle had been opened to cultivation. In 1965, 88 percent of banana farms were less than 100 hectares (250 acres) in size, controlling just under 50 percent of the land in banana production.[76] Because of the relatively large number of smaller producers, income from the banana boom, though still concentrated in relatively few hands, was not nearly as concentrated as it had been during the cacao boom.

Banana production demanded much greater infrastructural development than cacao production. Bananas, unlike cacao, are harvested throughout the year and are sufficiently perishable that they cannot be stored for longer than very short periods of time. The successful expansion of banana exports required a reliable, all-season system of transportation. River transportation, the means by which most cacao had traditionally reached market, was neither sufficiently reliable nor sufficiently extensive to accommodate the growth of banana exports. In Central America, where foreign producers owned and operated extensive plantations, the necessary infrastructural development was typically financed by the producers themselves. In contrast, foreign producers played a relatively minor role in Ecuador's banana boom. In addition to United Fruit's operations at Tenguel, there were several foreign-owned operations, but, collectively, foreign-owned production probably accounted for less than 15 percent of total exportable production.[77] Without private foreign investment, the infrastructural development essential to the expansion of the banana industry was undertaken by the public sector. Extensive development of roads and ports, begun during the Galo Plaza administration (1948–1952), was financed largely through loans from the United States and the World Bank. Between 1944 and 1967, for example, 3,500 kilometers (2,175 miles) were added to the road system—an increase of almost 50 percent.[78] Liberal credit was also made available to banana producers through the government's Banco de Fomento. Between 1948 and 1951, nearly 1,000 colonists in the Santo Domingo and Esmeraldas areas received loans financing the planting of some 10,000 hectares (25,000 acres) of new land in bananas.[79] Indicative of the small-producer orientation, no single loan was greater than 50,000 sucres (roughly US$3,700).[80]

Both the nature of banana production and the extent of government direction ensured that the impact of the banana export boom on the Ecuadorian economy and society was far greater than had been the case during the cacao boom. The much greater proportion of smaller producers allowed for an increased diffusion of banana income beyond the coastal elites to other sectors of the society. Consumption demands from the small but growing middle class provided a stimulus to domestic agricultural production, which was concentrated in the sierra. Between 1950 and 1952, agricultural production for domestic consumption rose by 25 percent.[81] Politics became less conflictual. Government expenditures continued to play an important political role in mediating among regional demands for expenditures, but, at least during the early 1950s, relatively large public revenues reduced the level of conflict. Military spending, such a large proportion of the government budget during the liberal period during which civil wars were repeatedly erupting, was sharply reduced, thus allowing the governments greater flexibility to respond to expenditure demands. This, and the increased availability of foreign capital, allowed for the successful undertaking of an extensive public program of infrastructural development, which opened up vast new areas to production.

The growth of banana exports also stimulated large population shifts from the sierra to the coast. The flow of migrants from the highlands, hindered during the cacao boom by legal restrictions and sharply reduced by the lack of employment following its collapse, resumed during the banana boom in even larger numbers. Between 1942 and 1962, the population of Ecuador increased by 45 percent, but the population of the coast increased by more than 100 percent. Migration also took place within the coast, in response to both the increased economic growth of Guayaquil and the later export instability, which displaced numerous small producers. The population of Guayas province, in which the city of Guayaquil is located, increased by 135 percent.[82] And between 1930 and 1962, Guayaquil's population overall increased by 340 percent, from 116,047 to 507,000 inhabitants.[83] As late as 1975, at least 60 percent of Guayaquil's population consisted of first-generation immigrants.[84] Hence the coast had not only become the locus of economic power in Ecuador; it was also rapidly becoming the most populated region—a change that held important electoral implications.

Despite these differences between the cacao and banana booms, by the mid-1950s there were signs that banana exports might repeat the pattern of collapse established earlier by cacao. Both disease and renewed competition from Central American producers threatened to bring an abrupt end to the period of banana-led prosperity. The Sigatoka leaf blight had reached epidemic proportions in the Esmeraldas area by 1952 and began to spread south, and Panama disease began to make inroads into the banana-producing areas in the southern part of the country. Unlike the diseases that had devastated the cacao plantations, however, those afflicting the banana plant merely slowed the rate of growth of export volume from 25 percent per year between 1950 and 1955 to 12 percent per year between 1955 and 1960, but they did not seriously reduce banana exports except during brief periods.[85] Government-sponsored spraying programs proved to be cost effective against Sigatoka. No controls were available for Panama disease, but, in the short run, the availability of disease-free land in other areas of the coast and the short maturation period of the banana plant (eleven months as opposed to five to seven years for cacao) allowed for rapid production shifts. In the longer run, banana growers were able to take advantage of the new Cavendish varieties of banana, which were resistant to Panama disease.

Ecuador's banana prosperity was more seriously affected by world market conditions than by disease. Rising banana exports from the recovering Central American producers combined with relatively sluggish world demand in the latter half of the 1950s to depress world market prices for Ecuadorian bananas, thus sharply slowing the rate of growth of export earnings.[86] The saturation of the world market for bananas also increased revenue instability inasmuch as production changes rapidly translated into price fluctuations.[87] Accustomed to a steady diet of rapidly growing export earnings, the Ecuadorian economy did not adjust easily to the period of relative stagnation and increased instability that set in after 1955. The rate of economic growth slowed; import demands outraced the earning ability of exports, leading to balance-of-payments problems; and government revenues were constrained.

THE POLITICS OF PROSPERITY

Although the political changes accompanying the banana boom were perhaps not as immediately dramatic as the cacao-financed liberal revolution, bananas did far more than just underwrite a brief period of political stability. The structural and demographic changes brought about by the banana boom profoundly influenced subsequent political development in ways that did not occur following the cacao boom.

The demise of Liberal party hegemony after 1925 ushered in a period of acute political instability. Both the liberals and the conservatives were discredited, and the economic stagnation following the collapse of the cacao boom heightened tensions among regional elites. New political contenders, such as the urban marginal workers and public-sector employees, though still small in numbers, contributed to an increase in the volatility of politics. In an economy with limited opportunities for mobility in the private sector, the state became an increasingly valuable prize, offering opportunities for economic gain not available elsewhere. And the limited revenues accessible to the state exacerbated political conflict by greatly restricting its ability to satisfy all those who made demands for public expenditures. It was not surprising that in the twenty-three years between 1925 and 1948 there were twenty-seven governments, for an average of one president every ten months. Of the total, "only three originated in direct popular (albeit fraudulent) elections; twelve were made up of interim presidents, . . . eight were dictatorships, and four were elected by constituent assembly."[88]

Banana boom prosperity established the conditions for a twelve-year period of political stability, a period all the more remarkable by contrast to the turbulent years preceding it. In 1948 Galo Plaza Lasso, son of the former liberal president Leonidas Plaza, was elected president in a closely contested election. Committed to modernizing the Ecuadorian economy through a program of state-led development, Galo Plaza saw the strengthening of constitutional government as a prerequisite to economic modernization. In many ways he was ideally suited to the task. The son of an illustrious liberal, Plaza also had family ties to one of the most influential sierra families. Beyond this, he actively sought to encourage political stability by incorporating all the major political groups into his cabinet. Educated in the United States, and Ecuador's ambassador to that country from 1944 to 1946, he used his personal connections to secure U.S. assistance in developing the banana industry. His demonstration of leadership following a series of natural disasters, including the worst earthquake in Ecuador's history, helped establish his popularity. He remained aloof from partisan politics despite his distaste for Ecuador's emerging populism and his personal animosity toward its two leaders. However, Plaza's successful completion of his four-year term and the ensuing democratic transition—the first in twenty-eight years—was, as he readily acknowledged, made possible more by the banana boom than by his own personal qualities.[89]

Galo Plaza was followed in office by two constitutionally elected presidents, José María Velasco Ibarra and Camilo Ponce Enríquez. Both presidents completed their four-year terms, leading observers to make "confident predictions that 'Ecuador had overcome the stage of coup d'états and military intervention in politics'—predictions belied by the events of the next six years."[90] With the stagnation of the export boom in the latter half of the 1950s, Ecuadorian politics reverted to a familiar pattern of instability. Yet with the economic and social changes accompanying the growth of the export sector, some new ingredients were added to the traditional recipe for instability. In particular, the loss of legitimacy by both the liberal and the conservative parties, the failure of strong alternative parties to emerge, and the rising (though still very low) levels of political participation changed the traditional character of politics. As one observer has commented:

Given the continuing debility of the country's political institutions in the face of rising levels of political participation and the general absence of elite or mass belief in the legitimacy of the political system, the stability of that system varied according to the vagaries of the international market for primary products.[91]

In short, the cacao and banana booms had set the stage for the emergence of populism in Ecuador. In contrast to what had occurred in other more advanced countries of Latin America, where populist movements had developed out of the structural changes accompanying import-substitution industrialization, Ecuadorian populism emerged from the economic and demographic changes initiated by cacao and completed by bananas.[92]

NOTES

1. Georg Maier, "Presidential Succession in Ecuador, 1830–1970," *Journal of Interamerican Studies and World Affairs*, 13, 3–4 (July-October 1971):490.

2. For an examination of the relationship between economic fluctuations and political instability in Latin America, see Warren Dean, "Latin American Golpes and Economic Fluctuations, 1823–1966," *Social Science Quarterly*, 51, 1 (June 1970):70–80.

3. Linda Alexander Rodríguez, *The Search for Public Policy: Regional Politics and Government Finances in Ecuador, 1830–1940* (Berkeley: University of California Press, 1985), Appendix A, pp. 178–183, and Appendix D, pp. 191–193. It is worth noting that despite their name, "panama" hats have always been an Ecuadorian product. In addition, tagua nuts were a source of artificial ivory for button manufacture.

4. Eduardo Arcila Farías, *Comercio Entre Venezuela Y México en los Siglos XVII y XVIII* (México: El Colegio de México, 1950), p. 41.

5. Lois Crawford de Roberts, *El Ecuador en la Epoca Cacaotera* (Quito: Editorial Universitaria, 1980), p. 34. This is the Spanish translation of a revised version of Lois Weinman's "Ecuador and Cacao: Domestic Response to the Boom-Collapse Monoexport Cycle" (Ph.D. dissertation, University of California, Los Angeles, 1970).

6. It is ironic that Ecuadorian cacao was regarded as inferior to Venezuelan cacao in Mexico, the principal market for cacao in the New World during the seventeenth century. Upper-class Mexicans drank cacao without sugar; for this reason the sweeter Venezuelan variety was preferred. Lower-class Mexicans mixed strong bitter Ecuadorian arriba cacao with cheap sugar. Europeans, who likewise mixed their cacao with sugar in drinks or chocolate, also preferred the bitter, but more flavorful, arriba. (See Arcila Farías, *Comercio*, pp. 42–43.)

7. Crawford de Roberts, *El Ecuador*, p. 56.

8. There is little direct evidence of foreign investment in cacao, but William Glade has estimated that in 1914 less than 1 percent of total British

and U.S. investment in Latin America was in Ecuador. All of the U.S. investment in Ecuador was in mining and railways. Some German capital was invested in cacao, but the amounts were probably very small. See William P. Glade, *The Latin American Economies: A Study of Their Institutional Evolution* (New York: Van Nostrand, 1969), pp. 216–224.

9. See Crawford de Roberts, *El Ecuador*, p. 54. See also Andrés Guerrero, *Los Oligarcas del Cacao* (Quito: Editorial el Conejo, 1983).

10. Crawford de Roberts, *El Ecuador*, p. 78; and Gustavo Cosse, *Estado y Agro en el Ecuador* (Quito: Corporación Editora Nacional, 1984), p. 23. In this period, a sucre was worth approximately US $0.40.

11. Population figures from this period are not particularly reliable, and direct indicators of migration do not exist. Crawford de Roberts writes that "during the period of expansion, [the coastal population] did not grow significantly because of either internal or external migrations" (*El Ecuador*, p. 76). Alexander Rodríguez claims that "in 1830, about 85 percent of the population lived in the sierra. The century that followed witnessed extensive migrations to the coast" (*The Search*, p. 27).

12. Frederick B. Pike, *The United States and the Andean Republics: Peru, Bolivia, and Ecuador* (Cambridge: Harvard University Press, 1977), p. 148.

13. Alexander Rodríguez, *The Search*, Appendix H, pp. 204–205.

14. Amparo Menéndez-Carrión, "The 1952–1978 Presidential Elections and Guayaquil's Suburbio: A Micro-Analysis of Voting Behaviour in a Context of Social Control" (Ph.D. dissertation, The John's Hopkins University, 1985), p. 20.

15. Alexander Rodríguez, *The Search*, p. 23.

16. Ibid., Appendix D, pp. 191–192.

17. V. D. Wickizer, *Coffee, Tea and Cocoa: An Economic and Political Analysis* (Stanford, Calif.: Stanford University Press, 1951), p. 265.

18. Crawford de Roberts, *El Ecuador*, Appendix A, Tables 4A and Table 4B, pp. 247–250.

19. Guerrero, *Los Oligarcas*, p. 95.

20. See Oscar Efren Reyes, *Breve Historia General del Ecuador* (Quito: Decima Cuarta edición, n.d.), Tomo II–III, pp. 197–203, for a representative, if somewhat eulogistic, account of the accomplishments of Eloy Alfaro.

21. Reyes, *Breve Historia*, pp. 175–176.

22. Osvaldo Hurtado, *Political Power in Ecuador* (Boulder, Colo: Westview Press, 1985), p. 113.

23. Reyes, *Breve Historia*, p. 187.

24. Alexander Rodríguez, *The Search*, p. 46. Similar periods of disintegration of national authority were 1834–1835, 1859–1861, and 1883.

25. Hurtado comments in *Political Power* that "the interests of Guayaquil merchants were never better served than during the Progresista period" (p. 154).

26. Alexander Rodríguez, *The Search*, p. 44.

27. Pike, *The United States*, p. 151.

28. Crawford de Roberts, in *El Ecuador*, reports 38 percent (p. 128); Alexander Rodríguez, in *The Search*, reports 43 percent (p. 224).

29. Pike, *The United States*, p. 156.

30. Crawford de Roberts, *El Ecuador*, pp. 134–136.

31. Glade, *The Latin American Economies*, p. 213.

32. Alexander Rodríguez, *The Search*, p. 50.

33. Reyes, *Breve Historia*, p. 228.

34. Hurtado, *Political Power*, p. 115.

35. Pike, *The United States*, p. 153.

36. Alexander Rodríguez, *The Search*, p. 49.

37. Reyes, *Breve Historia*, p. 246.

38. Crawford de Roberts, *El Ecuador*, p. 130.

39. Darío C. Guevara, *Juan Benigno Vela, titán del Liberalismo Radical ecuatoriano* (Ambato, 1949), p. 243; quoted in Pike, *The United States*, p. 143.

40. Hurtado, *Political Power*, p. 115.

41. Alexander Rodríguez, *The Search*, Appendix L, pp. 224–225.

42. Glade, *The Latin American Economies*, pp. 97–109.

43. Alexander Rodríguez, *The Search*, pp. 92, 95.

44. Dana Munro, Office of Foreign Trade Adviser, Department of State, "The Ability of Ecuador to Resume the Service of Her Foreign Debt," File 822, 51/348 (February 3, 1920); quoted in Crawford de Roberts, *El Ecuador*, p. 124.

45. Alexander Rodríguez, *The Search*, pp. 94–96.

46. Ecuador, Ministerio de Hacienda, *Informe* (1922), p. 5; quoted in Crawford de Roberts, *El Ecuador*, p. 132.

47. Alexander Rodríguez, *The Search*, Appendix M, pp. 228–230.

48. Ibid., Table 29, p. 116.

49. In 1914, Ecuador suspended the convertibility of its currency to gold, as did many other countries. But the congress allowed banks to increase the money supply in proportion to metallic reserves *and* government debt. This meant that as government borrowed heavily, the money supply increased without any corresponding increases in real output, thus fueling inflation.

50. John Samuel Fitch, *The Military Coup D'Etat as a Political Process: Ecuador, 1948–1966* (Baltimore: The Johns Hopkins University Press, 1977), p. 16. The discussion in this book of the changing institutional character of the Ecuadorian military follows that in Fitch.

51. Fitch, *The Military*, pp. 15, 16.

52. Augusto Varas and Fernando Bustamante, *Fuerzas Armadas y Política en el Ecuador* (Quito: Ediciónes Latinoamérica, 1978), Anexo II, Cuadro 15, p. 179.

53. Varas and Bustamante, *Fuerzas Armadas*, Anexo II, Cuadro 14, p. 177.

54. Alexander Rodríguez, *The Search*, p. 124.

55. Alfredo Pareja Diezcanseco, *Ecuador: La Republica de 1830 a Nuestros Días* (Quito: Editorial Universitaria, 1979), p. 350.

56. Alexander Rodríguez, *The Search*, pp. 125–162.

57. Ibid., Appendix L, pp. 226.

58. Reyes, *Breve Historia,* p. 273. Reyes notes that in one year Guayaquil received 3 million sucres for sanitation expenditures—that is, approximately 40 percent of the public-works budget.

59. Ibid., p. 272.

60. Pareja Diezcanseco, *Ecuador: La Republica,* p. 484.

61. Reyes, *Breve Historia,* pp. 259–260.

62. Alexander Rodríguez, *The Search,* pp. 160–161.

63. Ibid., p. 168.

64. See Georg Maier, "The Boundary Dispute Between Ecuador and Peru," *American Journal of International Law,* 63 (1969):28–46.

65. In 1960, then President Velasco Ibarra declared the Rio Protocol nullified.

66. For a discussion of the degree of industrialization accompanying the cacao and banana booms, see Catherine Conaghan, "Industrialists and the Reformist Interregnum: Dominant Class Behavior and Ideology in Ecuador, 1972–1979" (Ph.D. dissertation, Yale University, 1983), pp. 55–70; and Fernando Velasco, *Ecuador: Subdesarrollo y Dependencia* (Quito: Editorial El Conejo), 1983.

67. Calculated from Jean-Paul Valles, *The World Market for Bananas, 1964–72* (New York: Praeger Publishers, 1968), Table 7, pp. 12–14; and Alexander Rodríguez, *The Search,* Appendix G, p. 200. See also Moritz Thomsen, *The Farm on the River of Emeralds* (Boston: Houghton Mifflin, 1978), pp. 49–56, for a wonderfully rich, if perhaps not altogether faithful, account of some of the effects of the banana boom on Esmeraldas.

68. James J. Parsons, "Bananas in Ecuador: A New Chapter in the History of Tropical Agriculture," *Economic Geography,* 33, 3 (July 1957): 203–204.

69. Calculated on the basis of Valles, *The World Market,* Table 42, p. 123.

70. Ralph J. Watkins, *Expanding Ecuador's Exports* (New York: Praeger Publishers, 1967), Statistical Appendix, Table 2, p. 313.

71. Calculated on the basis of Banco Central del Ecuador, *Series Estadísticas Básicas* (Quito, 1977), Table 7.8, p. 82.

72. Alexander Rodríguez, *The Search,* Appendix C, pp. 188–189.

73. Stacy May and Galo Plaza, *The United Fruit Company in Latin America* (Washington, D.C.: National Planning Association, 1958), pp. 170, 174.

74. Cesar Herrera Vásconez, "El Cultivo del Banano en el Ecuador" (unpublished manuscript, 1963); cited in M. R. Redclift, *Agrarian Reform and Peasant Organization on the Ecuadorian Coast* (London: The Athlone Press, 1978), Table 7, p. 50. Producers with farms between 100 and 500 hectares (between 250 and 1,200 acres) in size occupied 36 percent of the land in banana production.

75. Watkins, *Expanding Ecuador's Exports,* p. 16.

76. Redclift, *Agrarian Reform,* p. 50. Redclift argues that many of the beneficiaries of official colonization programs in the Santo Domingo area

were in fact urban professionals and military officers from Quito, not poor farmers.

77. Parsons, "Bananas," pp. 203, 213–214.

78. Anne Collin Delavaud et al., *Atlas del Ecuador* (Paris: Les Editions J. A., 1982), p. 60.

79. Parsons, "Bananans," p. 206.

80. Germánico Salgado, "Lo que Fuimos y lo que Somos," in Gerhard Drekonja, ed., *Ecuador, Hoy* (Bogotá: Siglo Veintiuno Editores de Colombia, 1981), p. 31.

81. Howard Handelman, "Ecuadorian Agrarian Reform: The Politics of Limited Change" (Hanover: American Universities Field Staff Reports, No. 49, 1980), p. 5; and Fitch, *The Military Coup*, fn. 7, p. 196.

82. Alexander Rodríguez, *The Search*, Appendix H, pp. 206–207.

83. Amparo Menéndez-Carríon, "The 1952–1978 Presidential Elections and Guayaquil's Suburbio: A Micro-Analysis of Voting Behavior in a Context of Social Control" (Ph.D. dissertation, The Johns Hopkins University, 1985), Table 1, p. 22.

84. Redclift, *Agrarian Reform*, p. 52.

85. Calculated on the basis of Valles, *The World Market*, Table 76, p. 211.

86. Ibid.

87. See Charles R. Gobson, *Foreign Trade in the Economic Development of Small Nations* (New York: Praeger Publishers, 1971). Gibson estimates that Ecuador's concentration of commodity exports was one of the highest in the world (p. 173). In 1957, only 7 countries out of a total of 62 had a higher degree of export concentration. Thus, changes in banana earnings had large effects on both the public and private sectors of the economy.

88. Hurtado, *Political Power*, p. 122.

89. Galo Plaza, *Problems of Democracy in Latin America* (Chapel Hill: University of North Carolina Press, 1957).

90. Fitch, *The Military Coup*, p. 149.

91. Ibid., p. 150.

92. José María Velasco Ibarra, generally acknowledged to be Ecuador's first populist leader, initially won election to the presidency in 1933. But the proportion of the population voting in this election was hardly sufficient to term this a "populist victory." Populism did not emerge as a movement with mass-based appeal until the middle to late 1940s (see Chapter 4).

4

The Politics of Limited Participation: Populist Experiments and the Role of the Military

Historically, political participation in Ecuador has been restricted to a tiny fraction of the population. However, social and demographic changes, begun during the cacao boom and accelerated by the banana boom, built pressures for an expansion of participation. Ecuadorian elites responded to these changes, and to the loss of electoral appeal by their traditional parties, first by introducing legal restrictions to participation and, second, by sponsoring alternative candidates such as Ecuador's legendary figure, José María Velasco Ibarra, widely regarded as the country's first populist, who held office five times between 1933 and 1980.

Thus defined in terms of the political life of its preeminent leader, Ecuadorian populism spanned nearly fifty years. But it was not until the 1950s, when the growth of Guayaquil's lower-class population made this a pivotal electoral group, that populist movements were able to establish themselves. Superficially resembling populist movements elsewhere in South America in their charismatic leadership and their appeal to sectors of the population previously excluded from electoral participation, Ecuadorian populist movements are distinguished by their development in a political system with highly restricted participation and by their relative absence of reformist policies. Before 1979, for example, no more than 18 percent of the population had ever voted in a presidential election. Most socioeconomic reforms were implemented not by populist governments but by the military junta, which held power from 1963 to 1966. Some of these differences are explained by the late emergence of industrialization and urbanization in Ecuador; others are explained by the traditional characteristics of Ecuadorian politics such as regionalism and the dependence of the state on the export sector for revenue.

POLITICAL PARTICIPATION

Most of Ecuador's population has been largely untouched by the parade of different governments through Quito. Even the bitter struggles between liberals and conservatives marking the turn of the century had little effect on the lives of most citizens. The actual policies of liberal and conservative governments differed little, thus lending support to Osvaldo's Hurtado's contention that "historical data seem . . . to support the thesis that coastal merchants and highland latifundistas participated jointly in the exercise of power from the earliest days of the republic."[1] The mass of the population did not participate. As a resut, the principal function of politics has been that of mediating inter-elite conflicts, most of which originated in regional antagonisms, personal rivalries, and differences over the proper relationship between church and state. Ecuadorian politics was a profoundly elitist politics.

In the early years of the republic, the restriction of political participation to small groups of highland and coastal elites was achieved largely without recourse to formal constitutional limitations. The low level of economic development, the highly concentrated distribution of income and wealth, the large, non-Spanish-speaking indigenous population, and the predominantly agrarian economy provided natural impediments to the expansion of participation. In this setting, the influence of patron and priest, particularly in the sierra where most of the population resided, was a remarkably effective alternative to more formal sanctions. For example, barely 3 percent of the population voted in the presidential elections of 1888.[2] To be sure, there were challenges by excluded groups to elite domination of the political system, which, given the exclusion of these groups from electoral participation, took the form of uprisings and strikes. These occurred periodically, primarily in response to exploitative conditions. But given the control exercised by the hacendado, the isolation of most uprisings, and their lack of organization, such protests did not constitute a serious threat to elite control and were crushed without significant political concessions.

By the early 1930s, however, in spite of structural obstacles to mass participation, the economic dislocation caused by the cacao crisis and the ensuing world depression created the conditions needed to break the hegemony of the traditional parties. The conservatives were still weakened and discredited in the aftermath of the reaction to García Moreno; the liberals were still tainted by the widespread perception that they had sold out to coastal financial interests. In spite of the efforts of both parties after 1925 to create organizations, both remained personalistic creations. Both had flourished under the leadership of particularly charismatic leaders; without such leaders neither party could have demonstrated much electoral appeal.[3] Although landowners and the export elites remained a significant political force, the traditional electoral vehicles for their interests were not able to capture the presidency again for any significant period.

Traditional forms of elite control over mass participation had weakened in the aftermath of the cacao crash. Popular uprisings broke out on the coast and in the sierra, and rates of electoral participation began to rise. In November 1922, a protest over working conditions and low wages by railroad workers in Guayaquil precipitated a series of strikes by other groups of coastal workers that culminated in a mass demonstration involving 10,000 participants. Unaccustomed to mass protest and alarmed by such widespread display of discontent, the government violently overreacted, killing an estimated 1,000 workers.[4] A *campesino* uprising near Ambato in 1923 evoked a similar response from the authorities. By 1924, the participation rate in presidential elections had risen sharply from 3 to 11 percent.[5] For the first time, Ecuadorian elites had to confront the potential threat posed by the largely disenfranchised masses. At a Liberal party assembly in Quito following the 1923 campesino uprising, noted Ecuadorian Indianist Pío Jaramillo Alvarado undoubtedly reflected the concern of many elites when he commented that if a revolution was not made from above by a strong government, the masses would surely make one from below.[6]

Ecuadorian elites responded to this threat from the masses, and to the general discontent expressed by the lower-middle class, by pursuing a strategy that granted moderate social reform legislation while at the same time formally restricting legal channels for political participation.[7] Following the July 1925 military coup, the government introduced a series of progressive measures, such as the establishment in 1926 of a Ministry of Labor and Social Welfare. These reformist measures were consolidated in the constitution of 1929 (still considered one of Ecuador's most progressive), which contained the first labor legislation recognizing the rights of workers with respect to issues such as the length of the working day and a minimum wage. Such legislation, if enforced, would primarily have benefited the urban working class, still a very small fraction of the population but a fraction with considerable potential for organized protest. Promulgated several years later, in 1937, was a Law of Communes, which legally recognized the existing Indian communities and, in several instances, returned to them small amounts of land.[8] But this legislation, like the earlier labor legislation, remained largely unimplemented.

At the same time that the 1929 constitution established important rights for lower-class groups in society, it created a series of legal obstacles hindering the ability of these groups to effectively represent their interests. An upper chamber in the legislature was created, composed of senators elected by the respective provincial councils and fifteen senators elected by various functional associations representing the major interest groups in society. Labor was awarded one senator and the campesinos were awarded two; in addition, one senator was designated as guardian of the interests of the indigenous population. Although the system of functional representation formally extended participation to some middle- and lower-class groups, the net effect was actually an increased representation of traditional interests in the legislature, inasmuch as the selection of functional senators was made through elite-dominated interest associations.

The 1929 constitution also marked the formal extension of the franchise to women in Ecuador, an occasion widely celebrated by Ecuadorians as evidence of an early—and progressive—commitment to universal suffrage. But literacy restrictions on voting remained in effect and were enforced with new vigor. In a country with a large poor population, and one in which a substantial proportion of that population's first language was Quichua, not Spanish, it is hardly surprising that a majority of Ecuadorians, male and female, could not vote. Although literacy figures are not available for the 1920s, approximately 65 percent of the adult population was still classified as illiterate even in the early 1930s.[9] But concern over rising participation among even the literate population led to numerous technical restrictions on voting in the 1929 Law of Elections. All voters were required to register in person for each election, with registration possible only "during working hours and not at the work place" for a ten-day period preceding each election.[10] A registration fee was reintroduced for the first time since 1861. Residency requirements allowed registered voters to vote only in the electoral district in which they had originally registered, thus imposing a serious obstacle to participation for individuals who had migrated either to urban areas or to the coast. These migrants, of course, were precisely those who might have been expected to be least subject to traditional control.

The effect of these numerous restrictions on electoral participation was apparent by the early 1930s. In spite of some increase in the population of potentially eligible voters due to the inclusion of literate

TABLE 4.1
Participation rates in Ecuadorian presidential elections
(percentage of the population)

Year	Participation Rate	President
1888	3.0	Antonio Flores Jijón
1924	11.0	Gonzalo S. Córdova
1931	3.1	Neptalí Bonifaz Ascázubi
1932	4.2	Juan de Diós Martinez Mera
1933	3.1	José María Velasco Ibarra
1948	9.1	Galo Plaza Lasso
1952	10.8	José María Velasco Ibarra
1956	15.8	Camilo Ponce Enriquez
1960	17.8	José María Velasco Ibarra
1966	11.0	Otto Arosemena Gómez
1968	14.7	José María Velasco Ibarra
1978	21.0	Jaime Roldós Aguilera
1984	31.0	León Febres Cordero

SOURCE: 1888-1933: Rafael Quintero, *El Mito del Populismo en el Ecuador* (Quito: FLACSO Editores, 1980), p. 101, 236; 1948-1968: John D. Martz, *Ecuador: Conflicting Political Culture and the Quest for Progress* (Boston: Allyn and Bacon, 1972), p. 128; 1952 and 1978: Amparo Menéndez-Carrión, "The 1952-1978 Presidential Elections and Guayaquil's Suburbio: A Micro-Analysis of Voting Behavior in the Context of Social Control" (Ph.D. dissertation, The Johns Hopkins University, 1985), p. 158; 1984: The official vote total was reported in *Hoy* (June 19, 1984), and the estimated 1984 population was taken from *Boletín Anuario 1984*, No. 7, (Quito: Banco Central del Ecuador), p. 186.

women, by 1933 only 60 percent of the small eligible population was registered and only 27 percent of the registered voters were actually voting.[11] As Table 4.1 illustrates, the percentage of the population voting contracted sharply in the 1930s relative to earlier years. Ironically, the evidence suggests that the extension of the franchise to women also increased the electoral influence of the elites, particularly that of the Conservative party.[12] Virtually all literate women were upper class, and more than twice as many women registered to vote in the sierra, the stronghold of conservatism, than on the coast.[13]

The elections during the early 1930s provide a graphic illustration of both the electoral stalemate that had developed between the Liberal and Conservative parties, and the way in which the elites nevertheless were able to retain control over the elections, aided in considerable part by the recently established electoral restrictions. Following Ayora's resignation in 1931, the Conservative party, unable to field a candidate of its own but determined not to let the liberals recapture the presidency, organized an alternative electoral vehicle, the Compactación Obrera Nacional (National Workers Compact), in which liberals and socialists as well as sierra artisans, campesinos, and small-business people were represented. Through this organization, the conservatives achieved the election in 1931 of their candidate, Neptalí Bonifaz, a sierra landowner. In one of the country's few free elections, the conservative victory was not surprising given that more than 60 percent of the electorate was located in the sierra and dissident liberal and socialist candidates split the coastal vote. But Bonifaz's tenure was short. He faced immediate opposition from a liberal-dominated legislature that voted to disqualify him from the presidency, thereby precipitating another civil war. Four battalions from the Quito garrison took to the streets in support of the president and the constitution, and provincial units arrived in defense of the liberal legislature, ultimately driving Bonifaz supporters from the capital. The "Four-Days War," as it became known, left more than a thousand dead and the country in disarray.[14]

Although chastened by the carnage, Ecuadorian elites again failed to find a solution to the loss of hegemony by the traditional parties. In 1932, the liberals secured the election to the presidency of Guayaquil businessman Juan de Díos Martínez Mera in a election widely regarded as fraudulent. In addition to the bitter opposition he faced from conservatives who felt the election had been stolen from them, Martínez Mera was a personally unpopular individual who engendered immediate and widespread opposition to his presidency. Congressional opposition (led this time by Bonifaz supporter and president of the Chamber of Deputies, José María Velasco Ibarra), the withdrawal of liberal support, and renewed popular insurrection in the streets of Quito led to Martínez Mera's resignation after only three months in office. New elections were called for in 1933.

The conservatives again resorted to the strategy of mobilizing support for a candidate through an alternative electoral vehicle, the "Junta Nacional del Sufragio Libre" (National Council for Free Suffrage).[15] Both the Liberal party and the Socialist party were invited to participate but declined, leaving the conservatives in control. The junta selected Velasco Ibarra as its candidate. This charismatic individual, who had discovered his powers of oratory in the legislature, conducted the first campaign tour the country had ever witnessed, drawing enthusiastic crowds at every stop. Even in Guayaquil, he attracted large groups of people, leading some to conclude that the era of acute regional divisiveness was past.[16] With strong backing from the Conservative party and the Church, Velasco Ibarra triumphed in the 1933 elections, winning 80 percent of the total vote.

ECUADORIAN POPULISM

Velasco's Ibarra's victory in 1933 has been widely viewed as marking the emergence of populism in Ecuador.[17] Rising popular discontent, the economic isolation produced by the world depression, and the general discrediting of the traditional parties were seen as having created an opportunity for a different politics incorporating previously excluded groups—in particular, the growing population of marginal workers in Guayaquil. Certainly this was the pattern in other countries in Latin America, where the period between the Great Depression and World War II saw the emergence of populist movements such as those led by Peron in Argentina, Vargas in Brazil, and the Radical governments in Chile.

However, as Ecuadorian political scientist Rafael Quintero has convincingly argued, Velasco Ibarra's 1933 victory, although it represented a different style of electoral politics, did not signal his introduction of a new populist politics.[18] Even though his emergence shared some of the surface characteristics of populism as it was developing in other areas of Latin America, his first presidential victory had far more in common with traditional patterns of Ecuadorian politics. Though a strikingly charismatic leader who took his campaign to the people in a way not heretofore seen in Ecuador, Velasco Ibarra was essentially a Conservative party candidate, chosen to promote the interests of the highland elites. Notwithstanding his popular appeal, only 3 percent of the population voted. The lower-class coastal vote could not have been essential to this victory in which Velasco Ibarra won 80 percent of the total vote and 70 percent of the sierra vote. Not until later, when the banana boom had swelled the population of the coast, and that of Guayaquil's lower class in particular, could it be argued that a form of populism had emerged in Ecuador. In the 1950s, two uniquely Ecuadorian populist movements emerged: "velasquismo," under the leadership of José María Velasco Ibarra; and the "Concentración de Fuerzas Populares" (Concentration of Popular Forces, of CFP), first under Carlos Guevara Moreno (1950–1960) and later under Asaad Bucaram (1962–1981). Yet neither movement was particularly incorporating nor particularly reformist, even by comparison with populist movements elsewhere in South America.

José María Velasco Ibarra: Perennial Figure of Ecuadorian Politics

José María Velasco Ibarra casts a long shadow over Ecuadorian politics. Born in Quito on March 19, 1893, to upper-middle-class parents (his father was an engineer who died when his son was only sixteen), he graduated in law from the Central University in 1922 after a brilliant academic career. He worked for the Quito city government for a brief period during which he began to gain a reputation as a political columnist for the newspaper *El Comercio* under the nom de plume "Labriolle." Between 1931 and 1932 he continued his studies at the University of Paris, from which he was called back to Ecuador to begin his extraordinary political career in the lower house of the legislature. Velasco Ibarra dominated Ecuadorian politics until 1972, occupying the presidency on five separate occasions during this period.[19]

A prolific writer, Velasco Ibarra was the author of numerous political books and articles during his career. Yet in spite of his writing, Velasco Ibarra's political ideology has remained something of a riddle. He defined himself as an eighteenth-century liberal, writing that he was an "individualist and opposed to the intervention of the state in the name of social justice."[20] Nevertheless, public-works projects multiplied during his administrations and the bureaucracy expanded at a rapid rate. Though a proponent of individual liberties, he assumed dictatorial powers on more than one occasion. He frequently expressed his distaste for all Ecuadorian political parties, arguing that he served at the will of the people, not as the representative of any party. He was particularly critical of the left, writing that "all the injustices which are committed in other countries in the name of conservatism are committed in Ecuador in the name of leftism."[21] His own organization, the "Federación Nacional de Velasquistas" (National Velasquista Federation), served only as an electoral vehicle, organized for him by others. Yet at different times during his political career he was perfectly willing to be sponsored as the candidate of conservatives, leftists, or liberals.

Velasco Ibarra was an extraordinarily gifted orator whose boast— "give me a balcony and the people are mine"—was not entirely without foundation. Unprecedented crowds greeted his campaign tours around the country, contributing no doubt to Velasco Ibarra's perception of himself as uniquely qualified to interpret the desires of the Ecuadorian people. His desire for the presidency and his conviction that he alone could lead the country out of chaos led him to entertain whatever political alliance offered the greatest probability of his winning office, or of his remaining in power once elected. Yet in spite of his convictions, most Velasco Ibarra administrations ended with the country in greater disarray than when he had assumed office. Although he served as president on five separate occasions, Velasco Ibarra managed to complete his constitutional term only once. His popularity as a campaigner was never equalled by his abilities as an administrator.

Unlike the presidents before him, Velasco Ibarra brought politics to the people. He was the first presidential candidate to make countrywide appearances a standard feature of his campaigns. He repeatedly affirmed his commitment to freedom of suffrage, responding on one occasion to criticism that velasquismo had no doctrine by asking, "Do you think that working and fighting so that freedom of suffrage might become a definitive reality in the Republic of Ecuador is not having a doctrine?"[22] Certainly Velasco Ibarra provided previously excluded groups with a sense of incorporation into national political life. As one Indian leader in the late 1960s is reputed to have commented:

> Of course, as a political group, we peasants have been incorporated into the National Velasquista Federation—the Indians, the community in general—because this commune was created by Dr. Velasco Ibarra. So we will always be Velasquistas because he has shown us the way, he has helped us to see things better. But other presidents don't care how we live.[23]

But in spite of Velasco Ibarra's appeal to previously excluded groups and his avowed commitment to freedom of suffrage, no legislation to expand the electorate was passed during his administrations. Nor did he ever manage to implement significant structural reforms.

Velasco Ibarra's support after 1950 came from popular groups to whom he promised public-works projects, from middle-class professionals to whom he offered the prospect of public-sector employment, and from significant sectors of the elites who, unable to ensure the victory of their own candidates, saw in Velasco Ibarra no serious threat to their interests. Once in office, Velasco Ibarra would feverishly embark on ambitious public works programs, initiating the construction of roads, bridges, electric plants, and schools. He expanded the national bureaucracy at the same time that he multiplied the number of autonomous agencies to serve regional and provincial needs. But like other presidents before him, Velasco Ibarra was trapped between large demands for expenditures and a limited ability to satisfy them. It is not coincidental that the only presidential term he successfully completed was that from 1952 to 1956, at the height of the banana boom.

Other factors also contributed to Velasco Ibarra's inability to retain support for his presidencies, not the least of which was the personality of this complex individual. Velasco Ibarra considered himself above politics, as evidenced by his disdain for administrative detail, his rejection of political parties, and his frequent absences from the country. Indeed, prior to 1960 he had spent only eight of the preceding twenty-six years in the country, earning himself the sobriquet "El Gran Ausente" (The Great Absentee). Often exiled, he would flee to Colombia, Chile, or Argentina, where he established residency until called back to Ecuador by "the people." His aloofness from politics undoubtedly enhanced his appeal, given the impression he made as an individual without ties to any particular group in Ecuadorian society. At the same time, though, Velasco Ibarra's distance from politics and his lack of specific vision turned his followers into a particularly opportunistic lot, likely to desert this leader as soon as they perceived better opportunities elsewhere. Faced on several occasions with massive defection of his civilian supporters, Velasco Ibarra remained in office only through his appeals to the military, which he took care to favor with large budgetary appropriations during his administrations. But in spite of his largesse, Velasco Ibarra was not a military man and could never rely on the certain loyalty of the military. Indeed, it was a lack of military support in 1935 that caused his downfall and a series of military coups that deposed him in 1947, 1961, and 1972.

The Concentration of Popular Forces

Unlike velasquismo, Ecuador's second populist movement—the Concentration of Popular Forces (CFP)—was urban and coastal in origin, finding its support in the growing population of marginal workers in Guayaquil. Between 1950 and 1962, the total population of Guayaquil grew at an annual rate of 5.6 percent, with lower-class groups growing at much higher rates.[24] Although voting participation rates did not directly parallel rates of population growth, between 1952 and 1984 Guayaquil was nevertheless a consistently important contributor to populist victories.[25] Not surprisingly, given the demographic shifts that occurred during the banana boom, Velasco Ibarra's presidential victories in the same period also drew heavily on support from Guayaquil voters.

The CFP was formally established on July 9, 1950, by a group of individuals of diverse ideological and social backgrounds from which Carlos Guevara Moreno quickly emerged as leader.[26] Son of a schoolteacher, Guevara Moreno was born in 1911 in the small highland town of Licto, near Riobamba. His father took a job as headmaster in Guayaquil when Guevara Moreno was still young, and the family moved to that city.

Guevara Moreno received his first taste of political involvement as a member of the leftist student organization "Fracción Universitaria Izquierdista" (Leftist University Fraction) while at the University of Guayaquil. Expelled from the university by its rector, Carlos Arroyo del Río, for participation in a campus strike, Guevara Moreno was sent by his father to study in France. While in Europe, he apparently joined the Communist party but was expelled, later participating in the Spanish civil war with the International Brigade. He returned to Ecuador in 1939 in time to witness the 1940 presidential elections, which Velasco Ibarra lost through fraud to Carlos Arroyo del Río. Apparently incensed over the victory of his former nemesis, Guevara Moreno arranged a coup against Arroyo del Río in favor of Velasco Ibarra. The attempt failed, and both Guevara Moreno and Velasco Ibarra were sent into exile in Colombia. Although Velasco Ibarra continued on to Chile while Guevara Moreno remained in Colombia teaching secondary school for several years, the two stayed in close contact.

It was from Velasco Ibarra that Guevara Moreno received his real political training. In 1944, a political coalition of socialists, communists, conservatives, and a few dissident liberals—the "Alianza Democrática Ecuatoriana" (Ecuadorian Democratic Alliance)—led a successful revolt against Arroyo del Río, recalling Velasco Ibarra from exile to replace this unpopular president. Unanimously confirmed by a constituent assembly, Velasco Ibarra initially appointed Guevara Moreno his secretary of administration, and later his minister of government.

As minister of government, Guevara Moreno was charged with two important duties: the systematic persecution of his former colleagues on the Ecuadorian left, and the creation of an electoral vehicle to aid Velasco in the next presidential elections, scheduled for 1948. Guevara Moreno undertook the first task with considerable abandon and with little regard for constitutional guarantees of individual liberties. Leftists (many of whom had been instrumental in electing Velasco Ibarra but who he profoundly distrusted) were purged from the administration, students and factory workers were physically beaten, and opposition media were eliminated or suppressed.[27] Whatever influence the Ecuadorian left had accumulated during the 1930s and early 1940s was largely eliminated, leaving the conservatives as Velasco Ibarra's principal base of support.

To accomplish the task of creating an electoral vehicle for Velasco Ibarra, Guevara Moreno looked to Guayaquil, where he already had ties and where the growing lower-class population offered considerable opportunities for organization. In 1946, he began to work with the "Unión Popular Republicana" (Popular Republican Union), founded in Guayaquil in 1944 by the committed Velasco Ibarra supporter Rafael Mendoza Avilés, who at that time was mayor of the city.[28] The alliance was short-lived, however, as Velasco Ibarra, forced to pacify the conservatives disturbed by the increasing violations of civil liberties, sent Guevara Moreno to Chile in 1946 as ambassador.

Velasco himself lasted only another year, failing again to complete his term. With the erosion of his conservative support as these elites maneuvered to replace him with a president of their own choosing, Velasco Ibarra was forced into an increasing dependence on the military to remain in office. But a dispute with his minister of defense cost Velasco Ibarra his military support, and he was removed from office by a coup. He fled Ecuador for exile in Chile, leaving the country in a state of near anarchy and the public treasury exhausted by his efforts to retain the loyalty of his supporters, by his expansion of the bureaucracy, and by his refusal to concern himself with administrative detail.

With Velasco Ibarra in exile, Guevara Moreno returned to Guayaquil to continue his efforts to build a political machine. By 1950, he had managed to take over control of the "Union Popular Republicana," renaming it the "Concentración de Fuerzas Populares" (CFP) at the party's first convention on July 9 of that year. Ideologically, the new party was loosely defined, describing itself as "neither conservative, nor totalitarian, nor liberal, nor socialist, nor communist. . . . Its essence . . . is profoundly democratic, progressive, antifeudal, contrary to the caciquismo of cliques and influential bigwigs, republican, law-abiding and supportive of large-scale social and national transformation."[29] Its organization, on the other hand, was anything but loose. Structured in pyramidal fashion along the lines of the peronist movement in Argentina and led by the forceful Guevara Moreno, the CFP soon controlled local politics in Guayaquil. Nor were its ambitions limited to that city. From the beginning it aspired to become a national party, as evidenced by the inclusion of delegates from all but two provinces at its first convention.[30]

While continuing to denounce the left, the CFP became a major source of opposition to liberal president Galo Plaza. Its newspaper (El Momento) and radio station ("Radio Continental") carried scathing personal attacks on the president, whom the CFP considered the archetypal representative of the landowning oligarchy. An abortive coup launched in Guayaquil on July 15, 1950, with the assistance of a rebellious infantry battalion, culminated the CFP's vendetta against Plaza. Crushed within twenty-four hours, the insurrection resulted in Guevara Moreno's imprisonment, along with other leaders of the CFP, for fourteen months.

But imprisonment served only to increase Guevara Moreno's popularity; upon his release in 1951 he was elected mayor of Guayaquil with almost 50 percent of the vote in a four-way race. With the CFP now firmly in control of Guayaquil, the party voted to support Velasco, who at that time was in exile in Argentina, for president in the upcoming elections in 1952. But tensions were growing between the two populist leaders. Guevara Moreno feared the possible loss of his authority to "El Gran Ausente"; the latter had never easily tolerated even the hint of a rival. Velasco Ibarra's reception in Guayaquil from an overwhelmingly pro-CFP crowd upon his return from exile only increased the split. Arriving in Quito, Velasco Ibarra allegedly commented: "I do not owe anything to the CFP, or to the conservatives, or to anybody."[31] But in fact neither the CFP, which lacked a national base, nor Velasco Ibarra, who had no means of mobilizing the coastal electorate, could hope to win the presidential elections alone. The alliance, though increasingly fragile, did not openly rupture until after Velasco Ibarra's successful candidacy.[32] In December 1952, Guevara Moreno allegedly conspired to overthrow his former mentor, providing the latter with sufficient reason to send the CFP leader and several of his top political lieutenants into exile in Colombia. The break was now in the open, with Velasco Ibarra commenting in late 1953 that "for me the CFP is one of the worst evils surviving in Ecuador. It is a party of completely amoral people."[33]

Guevara Moreno returned to Guayaquil after nearly three years in exile to resume command of the CFP. After he only narrowly failed to win the 1955 election for mayor, the CFP chose Guevara Moreno as its candidate for the 1956 presidential elections. The moment looked favorable for the CFP to establish itself as a national force. The CFP had national recognition, Guevara Moreno's personal popularity was widespread, and, most important, Velasco was constitutionally prevented from presenting himself as a candidate. Like the 1952 presidential elections, this was clearly an opportunity for velasquismo and the CFP to join forces. But the personal antagonism between the two men was, if anything, worse than it had been in 1952. Velasco gave his support to Camilo Ponce Enríquez, who led the rightist coalition known as "Alianza Popular" (Popular Alliance) to a narrow victory over the second-place finisher, Liberal party candidate Raúl Clemente Huerta. And Guevara Moreno captured a convincing 58 percent of the Guayaquil vote, running third in this election, but the regional nature of the CFP was revealed in his inability to win more than 10.6 percent of the sierra vote.[34]

In November 1957, CFP candidate Luis Robles Plaza was elected mayor of Guayaquil with 73 percent of the vote. Shortly thereafter, however, the CFP's domination of Guayaquil politics began to weaken as the economic problems contributing to national political instability came to be reflected locally. Weaknesses in CFP control of the city became apparent with the outbreak in January 1958 of what was to be a six-month-long strike by municipal workers.[35] The CFP's ability to sustain support from its constituents depended critically on its ability to provide patronage and public works, both of which consumed scarce municipal income. By the late 1950s, Guayaquil's burgeoning population was making large demands for municipal services, but revenues were constrained by two factors. First, during the latter half of the 1950s, banana exports had stagnated, world prices for coffee and cacao had fallen, and national government income, which had increased at an annual rate of 11.3 percent between 1945 and 1955, had slowed to an annual rate of only 4.4 percent between 1955 and 1960.[36] Second, because local governments in Ecuador are heavily dependent on financial transfers from the national government, conservative highlander Camilo Ponce Enríquez's presidential victory in 1956 dried up funds for the CFP. In the 1959 mayoral elections, the fortunes of the CFP were at a low ebb, and Pedro Menéndez Gilbert, the candidate of the "Federación Nacional Velasquista" (National Velasquista Federation), defeated Guevara Moreno with 48 percent of the vote.[37]

The debility of the CFP favored another bid for the presidency by Velasco Ibarra, who was summoned once again from Buenos Aires by a reconstituted "Federación Nacional Velasquista" to run in the 1960 presidential elections. By contrast to his poor reception in 1952, he returned to a wildly enthusiastic crowd of supporters in Guayaquil—attributable in considerable part to the efforts of velasquista mayor Menéndez Gilbert, who had shrewdly taken advantage of the disarray into which the CFP had fallen to mobilize the *marginados* (urban lower class) on behalf of Velasco Ibarra. The CFP, struggling to retain its influence, backed leftist contender Antonio Parra, who polled less than 6 percent of the vote; Velasco Ibarra, on the other hand, won by the largest margin of his political career.

Velasco Ibarra lasted only fourteen months in office before falling victim to the political hazards facing any Ecuadorian executive. The economy deteriorated sharply in 1961. The dollar value of exports fell by 8 percent between 1960 and 1961, real GNP rose by only 1.5 percent, and per capita income fell. Estimated unemployment rose, and consumer prices, which had been relatively stable during the previous three years, began to increase.[38] Velasco Ibarra's own erratic economic policies contributed to the problems. Uncertainty and delay over a currency devaluation caused a massive flight of private capital. New taxes adopted to bolster declining government revenues increased domestic discontent, particularly among the middle and lower classes.

At the same time, demands for government spending were particularly high. Velasco Ibarra's campaign promises, always unrealistic, had been particularly inflated during this campaign. And given the near doubling of the vote since 1952, as well as Velasco Ibarra's unusually large margin of victory in the 1960s election, the incoming president faced far more claims for public employment from his supporters than he could possibly satisfy. Although thousands of government workers were dismissed so that jobs could be opened up for velasquistas, and although new agencies were created to increase the number of bureaucratic positions, there were simply too many claimants.

The regions also demanded assistance. Velasco Ibarra's policy of scattering appropriations about the country for public-works projects, many uncompleted for lack of sufficient funds, was strangely reminiscent of the "railroad politics" practiced by the liberals at the turn of the century and just as ineffective. Antagonism between the central government and the regions grew, leading Velasco Ibarra to comment in 1961 that "I have a real dread of Ecuador's municipalities."[39] When the leftist "Confederación de Trabajadores del Ecuador" (Ecuadorian Workers Confederation) called a general strike to protest deteriorating economic conditions on October 4, 1961, it was joined by five of the provinces.[40] Velasco Ibarra was able to call on the military to repress the strikers, but widespread loss of support for him signaled the end of his fourth presidency. On November 7, Velasco Ibarra was again deposed by the military; he was replaced in office by his vice-president, Carlos Julio Arosemena Monroy.

Between 1958 and 1962, the CFP, weakened by internal dissension and hostile national governments, faded in importance as a political actor. Apparently disillusioned with politics, Guevara Moreno resigned the directorship of the CFP shortly after the 1960 presidential election. He then left the country in 1963 for a seven-year period of self-imposed exile in Mexico, finished as a political force. But the leadership of the CFP was not long in a vacuum. Asaad Bucaram, born in Ambato in 1916 to Lebanese immigrant parents who moved shortly thereafter to Guayaquil, began to take control of the CFP in 1960 and was elected mayor of Guayaquil in 1962 with 45 percent of the vote.

As mayor, Bucaram was aided by highly favorable political and economic conditions. For the first time in the CFP's history, an individual who was not antagonistic toward the organization, Carlos Julio Arosemena Monroy, occupied the presidency. The economy recovered almost as rapidly as it had collapsed two years earlier (the dollar value of exports grew at an annual rate of 16 percent between 1961 and 1963), and municipal resources were relatively plentiful.[41] Bucaram effectively exploited the circumstances to build an organization loyal to him, earning a personal reputation for honesty and administrative ability. Unfortunately, his tenure in the mayor's office was brief. On learning of a military coup against Arosemena Monroy, Bucaram mobilized the CFP in defense of the president and the constitution. For his actions, Bucaram was deposed, jailed, and subsequently deported by the military government. He nevertheless managed to retain control of the CFP, the only partisan organization to maintain a presence in Guayaquil during the military government. When elections for a constituent assembly to return the country to democratic rule were held in 1966, Bucaram went to Quito as head of the CFP delegation and was elected vice-president of the assembly, thus notably increasing his stature as a national political figure.[42]

REFORMIST INITIATIVES:
THE 1963 MILITARY JUNTA

On July 11, 1963, the military overthrew the government of Carlos Julio Arosemena Monroy. Against the background of the recent Cuban revolution and U.S. preoccupation with the spread of leftist movements elsewhere in Latin America, the perception of a communist threat played a major role in military arguments for intervention, as it had in the wave of military coups taking place throughout Latin America during the early 1960s. An individual with a strong sense of nationalism, Arosemena Monroy attempted to pursue an independent foreign policy—in particular, by refusing under heavy pressure from the United States to break relations with Cuba. This effort, and his sympathy for domestic social reform, encouraged leftist protest within Ecuador. Opposition from Ecuador's traditional elites, though apparently a secondary factor in the coup decision, was particularly intense. The Guayaquil newspaper El Universo editorialized in favor of a coup, as did a public statement issued by the Conservative party.[43] A series of scandals involving the president's heavy drinking contributed to the sense that the government was losing control; his indecorous behavior at a state dinner honoring the visiting president of Grace Lines (a U.S. steamship company), with the diplomatic community in attendance, was the final straw for the military high command.

The military junta that assumed power in 1963 was the first such institutional intervention since 1925.[44] Both juntas espoused similarly reformist objectives. One of the leaders of the 1963 junta, Colonel Marcos Gándara, described the military's intervention as

> not merely a product of immediate or circumstantial causes. A long series of defects and errors obliged the armed forces to judge the

national reality and, consequently, to assume not only the responsibility to end the chaos and rectify mistaken paths, but also the responsibility to promote a new socioeconomic structure that would permt the State to comply with its function of serving the common interests of its citizens, thus laying the foundation for a true democracy.[45]

There were differences as well, however. In contrast to its predecessor of 1925, the 1963 junta was considerably more professional and possessed greater autonomy relative to civilian elites. After a highly favorable public reaction to its first year, this junta, rather than immediately handing over power to a civilian government, chose to remain in office until its reforms were firmly established.[46] But its activities during the first year had been largely confined to suppressing the left and to purging the administration of Arosemena supporters. As the 1963 junta began to implement its program of structural reforms, both the economy and the traditional elites turned against it.

The junta's reform program, strongly influenced by the Alliance for Progress and aided by the receipt of $84.5 million in aid from the United States, featured reorganization of the tax system and agrarian reform as its dual centerpiece.[47] A personal income tax was added to the corporate income tax, which had been introduced during the previous administration of Arosemena Monroy. More important, the junta also moved to centralize the existing inefficient system of taxation in which literally hundreds of different taxes directly financed the operations of various public entities, including a large number of autonomous public institutions, many located in Guayaquil. In 1964, a staggering 764 taxes were eliminated, with an additional 452 abolished during the next three years.[48] Although such a decentralized system of taxation was to the obvious advantage of regional interests, it greatly decreased the central government's control over public funds, thus contributing to its chronic problem with deficits.[49] The government's decree, which transferred revenue-collection responsibility from autonomous institutions to the Central Bank in Quito, sparked angry protests from Guayaquil elites who charged that coastal wealth was being robbed to support a parasitic central government. The protests provoked the junta to retaliate by imposing martial law, and the newspapers were ordered not to print "any news that might accentuate regionalism and aggravate the situation."[50]

The junta's agrarian reform program was embodied in the Agrarian Reform Law issued on July 11, 1964—not coincidentally, exactly one year following the overthrow of Arosemena Monroy. Land distribution in Ecuador was among the most unequal in South America, and agrarian reform proposals had been the object of heated discussion among Ecuador's landowning elites since 1960, when Velasco Ibarra appointed a National Agrarian Reform Commission to draw up potential legislation. Regional issues surfaced in that connection also. Even though the traditional highland landowners were most vehemently opposed, the coastal landed elites feared that legislation adopted in Quito would "make coastal landowners pay for the inefficiency of highland agriculture."[51] The 1964 Agrarian Reform Law, though denounced by the landed elites, was predictably not a serious threat to any but the most inefficient and politically less powerful landowners, particularly the southern highland hacendados. The major accomplishment of this law was the abolition of the highland semifeudal *huasipungo* labor system, which was already an embarrassment to many Ecuadorians inasmuch as their country was one of the last in South America to permit this practice.[52] Limits were placed on the maximum size of landholdings, but these limits were so flexible as to be virtually meaningless.

At the same time that both highland and coastal elites were antagonized by the junta's reform efforts, a softening occurred in the strong economy that had underlain the junta's first year. Real output, which had increased by a healthy 8 percent between 1963 and 1964, slowed to under 3 percent between 1964 and 1965—a percentage less than sufficient to keep per capita consumption from falling.[53] Government revenue increased by only 3 percent between 1964 and 1965, down from a 33 percent increase the preceding year.[54] Government deficits began to increase sharply, and in April 1965 the junta announced plans for an increase in import duties. The announcement touched off loud protests from the Quito and Guayaquil Chambers of Commerce, which, after rejecting a government compromise, organized a general strike in Guayaquil. The strike closed the city down, provoked a cabinet crisis, and ultimately won several wholesale concessions from the government.[55] In early 1966, the junta reiterated its plans to increase import duties, again provoking a general strike by the Guayaquil Chamber of Commerce—a strike that, supported by the Quito and Cuenca Chambers of Commerce and the coastal Chambers of Agriculture and Industry, as well as by labor and student groups, spread nationwide. Frustrated by its weak reform efforts, concerned about the damage to military prestige, and buffeted by adverse public opinion, the military relinquished power to a civilian interim president, Clemente Yerovi Indaburo, on March 29, 1966.

The 1963 junta's experience is illustrative for what it reveals about the difficulties of introducing even a moderate program of socioeconomic reforms into Ecuadorian society. Granted, the military government's fairly technocratic vision of government often clouded its judgment with respect to policy decisions and limited its ability, or willingness, to effectively mobilize potential support from either above or below for its policies. Nor was the economy particularly cooperative. But the main obstacle to reform proved to be the power and intransigence of elite groups organized through the chambers of production.

Elite opposition to the military's reform policies reached a high level, particularly from Guayaquil commercial and financial interests. Indeed, this, not popular protest, was the principal source of opposition to the junta.[56] Severely constraining the government's ability to introduce policies opposed by these elite groups was their control over government revenues and even over the country's economy. In the 1960s the Ecuadorian government was still heavily dependent on customs duties to generate approximately half of total revenues. As in the past, world market fluctuations were rapidly followed by domestic political instability. But 1965, the crisis year for the junta, did not correspond to a sharp downturn in export earnings. Rather, as Samuel Fitch has argued, the junta's economic difficulties appear to have been caused by the Guayaquil elites' refusal to process imports, the principal source of government customs revenue, and by the elites' movement of large sums of capital out of the country.[57] Supporting this thesis, customs revenue, which had risen by almost 12 percent between 1963 and 1964, decreased sharply by 8.5 percent in the following year.[58]

The junta also failed to mobilize support for its reforms from popular groups, the intended beneficiaries of many of its initiatives. In part, the lack of organized popular support was a direct result of the military's unwillingness either to use existing organizations or to mobilize its own organizations. For example, in 1965, when the strike organized by Guayaquil commercial interests shut down the city, the military refused offers of support from the CFP.[59] Similarly, peasant organizations could have been mobilized in support of the Agrarian Reform Law but for the military's fear of radicalizing the conflict. Nevertheless, the opportunities for mobilizing support from below would have been limited even if the military had been willing to undertake such mobilization. Ecuador's divided and personalistic populistic movements had bequeathed little in the way of mass-based organizations to subsequent reform efforts.

Meeting opposition from the country's elites and failing to secure support from below, the junta, not surprisingly, was accused of being a *dictablanda* (i.e., a milquetoast government) whose socioeconomic reforms were largely without substance.[60] Its policies came to resemble those of other Ecuadorian governments, with large expenditures going to education and public works. Without the necessity faced by civilian governments of dedicating a large share of the budget to ensure military loyalty, and—to its credit—willing to forego an unparalleled opportunity to increase the military's share, the 1963 junta was the first government since World War II to devote more money to education and public-works projects than to the Ministry of Defense. Unfortunately, in the absence of organizations linking the government to its intended beneficiaries, even the junta's increases in traditional spending probably failed to win it the support that might have been forthcoming for a civilian government. As with its 1925 predecessor, the junta's major accomplishment was reform of the tax system, which, though an important victory against entrenched regional interests, was not an accomplishment with widespread appeal.

ON THE EVE OF THE PETROLEUM ERA: THE FIFTH VELASQUISTA

With the reestablishment of electoral politics in 1966, following the junta's resignation, Bucaram returned to Guayaquil to contest the 1967 mayoral elections, sweeping to victory with 58 percent of the vote. He was again favored with large municipal revenues, which had resulted from a successful renegotiation of the municipal debt and from the tax reform carried out by the previous mayor.[61] While a member of the constituent assembly, Bucaram had also been able to secure passage of legislation granting the city of Guayaquil power to provide land titles to squatters in the *suburbios* of that city.[62] Armed with adequate revenues and this exceptional instrument for winning the loyalties of the marginados, Bucaram firmly consolidated his strength on the coast by successfully negotiating an alliance with the Liberal party. Poised to launch the CFP as a national political contender, Bucaram was frustrated in his ambitions by the return of Velasco Ibarra for his fifth presidential race.

Velasco Ibarra, recalled from exile in Argentina less than three months before the 1968 presidential elections to head his usual heterogeneous coalition of opportunistic supporters under the Federación Nacional Velasquista label, won a narrow victory with 283,350 votes over his two closest rivals, liberal Andrés Córdova and conservative Camilo Ponce Enríquez, who earned 264,312, and 259,833 votes, respectively. Though not initially favored to win the election, the aging Velasco Ibarra had conducted a fiery campaign in his usual style. But two factors in particular appear to have contributed to his inability to win a convincing mandate. His strength in Guayaquil was weakened by the CFP's support of Andrés Córdova. And a recent change in voting-registration procedures requiring all eligible voters to obtain a new *cédula* (identity card), ostensibly designed to facilitate voting by removing one step in the complicated process, appears to have constricted the electorate. With considerable justification, Velasco Ibarra contended that the real inspiration for the voting reform had been to reduce the voting participation of the lower class, an important component of his electoral support.[63] Certainly the proportion of registered voters eligible to vote dropped sharply relative to levels in the preceding two elections.[64]

Once in office, Velasco Ibarra found, as he is reputed to have commented on previous occasions, that "Ecuador is a difficult country to govern." Elected without a working majority in the congress, he entered into a short-lived pact with the liberals. A combination of mounting congressional opposition and a deteriorating export sector plunged the administration into near chaos. The value of exports fell by 15 percent in 1969 whereas the demand for imports remained strong, thus creating severe balance-of-payments problems.[65] Repeating the experience of previous velasquista administrations, budget deficits soared to record levels, driven principally by large increases in public spending. But in 1968, several additional ingredients were added to the traditional velasquista recipe for fiscal disaster. First, precisely in anticipation of a victory by Velasco Ibarra, the 1967 constitution had increased the number of autonomous public institutions. By early 1970 Velasco Ibarra was justifiably complaining that more than 50 percent of total tax revenues and some 1,300 public institutions were effectively outside of executive control.[66] Second, in 1968 regionalist interests in the congress had increased the earmarking of taxes for local projects, further reducing revenues for budgetary expenditures.[67] Third, mindful of his earlier experiences, Velasco Ibarra had designated a large share of the budget for the military in an effort to ensure its continued loyalty and to forestall a possible coup. And fourth, expectations triggered by the recent discovery of commercial quantities of petroleum in the northeastern region of the country contributed to large increases in both public- and private-sector spending.

Faced with a budget deficit of alarming proportions and frustrated by a congress that refused to consider his austerity proposals, Velasco Ibarra in early 1970 issued a series of emergency economic decrees designed to increase taxes and reduce expenditures. Particularly alarmed by an import tariff increase in the president's proposals, the Guayaquil Chamber of Congress appealed to the Supreme Court, which ruled against the constitutionality of the administration's tax proposals.[68] Opposed by congress and the courts, Velasco turned to the military,

Military support for Velasco Ibarra's 1970 assumption of dictatorial powers

which urged him to "assume dictatorial powers to save the country from total ruin."[69] In full agreement, he did so on June 22, 1970.

Following his assumption of dictatorial powers, Velasco Ibarra was able to stabilize public finances with the introduction of a 28 percent devaluation in the sucre, the establishment of a uniform sales tax, and the abolition of approximately half the autonomous public institutions. Together, these measures contributed to a healthy 25.6 percent increase in budgetary revenues.[70] With the closing of the universities and the deportation of opposition leaders such as Assad Bucaram, who was considered a certain victor in the scheduled 1972 presidential elections, popular protest against the government subsided. But the military, increasingly uneasy over the prospect of what it was convinced would be mismanagement of Ecuador's new petroleum wealth by traditional civilian politics, began to reassess its support for Velasco Ibarra and prepared to intervene. Guayaquil elites, particularly apprehensive over the prospect of a victory by returned CFP leader Assad Bucaram in democratic elections, strongly encouraged the military to act. Led by General Rodríguez Lara, the military seized power on February 15, 1972, this time arguing that "it would have to be different. . . . There would be no temporary interventions just in order to turn power over to the same old politicians, the same old parties. . . . This time it would be to totally transform the entire country."[71]

Velasco Ibarra again fled to Buenos Aires, where he remained until returning to Ecuador in 1979. He died in Quito on March 30 of that year at the age of eighty-six. Assad Bucaram kept alive his presidential ambitions until the next democratic elections in 1979 but was thwarted by the outgoing military. He died in November 1981 in Guayaquil. Neither velasquismo nor the CFP long survived its leader, thus closing a chapter of Ecuadorian populism as the petroleum era dawned.

A COMPARATIVE PERSPECTIVE

Highly restricted political participation and a relative absence of reformist policies were by no means uniquely characteristic of Ecuadorian politics. Indeed, such a description accurately characterizes most of the Latin American countries at the turn of the century. But beginning in the 1920s, structural changes, particularly industrialization and urbanization, in many of the more developed countries in the region created conditions conducive to an expansion of participation and the emergence of reformist, populist political movements. The same structural changes were not replicated in Ecuador. Dealt a near deathblow by the collapse of the cacao boom in the 1920s, the Ecuadorian economy did not begin to recover until the banana boom in the late 1940s, and industrialization did not begin to accelerate until the early 1960s. Although the political changes taking place in Ecuador during the period 1920–1960—notably, the erosion of legitimacy of the traditional parties as vehicles for elite domination of electoral politics, and the emergence of avowedly populist movements—bore some resemblance to political changes taking place elsewhere in the region, Ecuadorian populism was neither particularly incorporating nor particularly reformist.

In many of the Latin American countries, increasing urbanization created opportunities for those seeking political alternatives to rule by traditional elites. Early populists, such as Hipólito Yrigoyen in Argentina and Jorge Alessandri in Chile, first exploited these opportunities by appealing to urban lower-class and middle-class groups. Although their reformism was limited in that it had no major impact on the economy and society, these early populists did "pioneer a personalistic style of campaigning invoking mass support at the national level, thus opening political possibilities for the next generation."[72] Certainly one of their most important demands was for the incorporation of disenfranchised groups and the restitution of electoral rights. Thus, for example, Yrigoyen's "obrerismo" helped pave the way among the working classes for "peronismo," among other things by enfranchising the adult male population.[73] By the 1960s the electorate in most of the countries in which populism had flourished was approaching 30 to 50 percent of the population.[74]

The next generation of populists, who held power generally in the period between the Great Depression and the mid-1950s, won national office with organizations that were built on appeal to urban groups but, once installed, were also able to reach an accommodation with elements of the growing industrial class. The acceleration of industrialization taking place in this period, particularly in the import-substituting industries, provided further impetus to the urbanization of Latin America and created a class of industrialists whose orientation was more toward the domestic market than was that of their export-oriented predecessors. Although initiatives for reform did not necessarily originate with these industrialists, they were often more willing to accommodate reformist policies than were traditional elite groups. The reasons for their willingness could vary from a reluctant acceptance of reformist policies as distinctly preferable to more radical threats from the left, to an interest in expanding the domestic market through moderate programs of income redistribution. But whatever the reasons for support from these elites, the reformist alliance thus created produced a mix of policy outcomes favoring protected industrialization and social reforms directed toward its urban supporters—reforms such as higher wages, stronger unions, better housing, improved health, social security, and education. Although such reformist policies rarely matched the rhetoric of their proponents, they nevertheless went further than those implemented by other governments. As Paul Drake has noted: "While shying away from the necessary structural changes, populists captivated the masses not only with dashing slogans and psychic payoffs, but also with concrete benefits well in excess of those delivered by most other political systems."[75]

Ecuador has not followed the pattern observed elsewhere in the region. Certainly the populism there appears to have had more in common with the "early" populist experiments in South America than with their "later" variants. Both velasquismo and the CFP relied on highly charismatic leaders who could appeal to groups formerly excluded from electoral politics. But in contrast to the incorporating nature of "early" populism, the Ecuadorian electorate remained highly restricted despite the existence over a thirty-five-year period of two populist movements. As noted in one careful study of the period,

"The fact is, however, that in the 1952–1978 period governments were always elected by a minority of the adult population, 60 percent of whom did not cast a vote as late as the 1978 election."[76] Illiterates voted in the presidential elections for the first time in 1984, after the demise of both populist movements. In addition, Ecuador's populist governments were not particularly reformist, even by Latin American standards. Military, not populist, governments were responsible for most of the significant social and economic reforms introduced during the period.

The delayed emergence of industrialization in Ecuador is undoubtedly an important factor in explaining the different character of populism in this country. Whereas import-substituting industrialization proceeded rapidly in other countries in the region during the first half of the century, Ecuador, in spite of some limited early efforts to promote industrialization, continued to rely on the export of primary commodities. Not until 1957 were systematic efforts made to promote industrialization. The Industrial Development Law, issued during the administration of conservative President Camilo Ponce Enríquez, endeavored to encourage domestic industry through a variety of tax incentives. But it was under the 1963 military junta that state-directed industrialization policies received their strongest endorsement. In 1963, a development finance agency, the Corporación Financiera Nacional, modeled after similar agencies in Chile and Mexico, was established to provide funds for the development of industry. Issued in the following year was a revised version of the Industrial Development Law, which differed from the earlier version primarily in the increased generosity of its tax incentive provisions.

These state initiatives to promote industrialization came at a highly propitious time. Unlike Ecuador's experience in the 1920s, when the precipitous crash of the cacao market wiped out the fortunes of many of the cacao growers and left the domestic economy in a state of acute depression, the 1960s saw the banana boom stagnating but without threat of serious collapse. Export elites, recognizing that the spectacular growth of bananas in the 1950s was unlikely to be sustained into the 1960s and 1970s, were looking for ways to diversify their holdings. The domestic market, though still highly restricted, had undergone some expansion during the banana boom, making the production of a limited number of consumer goods relatively attractive. By the mid-1960s, industrialization had begun to accelerate in Ecuador. Manufacturing, which accounted for a roughly constant 15.5 percent share of gross domestic product between 1950 and 1960, rose sharply to 17 percent by 1970.[77] It was not until the 1970s that the share of output originating in manufacturing in Ecuador began to approach the levels prevailing in such countries as Brazil, Chile, and Argentina during the 1940s and 1950s. Further retarding the emergence of a reformist industrial class in Ecuador was the lack of differentiation of Ecuador's industrialists from other economic elites.[78]

Nor did Ecuadorian industrialization during the 1960s contribute greatly to the development of an urban working class. Although urbanization, particularly of Guayaquil, had begun during the cacao boom and accelerated during the banana boom, Ecuador remained a predominantly rural society. In 1960, 34 percent of the population was urban; by 1981 this figure had risen to 45 percent. By contrast, urbanization in many other countries in the region had begun earlier and progressed at a more rapid rate. In Peru and Brazil, just over 45 percent of the population was urban by 1960; in Argentina and Chile the corresponding figures were 74 and 68 percent, respectively. By 1980, more than 65 percent of the population in all of these countries was urban.[79] Nor was a large percentage of Ecuador's urban workers employed in industry. Drawn primarily into Guayaquil by economic changes associated with export production, most workers found employment in services, construction, or marginal occupations. Even the acceleration of industrialization during the 1960s did not have strong effects on employment. Although manufacturing production increased at an annual rate of 10 percent during 1965 to 1973, employment increased at a much lower rate of only 3 percent, considerably below the rate of growth of the urban population.[80]

It would be a mistake, however, to suggest that the failure of Ecuadorian populism to become particularly incorporating or reformist can be fully explained by the late development of industrialization and urbanization (see Table 4.2). Traditional features of Ecuadorian politics, notably regionalism and the heavy dependence of the state on the export sector for public revenues, also played an important role. Regionalism frustrated efforts to create national political organizations. Indeed, the existence of two competing populist movements, a factor unique to the Ecuadorian experience, reflected these regional divisions. Labor union members accounted for only a small percentage of the total labor force and were divided locally among numerous small independent unions. At the national level, three different labor federations competed for authority. Thus, mass-based political support for reformist programs was not forthcoming. Demands were fragmented and satisfied primarily as they had been since the founding of the republic—through public-works projects and employment opportunities in the growing state bureaucracy. The principal difference was that the modest expansion of participation had greatly increased

TABLE 4.2
Industrialization and urbanization in selected Latin American countries, 1940-1980
(in percentages)

Year	Ecuador	Brazil	Chile	Argentina	Peru	Latin America
			MANUFACTURING SHARE IN GDP			
1940	16.0[a]	15.0	11.8	22.7	---[b]	16.6
1950	16.0	21.2	23.1	23.7	14.2	18.7
1960	15.7	26.3	24.8	26.5	17.1	21.3
1970	16.8	28.4	27.2	28.0	21.1	25.1
1980	20.1	30.2	24.2	25.3	21.2	25.4
			AGRICULTURE SHARE IN GDP			
1940	38.3	21.4	13.0	23.2	---	25.1
1950	42.5	16.2	11.6	16.2	25.5	19.7
1960	39.0	13.4	9.8	14.9	24.4	17.1
1970	29.7	10.0	7.9	12.9	20.3	13.8
1980	21.1	7.3	7.7	12.9	13.3	11.2
			URBANIZATION[c]			
1940	17.0[d]	16.0	37.0	41.0	12.9	20.5
1950	17.8	20.3	42.6	49.9	18.1	28.8
1960	27.9	28.1	50.6	59.0	28.5	33.0
1970	35.3	39.5	60.6	66.3	40.3	41.5
1980	39.5	45.7	67.9	70.2	47.2	47.3

[a]Manufacturing figures for Ecuador include a large number of artisan producers as well as modern industrial enterprises.
[b]Not available.
[c]For all years, urban areas are defined as "clusters of population 20,000 and over," but the 1980 figures are from a different source and may not be directly comparable to the figures for 1940-1970.
[d]This figure is for 1938.

SOURCE: Manufacturing and agriculture figures from James W. Wilkie and Adam Perkal, eds., *Statistical Abstracts of Latin America*, Vol. 24 (Los Angeles: UCLA Latin American Center Publications, University of California, 1985), pp. 841, 839. Urbanization figures are from Ibid., Table 657 (1940-1970), p. 95, and Table 656 (1980), p. 94.

the number of claimants, making it even more difficult for governments to finance their budgets.

The state was also constrained by its heavy dependence on the export sector for revenues. This factor not only contributed to political instability; it also gave the country's economic elites, particularly Guayaquil's financial community, considerable ability to veto objectionable government policies through manipulation of foreign trade. Ironically, although industrialization held the potential in the long run to reduce the state's dependence on customs duties, in the short run the tax incentives adopted to promote industrialization—typically, exemption from import duties for capital goods and raw materials—cut into government revenues.

By the mid-1970s, however, the constellation of factors inhibiting the emergence of reformist politics had assumed a considerably more favorable pattern. Industrialization and urbanization continued to accelerate. The discovery of petroleum provided a powerful stimulus to the economy. A middle class began to emerge, and the domestic market broadened. Petroleum earnings, unlike those from earlier export booms, accrued directly to the state. Freed from the need to tax private economic activity in order to appropriate a share of the growth in income created by the export boom, the state enjoyed considerable autonomy relative to the country's elites.

NOTES

1. Osvaldo Hurtado, *Political Power in Ecuador* (Boulder, Colo.: Westview Press, 1985), p. 153.

2. Rafael Quintero, *El Mito Del Populismo en el Ecuador* (Quito: FLACSO Editores, 1980), p. 101.

3. Despite the debility of the traditional parties, leftist groups were not successful in organizing alternative parties. The Socialist party, for example, was organized in 1926, but it succumbed quickly to internal dissension, thus failing to become an important political force.

4. Osvaldo Hurtado and J. Herudek, *La Organización Popular en el Ecuador* (Quito: Instituto Ecuatoriano para el Desarrollo Popular, 1974), pp. 66–68.

5. Quintero, *El Mito*, p. 101.

6. Pío Jaramillo Alvarado, *La Asamblea Liberal y sus aspectos políticos* (Quito, 1924), p. xlvi; cited in Frederick B. Pike, *The United States and the Andean Republics* (Cambridge: Harvard University Press, 1977), p. 189.

7. See Ruth Berins Collier and David Collier, "Inducements Versus Constraints: Disaggregating Corporatism," *American Political Science Review*, 73, 4 (December 1979):967–986, for a general discussion of this type of political strategy.

8. Pike, *The United States*, p. 264.

9. Quintero, *El Mito*, Cuadro No. 27, p. 227.

10. Ibid., p. 230. The discussion of voting restrictions draws on pp. 230–237. Note also that Ecuadorian males were legally required to vote if qualified.

11. Ibid., Cuadro Nos. 28 and 29, pp. 232, 235, respectively.

12. George Blanksten, *Ecuador: Constitutions and Caudillos* (Berkeley: University of California Press, 1951), p. 74.

13. Quintero, *El Mito*, p. 244.

14. Oscar Efrén Reyes, *Breve Historia General del Ecuador*, Tomo II–III, Duodécima Edición (Quito, n.d.), p. 276.

15. Quintero, *El Mito*, p. 259.

16. George Maier, "The Impact of Velasquismo on the Ecuadorian Political System" (Ph.D. dissertation, Southern Illinois University, 1966), p. 178.

17. Populism is not easily defined because there have been so many variants; in general, however, populist movements can be classified as electoral movements involving a charismatic leader, a multiclass coalition drawing on urban middle- and lower-class groups, an interest in expanding the electorate, and a set of moderately reformist policies. See, for example, the essays by Michael Conniff and Paul Drake in Michael Conniff, *Latin American Populism in Comparative Perspective* (Albuquerque: University of New Mexico Press, 1982).

18. Quintero's *El Mito* is an essential contribution to the study of this period. See especially pp. 253–299.

19. Velasco Ibarra was elected president in 1933, 1952, 1960, and 1968. In 1944, he was appointed president by a constitutional convention. His third presidency (1952–1956) was the only one of five that he managed to complete without being overthrown.

20. José María Velasco Ibarra, *Conciencia o Barbarie* (Buenos Aires, 1938), p. 65; cited in Blanksten, *Ecuador*, p. 47.

21. Velasco Ibarra, *Conciencia o Barbarie*, p. 11.

22. José María Velasco Ibarra, *Obras Completas* (Quito: Editorial Lexigrama, 1974), Vol. XII-B, pp. 297–298; cited in Osvaldo Hurtado, *Political Power*, p. 342.

23. John Hammock and Jeffrey Ashe, *Hablan Los Lideres Campesinos* (Quito: Graficas Murillo, 1970), p. 90.

24. Recalculated from population figures in Amparo Menéndez-Carrión, "The 1952–1978 Presidential Elections and Guayaquil's Suburbio: A Micro-Analysis of Voting Behavior in a Context of Social Control" (Ph.D. dissertation, The Johns Hopkins University, 1985), Table I, p. 22.

25. Ibid., p. 217, 253. The populist vote in Guayaquil was never less than 53 percent of the total during the period 1952–1978. Quito's support for populist candidates was much less consistent (see Table VII, p. 255).

26. Lamentably, there is no biography of Carlos Guevara Moreno. The present discussion draws on a wide variety of sources, principally Maier, "The Impact," pp. 102–109; Marcelo Ortíz Villacís, *La Ideología Burguesa en el Ecuador* (Quito, 1977); John D. Martz, "The Regionalist Expression of Populism: Guayaquil and the CFP, 1948–1960," *Journal of Interamerican Studies and World Affairs*, 22, 3 (August 1980):297–314; and Amparo Menéndez-Carrión, "The 1952–1978 Presidential Elections," pp. 318–399.

27. Efrén Reyes, *Breve Historia*, p. 305.

28. *Bucaram: Historia de una Lucha* (Quito: Editorial El Conejo, 1981), p. 178.

29. Hurtado, *Political Power in Ecuador*, p. 205.

30. "La Convención del Partido del Pueblo," *Momento*, No. 38 (July 15, 1950); cited in Menéndez-Carrión, "The 1952–1978 Presidential Elections," fn. 35, p. 408.

31. Ortíz Villacís, *La Ideología*, p. 240.

32. Maier, in "The Impact," notes that Velasco was aided by the liberals' fear of a victory by reactionary conservative Ruperto Alarcón Falconí (pp. 211–212).

33. L. Maldonado Estrada, *Una Etapa Histórica en la Vida Nacional* (Quito: Editorial Rumiñauhui, 1954), p. 206; cited in Martz, "The Regionalist Expression," p. 303.

34. John D. Martz, *Ecuador: Conflicting Political Culture and the Quest for Progress* (Boston: Allyn and Bacon, 1972), p. 129.

35. Menéndez-Carrión, "The 1952–1978 Presidential Elections," pp. 356–358.

36. Calculated on the basis of Linda Alexander Rodríguez, *The Search for Public Policy: Regional Politics and Government Finances in Ecuador, 1830–1940* (Berkeley: University of California Press, 1985), Appendix K, pp. 220–221.

37. Menéndez-Carrión, "The 1952–1978 Presidential Elections," p. 363.

38. Banco Central del Ecuador, *Series de Estadísticas Básicas* (Quito, 1977) pp. 30, 49; and John Samuel Fitch, *The Military Coup D'Etat as a Political Process: Ecuador 1948–1966* (Baltimore: The Johns Hopkins University Press, 1977), p. 48.

39. Peter Pyne, "Presidential Caesarism in Latin America: Myth or Reality?" *Comparative Politics*, 9, 3 (April 1977):291.

40. Peter Pyne, "The Politics of Instability in Ecuador: The Overthrow of the President, 1961," *Journal of Latin American Studies*, 7, 1 (May 1975):116. Pyne also notes a regional bias among protesting provinces inasmuch as four of the five were in the sierra. Government investment under Velasco Ibarra showed a definite coastal bias, relative to that under his predecessor, conservative Ponce Enríquez.

41. Banco Central del Ecuador, *Series Estadísticas Básicas* (Quito, 1977), p. 48.

42. John D. Martz, "Populist Leadership and the Party Caudillo: Ecuador and the CFP, 1962–1981," *Studies in Comparative International Development*, 18, 3 (Fall 1983):29.

43. See Fitch, *The Military Coup*, p. 61, for a systematic review of the factors that led the military to intervene.

44. General Alberto Enríquez Gallo ruled as a military president from October 1937 to August 1938.

45. Junta Militar de Gobierno, *Plan Politico de la Junta Militar del Gobierno* (Quito: Talleres Gráficos Nacionales, 1963), pp. 3–4; cited in Fitch, *The Military Coup*, p. 66.

46. Fitch, *The Military Coup*, p. 67.

47. Pike, *The United States*, p. 316.

48. Ministerio de Finanzas, *Estadísticas Fiscales No. 1* (Quito, 1981), pp. 95, 96.

49. A compromise was reached in which numerous public entities received an earmarked percentage share of a large number of taxes and fees,

regardless of the entities' economic requirements. Although this compromise was still of benefit to the central government, a superior solution would have allocated revenues to regional institutions according to economic need. Thus, although the central government ran deficits every year between 1963 and 1969 (except for 1966), the autonomous agencies recorded a surplus in every one of those years. See Charles R. Gibson, *Foreign Trade in the Economic Development of Small Nations* (New York: Praeger Publishers, 1971), p. 57; *Estadísticas Fiscales No. 1*, p. 96; and World Bank, *The Current Economic Position and Prospects of Ecuador* (Washington, D.C.: The International Bank for Reconstruction and Development, 1973), pp. 67–68.

50. Maier, "The Impact," p. 235.

51. Howard Handelman, "Ecuadorian Agrarian Reform: The Politics of Limited Change" (Hanover: American University Field Staff Reports, No. 49, 1980), p. 7.

52. Ibid., p. 8. Under the *huasipungo* system, the peasant received a small plot of land and other benefits in exchange for virtually unpaid labor.

53. World Bank, *The Current Economic Position*, Statistical Appendix, Table 2.2.

54. Alexander Rodríguez, *The Search*, Appendix K, p. 221.

55. Fitch, *The Military Coup*, p. 69.

56. Ibid., p. 72. Note that the 1925 junta's relatively greater success in implementing policies antagonistic to the interests of the Guayaquil elites was greatly aided by the crash of the cacao boom. In contrast, although export earnings in the mid-1960s were somewhat stagnant, Ecuador had experienced none of the economic dislocation characterizing the 1920s.

57. Ibid., pp. 157–158.

58. Alexander Rodríguez, *The Search*, Appendix C, pp. 189–190. Total government revenues increased by 33 percent during the junta's first year, reflecting the effects of the tax reforms, but they increased by only 3 percent between 1964 and 1965, thus contributing to large public deficits.

59. Fitch, *The Military Coup*, p. 69.

60. "Dictablanda," literally "soft word," is a play on the Spanish for dictator, "dictadura" or "hard word."

61. Menéndez Carrión, "The 1952–1978 Presidential Elections," p. 380.

62. Ibid., p. 379.

63. Ibid., Table I, p. 158. See pp. 156–176 for a carefully reasoned discussion of this issue.

64. Freeman J. Wright, "The 1968 Ecuadorean Presidential Campaign," *Journal of Interamerican Economic Affairs*, 23, 4 (1981), p. 85.

65. Banco Central del Ecuador, *Cuentas Nacionales No. 2* (Quito, 1982), pp. 23, 60.

66. Martz, *Ecuador*, p. 82. Between 1968 and 1969, budgetary expenditures grew at an annual rate of 9 percent, whereas expenditures by the public administration (including the autonomous public institutions) grew at an annual rate of 22.6 percent. (The author's calculations were made on the basis of Ecuadorian national accounts statistics.)

67. *Estadísticas Fiscales No. 1*, p. 5.

68. Thomas E. Weil et al., *Area Handbook for Ecuador* (Washington, D.C.: Government Printing Office, 1973), p. 199.

69. Fitch, *The Military Coup*, p. 175.

70. *Estadísticas Fiscales No. 1*, pp. 6, 7.

71. Interview cited in Fitch, *The Military Coup*, p. 179.

72. Paul W. Drake, "Conclusion: Requiem for Populism," in Michael L. Conniff, ed., *Latin American Populism in Comparative Perspective* (Albuquerque: University of New Mexico Press, 1982), p. 237.

73. David Tamarin, "Yrigoyen and Perón: The Limits of Argentine Populism," in Conniff, *Latin American Populism*, p. 37.

74. Kenneth Ruddle and Phillip Gillette, eds., *Latin American Political Statistics* (Los Angeles: Latin American Center, 1972), pp. 105–114. Brazil is a notable exception, with just over 17 percent of the population voting in 1960.

75. Paul W. Drake, "Conclusion: Requiem for Populism?" in Conniff, *Latin American Populism*, p. 235.

76. Menéndez-Carrión, "The 1952–1978 Presidential Elections," p. 165.

77. World Bank, *The Current Economic Position*, Appendix Table 2-4. A large share of Ecuadorian manufacturing is taken up by traditional small-scale artisan production. Since 1960, however, most of the growth in the manufacturing sector has occurred in factory production.

78. Catherine Mary Conaghan, "Industrialists and the Reformist Interregnum: Dominant Class Behaviour and Ideology in Ecuador, 1972–1979" (Ph.D. dissertation, Yale University, 1983), pp. 78–85.

79. World Bank, *World Development Report 1983* (New York: Oxford University Press, 1983), Table 22, p. 190.

80. Manuel R. Agosin, "An Analysis of Ecuador's Industrial Development Law," *Journal of Developing Areas* 13, 3 (April 1979):264.

5

Black Gold:
The Petroleum Boom

The discovery of petroleum in the jungled regions of Ecuador's northern oriente in 1967 heralded the beginning of yet another export boom. Like cacao and bananas before it, petroleum brought an unprecedented surge of wealth to the country. But petroleum also differed in important respects from these earlier exports. The location of the petroleum fields in the Amazon region suggested that the infrastructural development from which the coast had benefited during earlier export booms would now take place in a region of the country largely untouched by either cacao or bananas. Petroleum also promised to radically alter the traditional role of the Ecuadorian state. Not only would the new wealth solve the immediate financial problems that had plagued Velasco Ibarra, but the state no longer had to rely on taxation of the private sector for revenue. With petroleum revenues accruing directly to the state, the autonomy of the public sector relative to private interest groups was greatly enhanced. Correspondingly, the traditionally dominant position of the coast in the national economy suffered a decline as petroleum shifted the locus of economic power toward Quito. In addition, for the first time foreign capital played a critical role in the development of Ecuadorian exports. The future of the petroleum boom depended not only on the performance of world markets but also on Ecuador's ability to attract the participation of foreign petroleum companies on terms it considered favorable.

EXPLORATION AND DISCOVERY

Petroleum exploration throughout the world by U.S. and European firms increased markedly in the 1920s following fears of an imminent and severe world shortage. Foreign petroleum companies—notably, Standard Oil of New Jersey and Royal Dutch-Shell—had operated in South America prior to this time but had concentrated their activities on the marketing of refined products rather than on exploration and production. Even as late as 1910, representatives of Standard Oil had commented with respect to direct investment in Peru that "it will be more profitable to buy production than to hunt for it, and to buy oil than to run the risks in this territory of producing it."[1] By the early 1920s, however, Standard and numerous other companies were involved in exploration and production throughout South America. By 1924, five countries—Argentina, Colombia, Ecuador, Peru, and Venezuela—were producing crude oil on a commercial basis.

Ecuadorian production of crude petroleum began when foreign firms with profitable operations on the northern Peruvian coast looked northward toward southern Ecuador for possible extensions of these fields. In 1917, Anglo-Ecuadorian Oilfields, Ltd., an affiliate of the British-owned Peruvian operator, Lobitos Oilfields Ltd., began production from fields discovered southwest of Guayaquil, on the Santa Elena peninsula. Standard Oil, through its Peruvian subsidiary, International Petroleum Company, also acquired concessions on the Ecuadorian coast but failed to find petroleum. Further exploration and development in the 1920s was discouraged by Anglo's low profitability relative to petroleum firms operating in other areas of South America, and by Standard's lack of success. Production from these coastal fields was never extensive. In 1929, Ecuador produced only 3,700 barrels per day of crude, or less than 1 percent of total South American output for that year.[2] In spite of Ecuador's small production of crude petroleum, however, even smaller domestic demand allowed the country to begin exporting petroleum in the 1930s. Although three small refineries built to supply the domestic market were in operation in Ecuador by the end of the 1920s, the largest of these, operated by Anglo, had a daily capacity of a mere 150 barrels.[3] In 1932, Ecuadorian exports of crude accounted for a pre-1972 high of nearly 30 percent of the total value of exports. But crude petroleum's contribution to export earnings steadily diminished after 1932 to around 1 percent by the 1950s.[4]

A second round of petroleum exploration in Ecuador was initiated in August 1937, when Shell received a concession contract covering nearly the entire oriente—namely, the part of Ecuador lying to the east of the Andes Mountains. Unlike the conditions encountered on the Ecuadorian coast, where access to the fields was relatively easy and the climate was dry, and where most petroleum had been found at depths of not more than 7 to 12 meters (23 to 39 feet), the oriente was an exceedingly difficult area for oil exploration and development.

Dense rain forest covered the entire region, and only mule trails linked the oriente to the highlands. Most communication was by river, but only a few rivers in the region allowed the transport of heavy equipment. Compounding the problem of difficult terrain, oriente petroleum appeared to lie at much greater depths than on the coast, and the formidable geographical barrier imposed by the Andes Mountains isolated the region from most potential markets.

Shell carried out an extensive program of reconnaissance work but chose to undertake no drilling, relinquishing one-half of its concession when operations ceased.[5] Even though the world oil market had recovered its profitability by the late 1930s, the uncertainties in the world market caused by World War II and the growing nationalist sentiment in Latin America undoubtedly dampened Shell's enthusiasm for what would certainly have been a costly drilling program.

Ecuador's attitude toward foreign oil companies reflected both the larger region's increased sense of nationalism and the Ecuadorian government's chronic need for revenues, particularly at a time when the government's access to foreign credit markets was severely restricted. During the 1930s, Argentina, Chile, Uruguay, and Bolivia all increased state control over their petroleum industries. At the end of the decade Mexico nationalized its petroleum industry. In Ecuador, the government of military officer General Alberto Enríquez Gallo proposed Ecuador's first petroleum legislation in 1937 and in the following year gave Anglo-Ecuadorian Oilfields fifteen days' notice of its intention to renegotiate the company's contract. The need to increase government revenues played an important role in this decision. Public spending between 1935 and 1938 had left the government with large obligations, unable to pay even the salaries of its employees. Anglo's offer to raise its royalty payments from 7 to 10 percent apparently satisfied the government as it provided the extra income needed to renegotiate a foreign loan.[6] Similarly, a bill submitted to the Ecuadorian congress in 1939 calling for the nationalization of domestic oil marketing lapsed after the government extracted loans from both Anglo and Shell.[7]

Immediately following World War II, renewed fears of a worldwide shortage of petroleum launched yet another round of exploration in Ecuador. In December 1948, Shell joined with Esso Standard Oil Company (formerly Jersey Standard) to begin a program of exploratory drilling on its remaining oriente holdings. Owing to the difficult terrain and the absence of roads, Shell's operation was completely airborne, the first such undertaking in the history of the oil industry and one of the most expensive. Two years later, the $40 million program was abandoned after six exploratory wells had failed to produce commercial quantities of petroleum: Five were drilled along the eastern edge of the Andes, and one was drilled on the far eastern border with Peru near Tiputini.[8] By this time, the immediate postwar shortage of petroleum had evaporated with the discovery of vast quantitites of inexpensive petroleum in the Middle-East, making continuation of the high-cost Ecuadorian operation relatively unattractive. Petroleum companies expressed no further interest in the Ecuadorian oriente except during a brief period in 1961, when two Canadian firms, operating as Minas y Petróleos del Ecuador, were awarded a 55-year, 4.5-million-hectare (11-million-acre) concession covering most of the former Shell holdings—at the time the largest independent oil holdings in the Western Hemisphere.[9] But in spite of four years of effort, Minas y Petróleos failed to arrange a satisfactory agreement for exploration of its concession.

Aside from the short-term financial benefit to Ecuadorian governments, the principal legacy from oil company operations in the oriente prior to 1964 was some limited infrastructural development. To service its operations, Shell had financed the construction of both the first road linking the highlands with the oriente and an airport at the oriente town of Mera in the eastern foothills of the Andes. The road, a precipice-hugging 107-kilometer (66-mile) feat of civil engineering between the highland city of Ambato and Mera, opened up a part of the region to some limited colonization and small-scale commercial agriculture.

Yet the oriente, a region accounting for just under one-half the total area of the country, remained largely undeveloped. Early Spanish attempts to settle the region had been largely frustrated by disease and the failure to discover precious metals, leaving only a scattering of tiny missionary settlements catering to a small population of isolated indigenous groups at places such as Archidona, Baeza, Tena, and San Francisco de Orellana. The largest oriente Indian group, the lowland Quechua, numbered about 27,000 in 1959; other oriente Indians probably totaled no more than 16,000.[10] Particularly following Ecuador's loss of more than half of its oriente territory to Peru in 1941, the military promoted some settlement of the region, but the numbers have never been significant. Colonists from the highlands, deterred by the lack of roads and limited economic possibilities, were never attracted in large numbers. As late as 1962, less than 2 percent of Ecuador's population resided in the oriente.[11] The economic importance of the oriente also remained marginal, with naranjilla, a fruit used domestically to make a refreshing drink, and beef cattle the only products of economic significance.

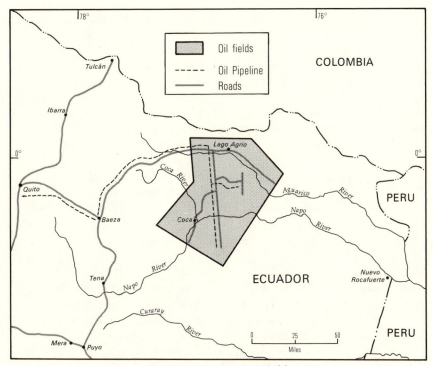

MAP 5.1   Oriente oilfields

In spite of the failure of the Spaniards to find gold or silver in the oriente, Ecuadorians from the time of the conquest had continued to dream of the hidden riches of the oriente. The failure to find petroleum in the 1930s and 1940s only embellished the myth with stories of the oil companies' unreported discoveries. The public expressions of outrage following President Galo Plaza's comment in the late 1940s, that "el Oriente es un mito" (the oriente is a myth), provided evidence of the depth of this belief. But not until 1967, when large deposits of petroleum were discovered in the northeastern corner of the region just south of the Colombian border (see Map 5.1), were there objective reasons for believing that Ecuadorians' long-cherished dreams might be realized. In mid-1963, a Texaco-Gulf consortium had discovered a large petroleum field at Orito in the Putomayo area of southern Colombia. Believing that this field extended south across the border into Ecuador, the consortium signed an agreement in March 1964 with the ruling military junta for a 1.4-million-hectare (3.5-million-acre) concession in the northeastern oriente. A year later, the consortium acquired a lease on an additional 650,000 hectares (1.6 million acres) from Minas y Petróleos. In 1965, the military government issued new petroleum legislation, the first since 1937. Perceived to be quite favorable, the new laws encouraged oil company exploration in Ecuador, particularly as Colombia was contemplating the nationalization of its petroleum industry and Peru was still embroiled in a bitter dispute with the International Petroleum Company.[12]

Operating in territory considered by one of the petroleum trade journals to be "one of the toughest operating areas in the world," Texaco-Gulf launched a costly exploration program that paid off three years later, on April 8, 1967, with the discovery of a large field of high-quality petroleum at Lago Agrio, just forty miles south of the Orito field in Colombia.[13] The consortium followed this find with a remarkable string of successes. By 1969, twelve of thirteen wells drilled had yielded commercial quantities of petroleum, an achievement reported as "one of the most spectacular wildcat success records in oil industry annals."[14]

Attracted by Texaco-Gulf's success rate in the Ecuadorian oriente, other foreign oil companies rushed to obtain concessions. But the same evidence of large deposits of petroleum also encouraged Ecuadorian governments to adopt a more nationalistic petroleum policy. In early 1969, motivated partly by nationalistic sentiment and partly by his desperate need for increased government revenues, Velasco Ibarra announced major revisions in the government's contract with Texaco-Gulf. According to the revised terms, the consortium would pay an advance of $11 million on royalties and concession rights, increase royalties from 6 to 11.5 percent, invest $35 million for roads and airports in the oriente, and return two-thirds of its original concession to the government, leaving the companies 485,000 hectares (1.2 million acres).[15] Though considerably stiffer than the original contract, the new terms do not appear to have seriously discouraged exploration, at least not as evidenced by subsequent bidding on Texaco-Gulf's relinquished acreage. By early 1971, more than twenty foreign companies were exploring for petroleum in Ecuador.[16]

The potentially large size of Ecuador's petroleum reserves convinced Texaco-Gulf of the feasibility of an Ecuadorian pipeline connecting Lago Agrio with the coastal port of Esmeraldas, a project the government had been forcefully advocating since the initial discovery. The only alternatives to this pipeline would have involved shipment through either Colombian or Peruvian territory. Given Ecuador's long history of territorial disputes with both of these countries, particularly with Peru, neither was an alternative the government viewed with any enthusiasm. Even the domestic route of the pipeline was not without controversy. On economic grounds

Esmeraldas was the logical termination point for the pipeline, but Guayaquil, fearing the creation of a rival to its own dominant position in the coastal economy, bitterly opposed the northern route, arguing that the pipeline should terminate in Guayaquil.[17] In mid-1972, notwithstanding Guayaquil's arguments, the pipeline was completed to Esmeraldas and Ecuador once again became a petroleum-exporting country, shipping 195,000 barrels per day by 1973.

ECONOMIC AND SOCIAL CHANGE

Petroleum revenues launched an unprecedented period of economic expansion. Economic growth accelerated rapidly into the 1970s. During the last half of the preceding decade, real output had increased at an annual rate of just over 4 percent. Between 1970 and 1975, the growth of real output jumped sharply to an annual rate of 11.4 percent. Although this rapid rate of growth was not sustained during the latter half of the 1970s, the economy nevertheless grew at an average annual rate in excess of 6 percent throughout the remainder of the decade.[18] Given rates of growth of population around 3.5 percent, well below the rate of growth of output, per capita income also rose rapidly. Formerly one of the poorest countries in South America, Ecuador by 1981 had attained a per capita income of $1,180, roughly equal to that of its neighbors Colombia and Peru.[19]

Like Ecuador's previous export booms in cacao and bananas, the petroleum boom accelerated economic growth through linkages to the domestic economy directly associated with the production of petroleum, and indirectly through state expenditure policies. But in contrast with earlier export booms, the direct effects of petroleum production were of short duration. Only during the early years when Texaco-Gulf and other oil companies were making large investments in exploration and development did the petroleum sector contribute directly and significantly to economic growth. Between 1970 and 1973, more than 60 percent of the growth of output was attributable to the growth of the petroleum sector.[20] Employment associated with exploration and development activities rose to a peak of nearly 6,000 workers, but it declined rapidly after 1971 as these activities slowed and the pipeline was completed.[21] From 1974 to 1982, the petroleum sector contributed barely 2 percent to the rate of growth of the economy.[22]

As in Ecuador's earlier experience with Shell, infrastructural development in the oriente was again the principal direct legacy of petroleum exploration and production, although this time on a far larger scale than during the 1930s and 1940s. Both road and airport construction helped to link the oriente to the highlands and to provide access to large areas of unsettled land within the region. Some of this construction occurred because of the oil companies' need to transport equipment and maintain access to pipelines; some was explicitly stipulated in contracts between the petroleum companies and the government. In 1971, Texaco-Gulf completed a 280-kilometer (175-mile) third-class road between Quito and Lago Agrio, the first road linking the highlands with the northern oriente and the first such road to extend beyond the eastern foothills. Extensions of this road south and east of Lago Agrio are currently opening up further areas of the oriente. By the 1980s, more than 1,000 kilometers (620 miles) of roads had been constructed in the oriente.

Colonization of the newly accessible region progressed at a rapid rate, following the initial discovery of petroleum. Even before the Quito–Lago Agrio road was completed, the military, fearing Colombian settlement of the region around the oilfields and a possible loss of sovereignty, had sponsored free flights from Quito for colonists. Although these early colonists were literally left at the end of the runway to fend for themselves, nearly 400 families had taken advantage of the military's offer by the time the flights were terminated in late 1970.[23] Since 1969, military conscripts have been encouraged to settle in the oriente as agricultural colonists, also for national security reasons. Most of these military settlements are small and isolated. The petroleum companies' need for unskilled workers also introduced approximately 10,000 people to the region, some small proportion of whom remained and acquired land for settlement.[24] It was only with the completion of the Quito–Lago Agrio road, however, that settlers arrived in large numbers. Between 1971 and 1978, approximately 6,000 families settled in the region, most from crowded regions of the sierra, such as the Loja area in southern Ecuador; others came from the earlier colonization zone around Santo Domingo, where they had failed either to acquire or to retain land.[25] By 1982, the population of the oriente had risen from less than 2 percent of the total population of the country to slightly more than 3 percent.[26] Although the absolute number of residents remained small, the oriente became the fastest growing region of the country.

In spite of increasing numbers of colonists, the economic importance of the oriente to the nation's economy, aside from petroleum, remains marginal. Most agricultural production is for local consumption. A limited amount of timber is exported to Quito; some coffee and cacao is produced in commercial quantities. But the distance from markets, both domestic and foreign, as well as the poor quality of communications place oriente production at a decided disadvantage relative to the coast. Most hopes for commercial agriculture rest on cattle ranching. Increasing urbanization, the petroleum-induced rise in per capita incomes, and the broadening of the domestic market have raised the internal demand for beef to the point where oriente production could profitably supplement established coastal production. A shift to cattle production, however, may result in a concentration of landholdings. Most settlers in the oriente acquired lots of between 50 and 100 hectares (120 to 240 acres), an area sufficient in most cases for crop production in the region but not for commercial cattle ranching. Thus, without careful government policy, some serious trade-offs could occur between more profitable oriente agriculture and the ability of the region to reduce population pressures in the sierra.

The principal linkage between petroleum and the Ecuadorian economy is provided by state expenditures. Indeed, in contrast to previous export booms, when the state had to tax the private sector in order to capture a share of the increase in export earnings, the petroleum boom is distinguished by the fact that virtually all of Ecuador's petroleum earnings accrue directly to the public sector. Thus, a characteristic of the petroleum boom is that the growth of government spending has closely paralleled the large increase in petroleum export earnings. Between 1973 and 1982, real public expenditures increased at an annual rate of 12 percent, rising as a share of gross domestic product from 22 percent to a high of nearly 33 percent.[27] The growth of government spending provided an important stimulus to urbanization, to expansion of the domestic market, and to industrialization. From 1974 through the end of the decade, two sectors—services (of which government services are the largest component) and manufacturing—accounted for more than three-quarters of the growth of GDP.

The pace of urbanization quickened during the petroleum boom as the rate of rural-to-urban migration increased. Booming urban construction industries and a depressed agricultural economy combined to draw workers into the cities. From 1974 to 1982, the urban portion of the population rose from 41 to just over 45 percent.[28] Both Guayaquil and Quito, Ecuador's two largest cities, grew at rapid rates, as did many of the smaller provincial cities. Quito's growth, in particular, was stimulated by expanding public-sector employment, which grew at an annual rate of 8.8 percent (from 150,552 employees in 1975 to 271,966 by 1982), and by an increased tendency for industry to locate in the nation's capital.[29] Spurred by both these factors, the Quito area began to grow at a slightly faster rate than its larger coastal rival, Guayaquil.[30]

The emergence of an urban middle and lower-middle class, significant both numerically and in terms of its purchasing power, was one consequence of rising per capita incomes and increasing urbanization during the petroleum boom. Professionals, office workers, and drivers, the mainstays of the new middle class, experienced the greatest income gains of all occupational groups between 1968 and 1975.[31] Though still quite restricted relative to other South American countries, the domestic market in Ecuador rapidly expanded, ranking consistently as "one of the fastest growing markets in Latin America throughout the decade of the 1970s."[32] Supermarkets, which in Quito numbered only one prior to 1970, multiplied, as did U.S.-style shopping centers. Consumer expenditures, corrected for inflationary price increases, doubled between 1972 and 1982.

Industry, the most dynamic sector after services, also expanded rapidly during the 1970s, growing at an annual rate of 11.5 percent during the latter half of the decade. Between 1970 and 1980, the share of manufacturing in GDP rose from 16.8 percent to just over 18 percent.[33] The primary stimulus to the expansion of industry was the broadening of the domestic market. Not only a continuation of government incentives for import-substitution industrialization begun in the mid-1960s but also an overvalued exchange rate that cheapened the price of imported raw materials and capital goods contributed to growth of the sector. Thus, most of the growth in Ecuadorian manufacturing was directed toward the expanding domestic market. The export of manufactures, though promoted by government policy, accounted for only 17 percent of the value of total manufacturing production in 1979. Semiprocessed cacao, which received heavy government subsidies, and petroleum derivatives contributed over three-quarters of the total value of Ecuador's manufactured exports.[34] Excluding these two products, manufactured exports never amounted to more than 9 percent of total exports.[35]

In spite of the growth of industry during the petroleum boom, Ecuador's manufacturing sector remained at an early stage of development, its contribution to gross domestic product by 1982 still well below the average for Latin America. Growth in industries producing for the domestic market was constrained by Ecuador's small population and by a highly unequal distribution of income only marginally altered in favor of the middle class by petroleum income. A World Bank study has estimated that approximately 60 percent of Ecuador's population fell below the absolute poverty line in 1975.[36] As a consequence, the principal domestic market for Ecuadorian industry was limited to urban middle- and upper-income consumers. In the absence of explicit policies to expand the domestic market or to promote the continued development of manufactured exports, the possibilities for continued growth of Ecuadorian industry are severely constricted.

Two additional problems that raise questions about the ability of Ecuadorian industry to sustain its role as a leading sector of the economy are its limited contribution to employment creation and its heavy reliance on imported inputs. Ecuadorian industry reflects the duality characteristic of the country's economy and society, with large numbers of small-scale, virtually artisan producers coexisting with a small number of large, modern industrial enterprises. Most of the growth in new manufacturing during the petroleum boom took place in the modern sector of industry, which, in part due to incentives provided by the industrial development law, relied heavily on imported capital equipment and raw materials. Because growth in the modern sector was capital intensive, employment increases in this sector were limited. Between 1974 and 1982, urban manufacturing employment as a share of the labor force fell slightly from 16.2 to 15 percent.[37] In addition, the manufacturing sector's heavy reliance on imported inputs, in combination with limited exports, resulted in the financing of industrial growth through petroleum earnings. Consequently, any decline in petroleum earnings now reduces the country's ability to import manufacturing inputs, thus also threatening the continued growth of the sector.

In spite of spectacular earnings from petroleum exports and the ensuing rapid growth of the domestic economy, Ecuador's petroleum boom ran into trouble almost as soon as it had begun. Petroleum export earnings, like those of any other export, are determined by the combination of world prices and export quantities. Thus, the crash of the cacao boom in the early 1920s came abruptly as world prices fell under pressure from expanding exports by other producing nations, and disease cut sharply into Ecuadorian exports. The banana boom, on the other hand, stagnated in the late 1950s and 1960s, primarily because of steady or falling world prices for the fruit; disease played only a minor role in slowing the rate of growth of exports. Although immune to disease, petroleum export volume proved highly susceptible to stagnant production and rising domestic consumption of petroleum products, both of which contributed to a secular decline in shipments after 1973, the first full year of production. Rapidly rising world prices more than offset these export declines until 1982, when prices also began to decline. The drop in prices contributed to a serious economic recession in that year, regarded by many as the worst since the 1920s and 1930s.

Petroleum differed from Ecuador's earlier exports in two important ways. First, as petroleum is an exhaustible resource, its long-term export performance depended on increases in reserves. Second, because Ecuador depended on the participation of foreign firms to do a large share of petroleum exploration and development, expansion of the country's petroleum reserves rested on the government's ability (and willingness) to attract foreign participation.

The failure of other companies to replicate Texaco-Gulf's success and the aggressively nationalistic petroleum policy pursued by the military government that took power in February of 1972 seriously discouraged exploration and development. By the end of 1976, only four companies held approximately 1 million hectares (2.5 million acres), down from approximately twice that many companies holding 6.5 hectares (16 million acres) in mid-1972.[38] In the absence of exploration and development to increase reserves, Ecuador's oriente production of crude stagnated. Between 1973 and 1975, production declined by 23 percent, rising slowly by 1979 to just slightly greater than the 1973 level, only to stagnate again until 1983.[39] Petroleum exports performed even worse, as steadily rising domestic consumption of petroleum derivatives took an increasingly large share of total production. Driven by rising incomes and artificially low internal prices, domestic consumption of gasoline rose at an annual rate in excess of 20 percent. In 1978, the domestic price of gasoline at the pump was equivalent to $0.18 per gallon, well below the estimated production cost of $0.43 per gallon.[40] Indicative of the increased domestic demand for gasoline, the number of automobiles in Ecuador increased rapidly, from 82,000 in 1970 to 223,000 by 1977.[41]

In spite of more or less steadily declining petroleum exports between 1973 and 1982 (see Table 5.1), sharply rising world petroleum prices during the 1970s, caused by OPEC's supply restrictions, generally maintained the rise in Ecuador's crude petroleum export earnings. From 1973 to 1980, the price of Ecuadorian crude increased by over 800 percent, from $3.97 per barrel to a high of $35.20 per barrel. By 1981, however, decreased demand on the part of the consuming nations and increased crude exports from the producing countries depressed world petroleum prices, causing the price of Ecuadorian crude to fall into the low $20 range by 1985 (and into the $10–$18 range in 1986).

Paralleling Ecuador's earlier experiences with cacao and bananas, both the economy and the government became heavily dependent on the performance of a single export. By 1982, petroleum exports accounted for 65 percent of all export earnings; the petroleum sector generated nearly 10 percent of the country's gross domestic product.

TABLE 5.1
Petroleum production, export prices, and government income, 1972-1984

Year	Production (1000 barrels)	Exports[a]	Export Price/Barrel (dollars)	Percent of Total Exports[b]	Government Petroleum Income[c] (dollars x 1000)
1972	27,629.0	24,961.6	2.37	18.5	24,733
1973	75,336.1	71,125.6	3.97	48.3	123,594
1974	63,851.2	59,233.1	13.38	64.9	432,690
1975	58,104.3	52,094.9	11.82	61.0	430,423
1976	67,650.4	61,509.9	11.99	56.4	447,490
1977	66,090.1	50,453.1	12.94	47.3	378,320
1978	73,264.2	44,799.1	12.48	42.8	516,280
1979	78,320.4	44,736.6	23.09	54.6	1,012,240
1980	74,769.4	39,588.9	35.20	62.0	1,344,720
1981	77,028.0	45,242.8	34.40	67.6	1,591,440
1982	77,089.6	43,075.1	32.49	64.8	1,841,270
1983	86,691.1	59,303.6	27.64	72.5	1,745,850
1984	93,879.7	61,346.0	27.35	70.0	---[d]

[a]Ecuador also exported some fuel oil, particularly following the completion of the Esmeraldas refinery in 1978. For this reason, the drop in exports between 1977 and 1978 is not as pronounced as the figures for crude petroleum exports indicate.
[b]Includes exports of crude petroleum and fuel oil.
[c]Government petroleum income is not equal to exports times the export price because the former includes other receipts such as royalties and exports of refined products. Sucre figures were converted to dollars on the basis of 25 sucres to the dollar for 1972-1981; 30 sucres for 1982; and 44.12 sucres for 1983.
[d]Not available.

SOURCE: Petroleum production, exports, and export prices for 1972-1984 were taken from Banco Central del Ecuador, *Memoria 1985*, (Quito, 1986), pp. 98, 191, 266. Petroleum exports as a share of total exports for 1972-1979 were taken from World Bank, *Ecuador: An Agenda for Recovery and Sustained Growth* (1984), Table 8-9, p. 175, and Table 3-4, p. 128; figures for 1980-1984 were calculated from Banco Central del Ecuador, *Memoria 1985*, (Quito, 1986), p. 264. Government petroleum income figures were taken from Ministerio de Finanzas, *Estadísticas Petroleras* (Quito, 1981), p. 13, and *Estadísticas de Ingresos Petroleros* (Quito, 1984), p. 10.

Whereas traditional exports, such as bananas and cacao, grew very slowly, only shrimp and fish products showed rapid growth. Indeed, by 1982 the latter had become the country's second most important export after petroleum, at a time when earnings from these two products accounted for 9 percent of total export earnings. Petroleum revenues also became the principal source of public revenues, rapidly displacing other sources of income. By 1982, petroleum revenues were financing approximately 40 percent of public-sector expenditures.[42] Thus, by the 1980s any change in petroleum earnings had profound consequences for both the public and private sectors of the Ecuadorian economy.

Despite large petroleum revenues, which grew at an annual rate of 35 percent between 1973 and 1982, the substantial public-sector surplus enjoyed during the first three years of the petroleum boom had evaporated by 1975 as the rate of growth of government expenditures outpaced revenues. Faced with growing public-sector deficits after 1975, governments had essentially three choices, any one or all of which could be adopted: Government expenditures could be reduced, revenues could be increased by raising taxes or by increasing petroleum exports, or funds could be borrowed. Governments during the petroleum boom were as loath as their predecessors to reduce expenditures if any alternative could be found. Efforts to increase nonpetroleum taxes also faced traditional obstacles; in fact, nonpetroleum revenues declined in relative terms. Increases in petroleum revenues involved seeking a delicate balance between the desire to avoid discouraging expanded participation by foreign petroleum companies and the need to increase taxes on petroleum. Raising the domestic prices of petroleum derivatives could also increase petroleum exports, but this option was regarded as a delicate political issue—in fact, one that most governments preferred to defer if at all possible. Not surprisingly, Ecuadorian governments followed traditional patterns of behavior, turning to increased public-sector borrowing as the easiest solution to the deficit problem, at least in the short run. But unlike, for example, the situation faced by liberal governments in the early 1900s, when access to the international credit market was largely blocked because of the country's poor credit rating, in the 1970s petroleum guaranteed Ecuador's access to private international banks eager to make loans to the governments of developing countries. From 1976 to 1979, Ecuador's public debt increased four and one-half times; from 1979 to 1983 the rate of borrowing slowed, but the debt nevertheless almost doubled.[43]

Thus, even though petroleum revenues continued to grow until 1983, the ability of Ecuadorian governments to sustain the rate of growth of expenditures became dependent on their continued access to the international banking system. By the end of 1982, international bankers, thrown into a panic by Mexico's threatened default on its large foreign debt, had closed the door to further borrowing by Ecuador. The government was faced with an acute economic—and political—crisis that forced it to adopt an austerity program involving most of the measures for reducing the deficit heretofore considered politically unacceptable.

NOTES

1. Mira Wilkens, *The Emergence of Multinational Enterprise: American Business Abroad from the Colonial Era to 1914* (Cambridge, Mass.: Harvard University Press, 1970), p. 64.

2. Mira Wilkens, "Multinational Oil Companies in South America in the 1920s: Argentina, Bolivia, Brazil, Chile, Colombia, Ecuador, and Peru," *Business History Review*, 48, 3 (Autumn 1974):427, Table 3.

3. Wilkens, "Multinational Oil," p. 422.

4. Linda Alexander Rodríguez, *The Search for Public Policy: Regional Politics and Government Finances in Ecuador, 1830–1940* (Berkeley: University of California Press, 1985), Appendix A, p. 181.

5. Frank J. Gardner, "Oriente: The Hottest New Latin Oil Patch in Years," *Oil and Gas Journal* (March 24, 1969):66.

6. George Philip, *Oil and Politics in Latin America: Nationalist Movements and State Companies* (Cambridge: Cambridge University Press, 1982), p. 51.

7. Philip, *Oil and Politics*, p. 51.

8. See Gardner, "Oriente," p. 66. The Shell/Standard failure to find petroleum has been called "one of the costliest failures in exploration in the history of the oil industry." See also Institute of Petroleum, *Oil: Latin America and the Caribbean* (London: Institute of Petroleum, 1968), p. 18; cited in R. J. Bromley, "Agricultural Colonization in the Upper Amazon Basin: The Impact of Oil Discoveries," *Tijdschrift Voor Economische En Sociale Geografie*, 63 (1972):280.

9. Gardner, "Oriente," p. 66.

10. Bromley, "Agricultural Colonization," p. 280.

11. Banco Central del Ecuador, *Boletín Anuario*, No. 7 (Quito, 1984), p. 187.

12. J. E. Rassmuss, "Increase in Oil Development Is in Prospect in Ecuador," *World Oil* (June 1966):148.

13. *Oil and Gas Journal* (April 24, 1967):70.

14. Gardner, "Oriente" (March 24, 1969):63.

15. *Oil and Gas Journal* (March 10, 1969):50; ibid. (March 24, 1969):66; and ibid. (July 14, 1969):39.

16. Frank J. Gardner, "Explorers Fan Out in Ecuador's Oriente," *Oil and Gas Journal* (July 12, 1971):49.

17. This conflict between Guayaquil and Esmeraldas is not without historical precedent. In the early 1600s, proposals from Quito to build a road to Esmeraldas were defeated by opposition from Guayaquil merchants and exporters, who feared the loss of their virtual monopoly on trade with the highlands. See John Leddy Phelan, *The Kingdom of Quito in the Seventeenth Century* (Madison: University of Wisconsin Press, 1967), pp. 3–22.

18. Banco Central del Ecuador, *Cuentas Nacionales No. 5* (Quito, 1983), Cuadro 3, pp. 15–16.

19. World Bank, *World Development Report 1983* (New York: Oxford University Press, 1983), Table 1, p. 148.

20. World Bank, *Ecuador: An Agenda for Recovery and Sustained Growth* (Washington, D.C.: The Bank for International Reconstruction and Development, 1984), p. 3.

21. Bromley, "Agricultural Colonization," p. 287.

22. World Bank, *An Agenda*, p. 3.

23. David Schodt, "Report on Colonization of the Northern Oriente," internal memorandum, U.S. Peace Corps—Ecuador (Quito, May 1970), p. 4.

24. Bromley, "Agricultural Colonization," p. 288.

25. Mario Hiraoka and Shozo Yamamoto, "Agricultural Development in the Upper Amazon of Ecuador," *Geographical Review*, 70, 4 (October 1980):427.

26. Banco Central del Ecuador, *Boletín Anuario*, No. 7, p. 188.

27. The author's calculations were made on the basis of Ecuadorian national accounts data.

28. Banco Central del Ecuador, *Boletín Anuario*, No. 7, p. 186.

29. Fidel Jaramillo B., "Estado: principal generador de empleo," *Hoy* (Quito, May 28, 1983), p. 2A.

30. Anne Collin Delavaud, *Atlas del Ecuador* (Paris: Les Ediciones J. A., 1982), pp. 64–68; and Banco Central del Ecuador, *Boletín Anuario*, No. 7, p. 186. Quito's growth rate exceeded that of Guayaquil only between 1962 and 1974, but Pichincha province (Quito) continued to grow faster than Guayas province (Guayaquil) from 1962 to 1982.

31. World Bank, *Ecuador: Development Problems and Prospects* (Washington, D.C.: The International Bank for Reconstruction and Development), 1979, p. 18.

32. Catherine Mary Conaghan, "Industrialists and the Reformist Interregnum: Dominant Class Behavior and Ideology in Ecuador, 1972–1979" (Ph.D. dissertation, Yale University, 1983), p. 185.

33. Calculated from World Bank, *An Agenda*, Table 2.2, p. 120.

34. Cristián Sepúlveda, *El Proceso de Industrialización Ecuatoriano* (Quito: Instituto de Investigaciones Económicas [Universidad Católica], 1983), p. 48.

35. Banco Central del Ecuador, *Cuentas*, No. 6, pp. 173–214.

36. World Bank, *Development Problems*, p. 21. The poverty line of $218 (1975 dollars) was calculated as that below which there was insufficient income to satisfy basic needs. Although this figure of 60 percent probably exaggerates the incidence of poverty, there is no question but that a large percentage of Ecuador's population can be considered absolutely poor.

37. Banco Central del Ecuador, *Boletín Anuario*, No. 7, pp. 192–193.

38. *Petroleum Economist* (October 1978):416.

39. Banco Central del Ecuador, *Boletín Anuario*, No. 7, p. 176.

40. *Petroleum Economist* (October 1978):418.

41. World Bank, *Development Problems*, Table 10.6, p. 637.

42. World Bank, *An Agenda*, p. 38.

43. Banco Central del Ecuador, *Memoria 1983*, p. 123.

6

The Military Returns to Power

The 1970s in Ecuador witnessed the conjuncture of several events that appeared to be highly conducive to the adoption of social and economic reform policies. Petroleum revenues provided the government with considerable resources for implementing its programs and relatively greater autonomy from entrenched economic elites. Import-substituting industrialization—stimulated by the 1957 Industrial Development Law, by its promotion under the 1964 military junta, and by expectations of petroleum-led economic prosperity—had accelerated, providing reformists with hope for the emergence of an ally from those elements of the industrial elite producing for the domestic market. Not least, a military government led by General Rodríguez Lara seized power in 1972, pronouncing itself in favor of socioeconomic reforms along the lines of the military government then in power in Peru. Yet, although the 1972 military government expanded the economic functions of the Ecuadorian state beyond that accomplished by any previous government, its achievements in the area of social reforms were limited, particularly in view of the generally propitious conditions surrounding the installation of this government. In January 1976, a centrist triumvirate of the three service commanders seized power from Rodríguez Lara, abandoning the reformist direction of that government and preparing to return power to the civilians.

MILITARY REFORM REVISITED: THE RODRIGUEZ LARA GOVERNMENT

The 1972 military government headed by General Rodríguez Lara carried forward the tradition of reformist military governments first established with the 1925 military junta. But unlike its predecessors, the military government in 1972 had the experience of a relatively recent attempt to govern, the examples of strong military governments elsewhere in Latin America committed to using the state to achieve their objectives, and unparalleled resources for implementing its plans.

The military's most recent attempt to govern, the 1963 junta, was widely regarded by both military and civilians as a failure. Stung by harsh public criticism in which the period of the military junta was castigated as a time when "the nation [was] scorned and reviled by the most incompetent of her sons: . . . the military dictators," the military was initially loath to intervene again.[1] But the bankrupt policies of the civilian governments during the intervening years, which threatened again to squander the opportunities for development created by an export boom, convinced most officers by 1972 that the military should once more occupy the government palace. However, because of the perceived failure of the 1963 junta to alter either the inegalitarian socioeconomic structure of the country or the traditional patterns of civilian politics, the military intervened in 1972 with an even greater commitment to these objectives. Nowhere was this renewed commitment more apparent than over the issue of nationalism. Still smarting over allegations that the 1963 military junta had forfeited the country's patrimony in exchange for foreign loans when, under pressure from the United States, it had unofficially abandoned former claims to a 200-mile territorial limit, the military in 1972 was determined to establish its nationalistic credentials.

State-led development was the cornerstone of the Rodríguez Lara government's plan to transform Ecuadorian society. The development plan for 1973–1977 stated that to achieve the government's objectives, Ecuador required "a more decisive intervention by the State in the economy, as much to consolidate already initiated basic reforms . . . as to promote new reforms necessary to expand the potential for national development. The strategy implies transferring to the Public Sector those fundamental decisions that affect the economy and Ecuadorian society, those that today reside in foreign centers." Most important, the military wanted the state to move beyond its traditional role as provider of services such as public works and education to direct involvement in production. As noted in the plan, "The direct participation of the State in the productive process through the introduction of basic industries, which implies that the Public Sector should adopt a very active stance in the promotion of enterprises, is of fundamental importance."[2] State intervention in the financial sector was also advocated as a means of channeling petroleum revenues toward priority areas of the economy. At the same time, the plan emphasized that increased state intervention was to complement, not substitute for, the private sector of the economy, arguing that "more intense Public Sector participation in these areas will permit greater assistance to the Private Sector."[3]

Prior to the 1970s, although the Ecuadorian state was large relative to similarly situated countries in Latin America, its principal activities were limited to traditional functions such as the provision of public works and education. The few public enterprises that did exist, such as the Fábrica de Abonos del Estado (State Fertilizer Factory), had been established to meet a specific need (in this case the acute shortage of fertilizer during World War II), not out of a commitment to state-led economic development as was now being proposed. During the fifth Velasco Ibarra administration several additional public enterprises were created, but by 1972 all public enterprises still contributed less than 2 percent of the total value of final goods and services (GDP).

Between 1972 and 1979, approximately fifteen additional public enterprises were established, and many of the existing enterprises received large increases in funding. Both nationalization, such as the takeover of bankrupt Ecuatoriana Airlines, and the creation of new public enterprises, such as the Ecuadorian State Petroleum Company (CEPE), were part of the state's policies. Nationalization, particularly with respect to failing industries, accounted for a large number of the enterprises created during this period. In addition, the military established a number of enterprises to service its own needs. Value added by public enterprises as a share of GDP rose from 2 percent in 1972 to 12 percent by 1983. Most of this growth occurred in the petroleum, transport, communications, and public utility industries.[4]

Similarly, public financial institutions grew in importance during the 1970s. In the period from 1968 to the present, a clear shift has occurred in financial intermediation away from the private institutions toward state banks and private nonbank financial institutions. A large part of this shift can be explained in terms of the allocation of petroleum revenues to public financial institutions; the remainder can be accounted for by the expansion of public-sector borrowing requirements as well as by government interest rate and credit restrictions, which have retarded the growth of private bank deposits. In 1968, public financial institutions accounted for 26 percent of total deposits and 36 percent of the total domestic credit supply; by 1981, these figures were 40 percent and 55 percent, respectively.[5] The public financial institutions have served, among other things, as a channel for state investment, specifically as minority shareholders in mixed enterprises. By 1974, the Corporación Financiera Nacional, one of the public financial institutions, was a shareholder in twenty-eight firms.[6]

TABLE 6.1
Allocation of petroleum revenues within the public sector, 1972-1983
(in percentage shares)

Year	Budget[a]	Other Public Administration	Public Enterprises	Public Financial Institutions	Public Sector[b]
1972	55	43	1	0	100
1973	60	32	2	5	100
1974	35	60	1	4	100
1975	28	61	7	4	100
1976	30	57	8	4	100
1977	26	61	10	3	100
1978	21	64	12	2	100
1979	18	56	24	2	100
1980	34	41	15	10	100
1981	44	31	16	9	100
1982	45	28	16	12	100
1983	42	35	13	11	100

[a]The budget refers to the official document submitted by the president to the legislature for its consideration. The public administration includes the national government budget, local governments, social security, the semi-autonomous institutions, and special funds.
[b]Subtotals may not add up to 100 due to rounding error.

SOURCE: Calculated from *Estadísticas Petroleras* and *Estadísticas de Ingresos Petroleros* (Quito : Ministerio de Finanzas, 1981 and 1984 respectively).

Petroleum revenues made possible the expanded state role envisaged by the military, and it was in the area of petroleum policy that the Rodríguez government sought hardest to establish its nationalistic credentials. (See Table 6.1 for a breakdown of revenue allocations.) Not surprisingly, these two objectives were potentially conflictual. In February 1972, Navy Captain Gustavo Jarrín Ampudia was appointed minister of natural resources. A former head of the Naval Academy, Jarrín was a determined nationalist, influenced in his attitude toward petroleum policy by the Brazilian state oil company Petrobrás and somewhat radicalized by the Navy's direct involvement in the 1971 conflict with U.S. tuna fishing boats over Ecuador's 200-mile territorial limit.[7] Jarrín adopted a relatively hard line toward the petroleum companies, apparently in the belief that if his policies slowed production this was not an altogether undesirable outcome, as it slowed the inflationary impact of petroleum on the Ecuadorian economy and banked reserves for a time when prices would be higher. In June 1972, he issued a decree making the 1971 petroleum legislation retroactive. Companies that had obtained concessions prior to 1971 were required to renegotiate their concession contracts. Negotiations dragged on well into 1973, creating an uncertainty that contributed to the withdrawal of a number of smaller companies and a virtual cessation of all exploration activities. Finally, in August 1973 the government reached an agreement with Texaco-Gulf. In 1972 the Ecuadorian State Petroleum Company was established, and by 1974 it had acquired a 25 percent share of the Texaco-Gulf consortium.[8] In November 1973, Ecuador joined the Organization of Petroleum Exporting Countries (OPEC), hosting the June 1974 meeting of this organization in Quito. Jarrín, who had played a role within OPEC entirely out of proportion to the relative size of Ecuadorian production, was appointed president of the organization at the Quito meeting and was reelected at the following September meeting. Immediately following his reelection, Jarrín ordered an increase in Ecuador's petroleum levies and formally proposed that the government acquire a 51 percent interest in the Texaco-Gulf consortium, the sole remaining producer of any significance.[9]

Jarrín's appointment as president of OPEC marked the apogee of his career as minister of natural resources. Five months later he was dismissed from his post and sent as military attaché to the Ecuadorian embassy in London. Both domestic and international factors played a role in his fall from power and in the blunting of Ecuador's aggressive nationalism. The private sector, alarmed by what it viewed as increasing state intervention and fearing that the flight of foreign capital from the petroleum sector would quickly spread to other areas of the economy, lobbied for Jarrín's removal. In February 1973, the newspaper El Universo reported that "there are growing doubts about whether the Ecuadorian government has miscalculated."[10] A growing world surplus of petroleum during 1974 began to shift the balance of bargaining power from the government to Texaco-Gulf, increasing the domestic costs of Jarrín's policies. Pressure from the United States also appears to have been a factor. As George Philip reported, "Rumours circulated within the Ecuadorian Army to the effect that Washington would cut military aid unless Jarrín were removed from his post."[11] Certainly conservative groups, both the civilian ones and those within the military, were concerned about his increasingly antagonistic remarks toward the United States. Indeed, Jarrín's public remarks on September 25, 1974, in which he criticized a speech by President Ford before the United Nations General Assembly, appear to have precipitated his dismissal.[12]

Following Jarrín's dismissal, the Ecuadorian government's policy toward Texaco-Gulf moderated. Petroleum had greatly increased government revenues, but public expenditures had grown even more rapidly. Similarly, imports began to race ahead of exports. By 1975, both the public-sector accounts and the current account balance of trade were in deficit. Heavily dependent on petroleum earnings, the government witnessed the erosion of its bargaining power with respect to Texaco-Gulf as the growing surplus of petroleum on world markets turned into a glut by the middle of 1975. Jarrín's proposal to acquire a 51 percent interest in the consortium was quietly abandoned in the face of company threats to quit the country. Arguing that Ecuador's petroleum taxes were excessively high, specifically that they reduced profits to unacceptable levels, the companies pressured the government to make concessions, which it did in July 1975.[13] In spite of these concessions, Gulf, which unlike Texaco was obliged to sell most of its crude on the open market, asked for its own nationalization in August 1976, claiming that the government's policies prevented the company from earning "a reasonable profit on its large unrecovered capital investment."[14] By the end of the year Gulf's assets had passed to CEPE, which now had a 62.5 percent share of the consortium. Relations between the government and Texaco improved markedly.

Nevertheless, in spite of Jarrín's personal setbacks and the government's retreat to a less aggressively nationalistic petroleum policy, his actions as minister of natural resources had left their marks. Not the least of these was the establishment of the state petroleum company, CEPE, which he had managed to endow with a 25 percent share of the consortium. Ironically, in the face of a government that by now had little enthusiasm for nationalizing the companies, it was Gulf's determination to be nationalized that resulted in CEPE's acquisition of a greater share of the consortium than even Jarrín had proposed. But the tough line taken by Jarrín toward foreign investment in the petroleum sector and the continuing uncertainty surrounding subsequent petroleum policy contributed to the discouragement of further investment by other companies. The decision to price domestic sales of petroleum derivatives such as gasoline at artificially low levels was a major contributor to an accelerating domestic consumption that cut into the amount of petroleum available for export. The legacy of these nationalistic policies—stagnant petroleum production and falling export volume—was one that continued to plague the military government.

If the military was relatively united on the issue of nationalism and only somewhat less so in its desire to expand the role of the Ecuadorian state beyond its traditional functions, if not always on the extent to which these objectives should be pursued, there was considerably less agreement in the area of reformist social policy. Relatively moderate in his own views, Rodríguez Lara had to contend with two competing factions within the military, one advocating the Peruvian military model of radical social and economic reforms and the other favoring the Brazilian military model of extensive state intervention in the economy but with very limited emphasis given to reformist policies.[15] Although the military firmly established its claim to nationalism and expanded the role of the state in the private sector beyond that achieved by any preceding government, its accomplishments in the area of social and economic reform were limited. Disagreement within the military, its failure to establish an independent political base, and increasingly entrenched opposition from Ecuadorian elites resulted in policies that, though rhetorically radical, were moderate in outcome; in fact, they were not markedly different from the policies of the 1963 junta, the government's immediate military predecessor.

Declaring itself "revolutionary, nationalist and autonomous, social humanist, and disciplined," the military announced that it would "implant a true social justice [making] a profound effort to incorporate man into the community, facilitating his integral development and his self-realization." But to do so would have required nothing less than a "transcendent change in Ecuadorian society and economy."[16] Both agrarian reform and tax reform were seen as cornerstones of the military's reform policies; both were intended as major attacks on the prevailing unequal distribution of income and wealth.

Agrarian reform was held to be essential to the elimination of rural poverty and the expansion of the domestic market to the extent required for the successful development of import-substituting industries. As the 1973–1977 development plan put it:

> Once the concentration of land ownership, 'precarious' tenancy arrangements, and other forms of exploitation, are eliminated, an immediate redistribution of income in favour of the large peasant population will be possible which, due to increases in its purchasing power, will lead to the creation of a broad internal market for industrial production for popular consumption. . . . The agrarian structural change will thus be transformed into a basic motor capable of expanding the productive process and energizing the national economy.[17]

In spite of the rhetoric surrounding the Rodríguez Lara government's proposals for agrarian reform, the Agrarian Reform Law issued in October 1973 was in most respects a continuation of earlier legislation. A draft copy of the proposed legislation, modeled after the tough Peruvian agrarian reform law circulated in June, drew vehement opposition from landowners whose successful lobbying was attested to by the much milder final version. The principal difference between the 1973 law and the earlier legislation issued by the 1963 junta lay in the former's provisions for expropriation in the event that land was inefficiently cultivated. But vague language and a two-year moratorium on enforcement all but eliminated the threat of expropriation, leading the newspaper *El Expreso* to remark that the agrarian reform law "leaves the impression that it is not conceived as a revolutionary weapon, as many thought it should be, but as a tool of production."[18] Nevertheless, concern by landlords that the very vagueness of the legislation could also be used against them led to their successful demands for the resignation of Minister of Agriculture Guillermo Maldonado Lince, perceived to be one of the leading advocates of a tough policy.

Not surprisingly, the effect of the 1973 agrarian reform law was fairly limited. For the period 1973–1975, total land redistribution represented just 88,132 hectares (218,000 acres), or about 17 percent of established goals.[19] Not only was the threat to large landowners rather slight in terms of the total amount of land redistributed, but a considerable portion of this land had either been publicly owned or involved the transfer of huasipungo plots. By 1978 only 7 percent of the total land in farms on the coast and in the sierra had been redistributed.[20] By contrast, the more radical Peruvian agrarian reform law of 1968 specifically eliminated the "efficiently cultivated lands" loophole and was implemented immediately following its promulgation. By 1977, more than 6 million hectares (15 million acres) of land had been redistributed to more than 265,000 families.[21]

The principal effect of the Ecuadorian agrarian reforms on land tenure patterns was the virtual elmination of "precarious" forms of land tenure. There were some very moderate improvements in the distribution of land by size of holding, notably a decrease in the number of very large estates and an increase in the number of medium-sized farms. In spite of this, Ecuador's highly unequal distribution of land and the serious problem of the *minifundio* was essentially unchanged. As noted in Table 6.2, 73 percent of farms in 1954 were less than 5 hectares (12.4 acres) in size, accounting for just 7 percent of farm land. By 1981, according to recent estimates, 67 percent of farms were under 5 hectares, occupying 7 percent of farm land.[22] Not surprisingly, with so little change in the number of farmers with marginal holdings, rural poverty remained a serious problem, essentially blocking the military's efforts to use rising agricultural incomes to drive its strategy of import-substitution industrialization. Indeed, industrial growth and urbanization during this period appear to have been financed not by increasing agricultural income (which would have expanded the domestic market) but, rather, by depressing income in the agricultural sector in order to lower the costs of food for urban workers.

TABLE 6.2
Land distribution by size of farm, 1954, 1974, and 1981
(in percentages)

Farm Size (hectares)	Number of Farms			Area Occupied		
	1954	1974	1981[a]	1954	1974	1981[a]
0-5	73.1	66.7	66.9	7.2	6.7	7.3
5-20	16.7	18.6	18.2	9.4	11.8	14.2
20-100	8.1	12.6	1.6	19.0	33.5	40.3
>100	2.1	2.1	1.6	64.4	48.0	38.2

[a]Figures for 1981 are estimates based on the 1974 farm census and data on land redistribution and colonization between 1974 and 1981. Data on the effects of population growth and rural-urban migration on land distribution are not included.

SOURCE: Adapted from Rob Vos, "El modelo de desarrollo y el sector agrícola en Ecuador," *El Trimestre Económico*, Vol. 52, 4, No. 208 (Mexico, October-December 1985), p. 1114.

Tax reform, the remaining vehicle for the military's attack on social and economic inequality, fared little better than agrarian reform. The 1973–1977 development plan stated that it was necessary to distribute "tax burdens in a form more equitable and just through the imposition of a flexible and socially just system," arguing not only that this would improve the distribution of income but also that, by complementing petroleum revenues, it would allow the public sector to carry out an ambitious program of public investments.[23] Thus, both a more equal distribution of income and increased revenues from nonpetroleum sources were to be the goals of tax reform.

Ecuadorian governments have traditionally depended heavily on foreign trade taxes to finance a large share of total public-sector expenditures, a dependence that increased during the petroleum boom. Between 1973 and 1979, government petroleum income rose from 4 percent of GDP to just over 6 percent, whereas nonpetroleum revenues declined from 17 to 12 percent of GDP.[24] One consequence of the public sector's growing reliance on petroleum income was to make government revenues even more susceptible to fluctuations in the world price of this single export. In addition, as petroleum taxes were paid primarily by foreigners, the relative burden of taxes on Ecuadorians fell during the petroleum boom, indicating that the military's goal of increasing revenues from nonpetroleum sources was not met.

Whether the Rodríguez Lara government was able to change the distribution of the burden of nonpetroleum taxes such that the system became more equitable is difficult to assess, but the available evidence suggests that this goal, too, was not achieved. Income and property taxes, the principal instruments for income redistribution, declined in importance during the 1970s. For example, the number of persons paying income taxes decreased by about 6,600 over the period 1972–1976.[25] Thus, there is little evidence to suggest that the tax system had become a means for improving the position of the poor in Ecuadorian society.

THE RETREAT FROM POWER: THE MILITARY TRIUMVIRATE

By late 1975, the reformist efforts of the Rodríguez Lara government were largely exhausted and the political legitimacy of the regime was becoming increasingly tenuous. During the first two years of the petroleum boom, the large inflows of revenue had allowed the government to satisfy competing political demands by simply spending its way to legitimacy without making serious efforts to establish a base of support in civilian society. As Ecuador's petroleum earnings fell in 1975, owing to declining production and glutted world markets, the government was trapped between its inability to increase expenditures and the public's unwillingness to make reductions in the rich diet of petroleum revenues to which it had only recently become accustomed. By mid-1975, the Rodríguez Lara government was subject to increasingly harsh criticism from civilian political leaders, representatives of the private sector, and labor groups. On August 31, the armed forces chief of staff, General Raúl González Alvear, with the support of representatives of Ecuador's major political parties, launched an armed attack on the presidential palace, which he took at the cost of twenty lives, only to discover that Rodríguez Lara had earlier fled to Ambato. Failure to secure support from the rest of the military led to the defeat of this coup attempt. Nevertheless, the Rodríguez Lara government was on its way out. In early January 1976, the three service commanders notified Rodríguez Lara that he would have to resign, and a triumvirate headed by Rear Admiral Afredo Poveda Burbano took control.

Ironically, the military had fallen into the very difficulty for which it had excoriated previous governments. As the 1973–1975 development plan had warned:

> [Earlier] periods of boom which the country experienced were not sufficiently taken advantage of to develop and reform internal production, for different reasons which are ultimately explained by the country's social structure. The periods of relative bonanza were translated quickly into an economic instability manifested in balance of payments problems

and a fiscal deficit greater in magnitude than those which characterized the period preceding the boom.[26]

A severe balance-of-payments crisis had developed by the summer of 1975 as expenditures on imports increased at an explosive pace while export earnings stagnated.[27] With no short-run prospects for increasing exports, the government introduced an austerity program featuring severe import restrictions. In June automobile imports were suspended and credit restrictions established. By the end of August these measures were followed by additional restrictions on imports that, for example, raised the duties on nonessential goods by 60 percent.[28] The rate of increase of government spending, in which revenues from import duties still figured importantly, slowed abruptly from the 85 percent jump recorded the previous year, as the public sector recorded its first deficit since the start of the petroleum boom. As in past booms, government expenditures had risen at a heady rate, driven by the regime's efforts to satisfy all groups and by its lack of control over an increasingly decentralized public sector.[29]

Predictably, the government's austerity measures brought vehement protests from an already hostile private sector. Uneasy over what it viewed as increasing encroachment by the state into traditional areas of private economic activity, the private sector was particularly frustrated by its lack of access to policy formulation. The abolition of political parties had removed one avenue. The difference in social background between military officials and business elites reduced the latter's degree of influence relative to the level it had enjoyed during civilian administrations. For example, virtually no military officers were members of the elite social clubs of Guayaquil and Quito that "function as an important conduit for interaction among businessmen of all sorts."[30] The various chambers of industry, commerce, and agriculture became the primary vehicles for influence. But even these perceived themselves to be under attack. The Rodríguez Lara government had denied the functional representatives of the chambers of production the right to vote on the influential Monetary Board; it had also stopped subsidizing the Chambers of Agriculture on the grounds that they were unrepresentative institutions.[31]

As evidenced by its success in blocking the government's agrarian reform proposals, the private sector certainly retained influence. What it lost was its traditionally large influence over the formulation of policy and, as a result, could only react to policy initiatives from the bureaucracy. As one of the leading private-sector opponents of the regime, León Febres Cordero, director of the Guayaquil Chamber of Industry, complained:

> Is it possible by chance that one could demand a genuine participation
> by private enterprises for the accomplishment of developmental goals
> while pretending that we should not have a role in the organs of
> planning, credit, or monetary policy? . . . We cannot accept the assignment
> of great responsibilities without participation.[32]

Regionalism also clearly played a role in the debate over representation. Petroleum had not only shifted the locus of economic decisionmaking from the private sector to the public sector; it had also greatly enhanced the economic power of Quito relative to that of the coast. The overwhelming proportion of military officers with origins in the sierra contributed to a growing rift between the government and coastal economic elites.[33] When the military sought an accommodation with the coastal industrialists in a series of meetings held in January 1974, Quito newspapers warned highland readers in guarded language of the threat to their regional interests, noting that "the State should be above the interests and plans of private interests" and that "it would be better if the Government were one of vigorous authority, which could coordinate and set in order such interests in the function of the majority."[34]

The government's austerity measures, however, overcame any regional difference among economic elites, thus bringing the private sector together in opposition and catalyzing protests from other groups, such as the labor unions. The effect of significant import restrictions on an economy in which more than 90 percent of the investment in plant and equipment was made through imported capital goods reached far beyond denying luxury items to the upper class. Public statements from both the Quito and Guayaquil Chambers of Commerce and Industry attacked the import restrictions. The Junta Cívica, an umbrella organization of many of the country's political parties, joined in the criticism. All argued that the source of the country's economic problems was to be found in the government's poor management of its oil policy and excessive government spending.[35] Somewhat later, the trade unions joined the opposition, but on the grounds that the government had failed to deliver on its reformist promises, and successfully called for a nationwide one-day strike on November 13, 1975. Notably, this strike was important beyond its immediate show of opposition in that it was the first time Ecuador's three major labor unions had united. Under the label of the Unitary Workers Front (Frente Unitario de Trabajadores, or FUT), the strike had drawn together the Confederación de Trabajadores Ecuatorianos (CTE), the Central Ecuatoriana de Organizaciones Clasistas (CEDOC), and the Confederación

Ecuatoriana de Organizaciones Libres (CEOSEL), which collectively represented about 47 percent of the organized labor force.[36]

Facing widespread civilian opposition from both the left and the right, the various military factions came together against Rodríguez Lara. The military triumvirate that assumed power quickly announced its decision to return the country to civilian rule as rapidly as possible, abandoning all policies likely to cause any domestic political opposition. The emphasis of the agrarian reform program shifted in December 1977 with Agrarian Reform and Colonization Decree 2092, which established the new government's preference for policies to increase production on existing landholdings, and to colonize new lands, over those of redistribution. A desire to avoid further confrontation with landowning elites, together with growing food scarcities due to stagnant agricultural production, prompted the shift to an emphasis on production, which was promoted by the military as "rural capitalism." Similarly, colonization of unsettled lands was also clearly the less antagonistic option and, from the military's point of view, had the additional advantage of satisfying national security objectives by populating border regions, particularly those near the oilfields adjoining Colombia in the northern oriente.[37] With the abandonment of a redistributive agrarian reform program went efforts to link industrialization to a significant broadening of the domestic market. Deferring to industrial elites, the government made some attempts to redirect industrial policy toward export markets and to attract foreign capital. Regarding the latter point, the triumvirate retreated from the more nationalistic position of the Rodríguez Lara government, which had strongly supported the Andean Pact agreements regulating foreign investment. A revised Industrial Development Law, issued in 1976, provided incentives for both objectives. But the policy had limited success, reflecting in part the disagreement between sierra and coastal industrialists over the type and location of the new export industries that threatened the new rapprochement between industrialists and the military.[38] The coastal industrialists favored an industrialization strategy emphasizing processed agricultural exports, such as the semiprocessed cacao industry that had demonstrated such strong growth during the 1970s. The sierra industrialists, by contrast, advocated the development of a manufactured goods industry, based on the highlands and producing for the Andean Pact market.

Import restrictions were relaxed even though petroleum revenues had not increased appreciably and large balance-of-payments deficits persisted. Although the new minister of natural resources, Jaime Eduardo Semblantes, actively pursued new petroleum investment through policies he described as extensions of a "new pragmatism," increases in production were not sufficient to offset rising domestic consumption and exports fell steadily through 1979. As the efforts of the Rodríguez Lara government to increase revenue from non-petroleum sources had failed, the triumvirate—anxious to minimize the domestic political costs of the transition to civilian rule—turned increasingly to foreign borrowing to finance expenditures and the balance-of-payments deficit. From the beginning of 1976 to the end of 1979, when the triumvirate relinquished power, public external debt grew at an average annual rate of more than 50 percent, from $0.46 billion to $2.63 billion.[39]

Organized labor was the single group toward which the triumvirate adopted a fairly aggressive line.[40] Indeed, from organized labor's perspective the primary motivation for Rodríguez Lara's overthrow had been to break the growing power of the labor movement. The legal process of approving new labor unions ground to a halt. Minimum wages were frozen between 1976 and 1979, resulting in a decrease in the standards of living for large numbers of urban workers. Police were employed to repress strikers in a number of incidents between 1976 and 1978, the most notorious of which was the strike against the partly government-owned sugar mill Aztra that left between 20 and 100 workers dead. Then, in January 1979, on the eve of its departure from government and presumably unconcerned over future budgetary consequences, the military mandated a 33 percent increase in the minimum wage and the annual payment of an additional month's bonus salary to all public-sector employees.[41]

THE RETURN TO DEMOCRACY

The military bequeathed a mixed legacy to its civilian successor. On the one hand, to its credit, it supervised a transition to democracy in spite of repeated and determined efforts by conservative elites, as well as by some groups within the military, to derail the process. On the other hand, it left to the next government an economy in serious trouble and a series of politically difficult problems, such as the critical need to curb the escalating domestic consumption of gasoline, on which the outgoing military had simply refused to make decisions.

The conservatives favored an immediate transition, similar to those so frequently employed in Ecuador's past in which a constituent assembly, undoubtedly dominated by elite groups, would select the next president. The military, clinging to its desire to leave some mark on what it considered discredited civilian politics, sought to create a constitutional order that provided the new government with greater legitimacy and stability than past civilian governments had enjoyed. To this end the triumvirate supervised the drafting of two constitutions, one a revised version of the 1945 constitution, the other a new document. Both were submitted to popular vote on January 15, 1978. In spite of a forceful campaign led by Guayas (Guayaquil) Chamber of Industry president, León Febres Cordero, urging voters to reject the process by casting null votes, 75 percent of the voters chose one or the other of the two constitutions, thus also casting their support for the military's proposals for the transition.[42]

The winning constitution, the new document, was notable in several respects. It formally enfranchised the nation's illiterates, for the first time in Ecuador's history, thus promising to significantly expand the electorate. This provision, however, was not to take effect until August 1979, following the scheduled installation of the civilian government. In an effort to streamline and democratize the legislative process, a unicameral congress was to be created and functional representatives eliminated. The constitution also formally recognized four economic sectors: private, public, mixed, and communitarian. The last of these in particular evoked vocal opposition from the business sector, which viewed it as an attack on private property rights that would open the door to the kind of worker self-management recently introduced in Peru. To strengthen the mandate of the winning presidential candidate, a new electoral law was simultaneously promulgated, requiring a majority for victory and establishing provisions for a second round of elections should a majority not be obtained on the first round. To reduce the fragmentation of Ecuador's political parties, the electoral law stipulated that all parties receiving less than 5 percent of the vote in two successive elections would be denied official recognition.

Presidential elections were scheduled for July 16, 1978. In the face of a virtually assured victory by CFP leader Assad Bucaram, a man bitterly opposed by civilian and military elites, the latter's commitment to democratic procedure weakened. Twisting the constitutional requirement that presidents be Ecuadorian born, the military disqualified Bucaram on the grounds that his immigrant parents were not Ecuadorian at the time of his birth. The military further disregarded constitutional provisions by decreeing that all former presidents were ineligible for reelection. The new law of parties was also manipulated to disqualify two parties from sponsoring candidates: the populist Alfarista Radical Front (FRA) and the center-left Popular Democracy (DP), an alliance of the Christian Democrats and a progressive splinter of the Conservative party.[43]

With Bucaram removed from contention and military and civilian groups endeavoring to influence the outcome in other ways, the scheduled elections appeared to be a contest between two rightist candidates: former Quito mayor Sixto Durán Ballén and former Liberal party director Raúl Clemente Huerta Rendón. To the considerable surprise of most observers, the victors were CFP stand-in candidate Jaime Roldós Aguilera, a Guayaquil lawyer and nephew-in-law to Bucaram, and his Christian Democratic running mate Osvaldo Hurtado, a professor of political sociology at Quito's Catholic University and leader of the disqualified Popular Democracy party who ran on the CFP ticket. According to preliminary results, Roldós received a convincing 31 percent of the vote over rivals Durán and Huerta, who won 23 and 22 percent, respectively.

The victory by Roldós and Hurtado caused considerable unrest among Ecuador's political and economic elites, as well as within some elements of the military. Both men were deeply committed to redressing the social and economic inequalities so ingrained in Ecuadorian society. Osvaldo Hurtado's concerns for structural reforms in particular were widely known from his writings. For this reason, and because of his association with the Christian Democratic party, it was he whom the country's elites most distrusted. Yet in spite of accusations from the right casting Roldós and Hurtado as dangerous leftists who would lead the country down the road to ruin, neither was radical in his views. As Osvaldo Hurtado commented in 1979, "We realistically accept the fact that only moderate reforms are possible in this country and we propose no more than that. We will work entirely within the existing framework."[44] Roldós had already begun to distance himself from Bucaram, endeavoring to suggest that there was little substance to the CFP slogan "Roldós al presidente, Bucaram al poder" (Roldós to the Presidency, Bucaram to power). Although some groups undoubtedly believed that Roldós and Hurtado would attempt to shape their government along fairly radical lines, apparently what the elites genuinely feared was a continuation of their loss of access to government and their inability to participate directly in the formulation of public policy—the same issues that had proved so frustrating to them under the military governments.

Opposition from civilian elites and some groups of military officers stalled the transition process. Charges of fraud in the Roldós victory led to a lengthy recount that failed to change the outcome, in spite of strenuous efforts to do so. León Febres Cordero, speaking for the business elites of Guayaquil, called for a cancellation of the scheduled second round of elections, again advocating the selection of a constituent assembly to choose the next president. By September

1978, hard-liners within the military were reportedly on the verge of a coup, dissuaded ultimately only by Admiral Alfredo Poveda's personal commitment to the transition, by their fear that junior officers might not support the attempt, and by the Carter administration's clearly stated support for the return to democracy.[45] In spite of these efforts to overturn the process, the second round of elections was finally held on April 29, 1979. The Roldós and Hurtado team won with a convincing 62 percent of the vote in an election in which an unprecedented 21 percent of the population voted.

NOTES

1. *El Comercio* (November 22, 1966), cited in John Samuel Fitch, *The Military Coup as Political Process: Ecuador 1948–1966* (Baltimore: The Johns Hopkins University Press, 1977), p. 145.

2. *Plan Integral de Transformación y Desarrollo 1973–1977* (Resumen General, Quito: Editorial "Santo Domingo," 1973), p. 4, 5.

3. *Plan Integral,* p. 5.

4. Banco Central del Ecuador, *Cuentas de Las Empresas Publicas* (National Accounts Working Document, December 1984). These figures almost certainly understate the degree of state involvement in production, given that only those enterprises with 50 percent or greater state ownership are defined as public enterprises.

5. Rob Vos, "Financial Development, Problems of Capital Accumulation and Adjustment Policies in Ecuador, 1965–1982," Working Paper No. 9 (Subseries on Money, Finance, and Development) (The Hague: Institute of Social Studies, November 1983), p. 13.

6. Catherine Mary Conaghan, "Industrialists and the Reformist Interregnum: Dominant Class Behavior and Ideology in Ecuador, 1972–1979" (Ph.D. dissertation, Yale University, 1983), p. 133.

7. George Philip, "Oil and Politics in Ecuador, 1972–1976," Working Paper No. 1 (London: University of London, Institute of Latin American Studies, 1978), p. 5.

8. The CEPE was actually first established under the 1971 petroleum legislation but had to be legally reestablished in 1972.

9. José Vicente Zevallos, *El Estado Ecuatoriano y las Transnacionales Petroleras* (Quito: Ediciones de la Universidad Católica, 1981), p. 17.

10. Reported in Philip, "Oil and Politics in Ecuador," p. 9.

11. Ibid., p. 19.

12. Zevallos, *El Estado,* p. 17.

13. A lack of concrete data makes it difficult to assess the companies' claims. George Philip has concluded that "there is no reason to doubt that company profits in Ecuador between June 1974 and October 1975 were negligible or even negative" (*Oil and Politics in Latin America,* p. 285), whereas José Vicente Zevallos argues that petroleum taxes in Ecuador were equal to or less than those in other producing countries (*El Estado,* p. 20).

14. *Oil and Gas Journal* (January 10, 1977):51.

15. John Samuel Fitch, *The Military Coup D'Etat as a Political Process: Ecuador, 1948–1966* (Baltimore: The Johns Hopkins University Press, 1977), p. 182.

16. See *Filosofía y plan de acción del gobierno revolucionario y nacionalista del Ecuador: Lineamientos generales* (Quito, 1972), pp. 3–6; see also *Plan Integral*, p. 3.

17. *Plan Integral*, p. 4.

18. *El Expreso* (October 17, 1974); cited in Walter Spurrier, *Weekly Analysis*, No. 38 (September 20, 1974):157.

19. World Bank, *Ecuador: Development Problems and Prospects* (Washington, D.C.: The International Bank for Reconstruction and Development, 1979), p. 444. A hectare of land is approximately equal to 2.47 acres.

20. Carlos Luzuriaga and Clarence Zuvekas, Jr., *Income Distribution and Poverty in Rural Ecuador, 1950–1979* (Tempe: University of Arizona, Center for Latin American Studies, 1980), p. 167.

21. John Samuel Fitch, "Radical Military Regimes in Latin America: Revolution, Rhetoric, and Reality in Peru and Ecuador" (paper delivered at the 1977 Annual Meeting of the American Political Science Association, Washington, D.C., 1977), pp. 4, 5.

22. See Rob Vos, "El modelo de desarrollo y el sector agrícola en Ecuador, 1965–1982," *El Trimestre Económico*, Vol. 52 (4), No. 208 (México, October–December 1985):1114. See also Gustavo Cosse, *Estado y Agro en el Ecuador* (Quito: Corporación Editora Nacional, 1984), pp. 37–46.

23. *Plan Integral*, p. 5.

24. World Bank, *Ecuador: An Agenda for Recovery and Sustained Growth* (Washington, D.C.: The International Bank for Reconstruction and Development, 1984), p. 24.

25. World Bank, *Development Problems*, p. 87.

26. *Plan Integral*, p. 3.

27. Between 1974 and 1975, the current account plunged from a surplus of $22 million to a deficit of $239 million (World Bank, *An Agenda*, Table 3.1, p. 125).

28. Conaghan, "Industrialists," pp. 218–219.

29. David W. Schodt, "The Ecuadorian Public Sector During the Petroleum Period: 1972–1983," Technical Papers Series, No. 52 (Austin: University of Texas, Office for Public-Sector Studies, Institute of Latin American Studies, 1986), p. 19.

30. John Fitch reports that there were no military members in either the Club de la Union in Guayaquil or the Guayaquil Country Club, and that the Quito Tennis Club had only two or three military members (*The Military Coup*, p. 30). Evidence of the importance of elite social clubs has been gleaned from interviews with industrialists conducted by Catherine Mary Conaghan ("Industrialists," p. 244). Eighty-eight percent of her sample were members of these clubs.

31. *Weekly Analysis of Ecuadorian Issues* (February 15, 1974):26.

32. Speech by León Febres Cordero, in Conaghan, "Industrialists," p. 209. Febres Cordero's outspoken opposition to the military was apparently influenced by his incarceration in April 1973 on charges of tax evasion, as well as by his ideological differences and his clear aspirations toward the presidency.

33. Fitch, The Military Coup, p. 24. In the 1960s, 90 percent of all army cadets were from the sierra.

34. El Comercio (January 19, 1974) and El Tiempo (January 19, 1974), as cited in Weekly Analysis of Ecuadorian Issues (January 25, 1974):15, 16.

35. Conaghan, "Industrialists," pp. 220–221.

36. Nick D. Mills, Crisis, Conflicto y Consenso, Ecuador 1979–1984 (Quito: Corporación Editora Nacional, 1984), p. 129. Organized labor never represented more than 19 percent of workers during the 1970s.

37. It is true that the amounts of land adjudicated in 1976 and 1977 were the highest annual totals since 1964, but as Howard Handelman has noted, "This reflected the title transfer of property previously acquired by [the government], however, not an expansion of land redistribution." See "Ecuadorian Agrarian Reform: The Politics of Limited Change" (Hanover: American Universities Field Staff, No. 49, 1980), p. 10.

38. Conaghan, "Industrialists," pp. 227–232.

39. World Bank, An Agenda, Table 4.2, p. 140. Figures (based on author's calculations) are for disbursed debt only.

40. Análisis Semanal, 7, 42 (October 21, 1977).

41. Banco Central del Ecuador, Boletín Anuario, No. 7 (1984), p. 202.

42. John D. Martz, "The Quest for Popular Democracy in Ecuador," Current History, 78, 454 (February 1980):67.

43. Rightist elements within the military actually carried their opposition to the FRA further than this. On November 29, 1978, the leader of the FRA, Abdón Calderón, was gunned down in the streets of Guayaquil, and the responsibility for his assassination was traced to high levels of the military.

44. Interview with Osvaldo Hurtado, reported in Howard Handelman and Thomas G. Sanders, Military Government and the Movement Toward Democracy in South America (Bloomington: Indiana University Press, 1981), p. 54.

45. See Handelman and Saunders, Military Government, p. 46. As John Martz has noted, he was present at a briefing for Rosalyn Carter on the eve of her trip to Latin America, where it was explained to her that the reason for including Ecuador in her itinerary was to signal to a wavering Ecuadorian military the Carter administration's support for the return to democracy. See also "The Right Takes Command," Current History, 84 (February 1985):70.

7

Democratic Politics and Economic Austerity

In August 1979 the military withdrew from power, permitting a return to democracy and the election of the government of Jaime Roldós Aguilera and Osvaldo Hurtado. This government came into power with the most explicit program of social and economic reform yet witnessed in Ecuadorian politics, along with a serious commitment to its implementation. Yet this government also was largely unsuccessful in its efforts to implement a reformist program. Although it is true that the Roldós and Hurtado administrations were plagued by events entirely out of their control, such as the death of Roldós in 1981, a decline in the world price of oil, and an international recession, it is also true that neither administration was able to garner support for its policies either through an accommodation with the country's elites or through the organization of popular groups.

A LEGACY FOR REFORM

Roldós and Hurtado came into office with the slogan "La Fuerza de Cambio" (The Force of Change) and with what appeared to be relatively favorable circumstances for implementing the moderate reforms they had committed themselves to during the campaign. A strong popular mandate accompanied them into office, and the 1979 congressional election results suggested that center-left deputies would control a majority of the seats in the new 69-member unicameral assembly. The CFP had won 29 seats, and the Democratic Left (Izquierda Democrática, or ID), which had supported the Roldós/Hurtado ticket during the campaign, had won an additional 15 seats. The two men represented a new generation of political leaders. Deeply distrustful of the grand but insubstantial promises that had come to characterize Ecuadorian politics and determined to break with the "old style of government and of confronting national problems," they proposed a carefully executed programmatic politics, a broadening of democratic participation to "reverse the old patterns of power concentration," and a strengthening of democratic institutions.[1] Even though serious economic problems lay just below the surface of this optimism, these measures appeared somewhat less threatening in the wake of sharp increases in the world price of Ecuadorian crude in 1979 and 1980.

Nevertheless, even to Roldós and Hurtado it was clear that their goals would not be easily achieved. The new government had inherited a formidable array of problems, some deeply embedded in historical political and economic inequalities, others the direct legacy of policies pursued by the recent military governments, and some simply the result of eight years of rapid and relatively unplanned economic growth. The country's political history of elitist politics had left much of the population excluded from active political participation. While the economy had experienced sweeping changes, politics seemed to have remained mired in traditional patterns. The party system was fragmented and political identification highly personalistic. Most important, neither the populist nor the military governments had bequeathed an organized constituency for reformist politics to their successors. Without a doubt, one of the reasons for the failure of the reformist initiatives of the Rodríguez Lara government was its unwillingness to organize support from popular groups that stood to benefit from both its policies and from its inability to win support from elites. Agrarian reform, for example, which had been intended to benefit both peasants and those industrialists producing for the domestic market, foundered in part on a lack of effective support from either.

The policies followed by the Rodríguez Lara government and by the triumvirate also constituted a difficult legacy for the new democratic government. The failure to stimulate increased petroleum production remained a serious obstacle to continued economic growth. Although the triumvirate's policies had managed to reverse declines in production, by 1979 petroleum output had just barely recovered to 1973 levels. Petroleum exports, however, continued to decline as accelerating domestic consumption, fueled by the military's nationalistic policy of artificially low internal prices, took an increasing share of production. As shown in Table 5.1, crude exports by 1980 were only 56 percent of what they had been in 1973.

The combination of sluggish export earnings and rapidly rising imports, stimulated in part by an industrialization strategy favoring import incentives and in part simply by rising incomes, created growing balance-of-trade problems. Government policies to reduce the trade deficit were constrained by the heavy reliance of Ecuadorian industry on imported inputs. Measures such as devaluation or import restrictions would cost heavily in reduced domestic output and higher prices. Rather than pay this cost, the military had chosen to turn to foreign borrowing.

The failure of the military's agrarian reform program, as well as the policy of price ceilings on basic food commodities, took its toll on agricultural production. With the single exception of rice, which had received considerable state assistance, agricultural production for the domestic market between 1970 and 1980 actually declined an average of 2.4 percent annually.[2] The military's strategy of supplementing stagnant domestic production with subsidized food imports contributed to driving up public expenditures, thus further increasing the debt problem. All told, the incoming democratic government faced a public external debt of nearly $3 billion.

Lack of progress under the military in increasing tax revenues from nonpetroleum sources not only contributed to growing reliance on foreign borrowing; it also necessitated control of the rapidly rising public expenditures. But such control was complicated by the extensive earmarking of revenues and the increased decentralization of the public sector that occurred during the 1972–1979 period. By 1982 earmarking affected 52 percent of the government budget, and interest payments on the foreign debt accounted for an additional 26 percent of the budget.[3] Thus, almost 80 percent of the budget was legally committed even prior to the start of its formulation. And because of decentralization, this budget accounted for only 42 percent of public-sector expenditures in 1979, down from a high of 60 percent in 1968.[4]

In addition, although any civilian administration in Ecuador of necessity governs with one eye on the military, after the 1979 transition the military remained not just an important political actor but also an important economic one. Following its withdrawal from the government, the military retained more active control over public- and private-sector decisions than had ever been the case in the past. In contrast with the military's position before assuming power in 1972, it had (1) secured an allocation of petroleum revenues just under 23 percent of the total; (2) retained the power to name representatives to the Boards of Directors of the major state corporations, most of which had been created by the military; (3) established a virtual monopoly over the transportation sector through its extensive control of air and sea transport; (4) become a major shareholder in a wide variety of industries through investments made by the Directorship of Army Industries; and (5) secured guarantees with respect to the military's participation in the naming of the defense minister.[5]

Certainly Roldós and Hurtado had inherited an economy that had experienced profound changes during the petroleum boom, not the least of which was the dramatic increase in per capita incomes. But this improvement in average terms masked continued and serious economic inequalities. Poverty in general remained a serious problem, but rural poverty was particularly troubling given that 65 percent of the rural population had fallen below the poverty line as of 1979.[6] Both unemployment and underemployment were widespread, largely as a consequence of the stagnant agricultural sector and the capital-intensive nature of industrial growth. An urban construction boom had provided an outlet for some of this labor, but this boom could not be expected to continue as the rate of growth in the economy slackened. The continued and heavy dependence of the economy on a single export, petroleum, which in 1980 accounted for 62 percent of export earnings, held the country hostage to the performance of world markets for this product.

It was against this background that Roldós and Hurtado issued the first detailed statement of their plans. In April 1978, during the campaign, Hurtado presented a 21-point program to a national television audience. Following the inauguration of Roldós and Hurtado on August 10, 1979, a more detailed description of their agenda was delivered in the 1980–1984 national development plan. This document spelled out a firm commitment to strengthening the democratic system, held to be "the prime goal of the government"; economic development combining growth with equity, "giving primary attention to the agriculture sector"; and social justice, intended to provide "all Ecuadoreans with the opportunity to participate equitably in national wealth."[7] The plan argued that structural reforms would be necessary to achieve the administration's goals but that these would have to be implemented without "disrupting the equilibrium and harmony that should exist between efficient operation of the economic system and the advancement of social change."[8] Tax reform, as in the previous five-year plan, was intended both to augment public revenues and to promote a more equitable distribution of income. Agrarian reform, deemed essential to the administration's emphasis on the rural sector, was to take place under existing legislation. Administrative reforms were proposed to address the perceived problem that "the public sector has operated traditionally on behalf of private interests and not in relation to broader national goals that would benefit the entire society." Particular administrative problems identified included "the proliferation of public agencies and the formation of a fragmented public administration in which there is a total lack of coordination." Educational reforms were to place particular emphasis on literacy programs. Finally, a political reform was envisaged as a way of buttressing other reforms, making possible "a progressive displacement of national wealth, culture and political power away from minority elites" by promoting democracy through government support for expanding mass participation.[9]

The reformist goals of the new democratic government went largely unrealized; they were victims, first, to a political deadlock between the executive and the legislature and, second, to the severe economic crisis assailing the country by the beginning of 1981. Further compounding these problems were several events entirely out of the control of the government. On January 29, 1981, an armed clash with Peruvian troops on the southern border put the entire country on military alert. Though settled without a major escalation of the conflict, the crisis nevertheless diverted both attention and resources from the government's reformist initiatives. On May 24, 1981, President Roldós and his wife, along with the defense minister, General Marco Subía, were killed in an airplane crash in southern Ecuador. A final unexpected blow came in late 1982, when the new government of Osvaldo Hurtado, already under siege from the private sector and a struggling economy, was additionally burdened by the effects of devastating floods on agricultural production. Buffeted by misfortune, the two men had little chance to forge the kinds of political alliances they considered necessary for the success of their reformist initiatives.

DEMOCRATIC POLITICS, PART I: JAIME ROLDOS

Shortly after assuming office on August 10, 1979, President Jaime Roldós quickly learned what five-time former President Velasco Ibarra, in an uncharacteristic display of understatement, is reputed to have commented—namely, that "Ecuador is a difficult country to govern."[10] The congressional majority that had accompanied the new president into office quickly disintegrated as the CFP split into Roldós and Bucaram factions, reflecting both the growing personal animosity between the two men and, more fundamental, the split between traditional Ecuadorian populism and the new programmatic politics as articulated by Roldós and Hurtado.

Relations between CFP leader, Asaad Bucaram, and his standard bearer, Jaime Roldós, had steadily deteriorated throughout the course of the campaign. Although they had campaigned together before the first round of elections, the latter had demonstrated an increasing desire to step out from the shadow of his former mentor. Certainly

Political sign on Guayaquil street, "Bucaram with Roldós and Hurtado"

the two CFP leaders shared little ideological ground. Roldós's strong showing in the first round, his alliance with Osvaldo Hurtado and Julio César Trujillo's progressive Democracia Popular (DP) party, and his support from the center-left Izquierda Democrática (ID) party increased his political independence, thus further intensifying the rivalry. In a debate on national television three months before the second round, Roldós publicly declared his independence from Bucaram. Following Roldós's triumph in the second round, Bucaram, in one of the bewildering displays of ideological inconsistency so characteristic of traditional Ecuadorian politics, entered into negotiations with rightist politicians to try to block Roldós from taking office.[11] Failing in this effort, he successfully negotiated an understanding with conservative leader Rafael Armijos, giving Bucaram the votes he needed to win the election as president of the new Chamber of Representatives.[12] Bucaram's maneuvering left only 12 members of the 29-member CFP delegation still supporting Roldós. With this defection and only uncertain support from an ID already eyeing the 1984 elections, the stage was set for a confrontation between the president and an opposition congress (see Table 7.1).

TABLE 7.1
Ecuadorian political parties and seats in congress, 1979-1983

Party	Seats in Congress		
	August 1979	August 1980	August 1983
CFP (Bucaram)	29	17	4
CFP (Roldós)		12	11
Popular Democracy (DP)[a]		5	10
Democratic Left (ID)	15	12	12
Conservatives (PC)	10	8	7
Liberals (PL)	4	3	4
Social Christian (PSC)	3	2	2
Institutional Democratic Coalition (CID)	3	3	1
National Revolutionary party (PNR)	2	2	2
Popular Democratic Movement (MPD)	1	1	1
Broad Leftist Front (FADI)	1	1	1
Independent		2	3
Velasquismo	1	1	
People, Change and Democracy (PCD)[b]			1
National Integration Movement (MIN)[c]			7
Democratic party (DP)[d]			3

[a]The DP was not legally recognized during the 1979 elections. Its candidates ran with other parties, principally the CFP.
[b]Formed by Jaime Roldós after the 1979 congressional elections.
[c]A splinter group of CFP delegates.
[d]Formed in late 1979 by a group of dissident liberals under the leadership of Francisco Huerta Montalvo.

SOURCE: Adapted from Nick D. Mills, *Crisis, Conflicto, y Consenso* (Quito: Corporación Editora Nacional, 1984), Cuadro 1, pp. 55-56.

Even more than personal antagonism, however, the break between the two men represented a clash of political styles, initially played out in terms of the conflict between the legislature and the executive over spending legislation. Roldós's concerns for fiscal restraint, articulated most forcefully by Vice-President Hurtado, were not shared by the legislative majority. Responding to previously suppressed populist pressures for spending and encouraged by a near tripling of government petroleum revenues between 1978 and 1980, neither Bucaram nor many others cared to dwell on the subject of potential revenue constraints. An old-style populist politician with a largely regional base, Bucaram was primarily concerned with supplying patronage to his followers and providing immediate benefits, typically public works, to his lower-class Guayaquil supporters. Projects of broad national importance or those involving structural changes, such as many of the reforms proposed by Roldós and Hurtado, had never been part of Bucaram's political agenda, and now that his presidential ambitions had been thwarted they held even less appeal.

Never paragons of fiscal restraint themselves, the conservative politicians were usually quite willing to support Bucaram against the president if it meant they could block the administration's reformist initiatives and embarrass it fiscally without seriously threatening the economic interests of the country's economic elites. For example, the administration's tax reform proposals, which would have decreased taxes on lower-income groups while increasing the tax burden on the rich and on private businesses, drowned in a tide of spending and legislative opposition. Indeed, a congressional bill passed in November 1979 provided only for substantial tax reductions.[13] Like 38 of the 67 bills passed during the first six-month legislative session, it was vetoed by the president. But the veto was a limited weapon for an administration courting broad support, particularly when used to block expensive but popular proposals. Thus, although both Roldós and Hurtado strongly opposed the 1979 legislative proposal to immediately double the minimum wage, advocating instead a more fiscally responsible series of gradual increases, Roldós did not veto the bill. Private-sector groups, of course, added what they argued was an inflationary wage increase to the litany of their complaints against the government, even though some of the legislators who were closely identified with private business interests, such as former president Carlos Julio Arosemena Monroy, had supported the legislation.[14]

The conflict between Roldós and the congress continued into 1980, effectively derailing the administration's proposals for reform and eroding the widespread popular support with which the president had assumed office. Roldós sought desperately but unsuccessfully to forge a new alliance of center-left parties that would allow him to circumvent Bucaram's obstructionism and to move his program forward. Finally, threatening to hold a national plebiscite on a constitutional amendment to increase the power of the executive relative to the legislature, Roldós managed to assemble a majority coalition of the Democratic Left (ID), Popular Democracy (DP), and the Roldós faction of the CFP, all of which together elected ID deputy Raúl Baca Carbo president of congress. But while tensions between the president and the congress eased temporarily, the new progovernment alliance was unwieldy from the start, dependent on the equivocal participation of center-left deputies more united in their desire to end the stalemate between the executive and the legislature than in their support for the administration's program.

The economic problems lurking below the optimism with which the new government had taken office resurfaced by 1981. The world price of Ecuadorian crude began a sustained decline. Imports, relatively unconstrained since the triumvirate's austerity measures were discontinued, continued to exceed exports, putting increasing pressure on the already negative balance of payments. Public-sector deficits also rose sharply. Without increasing taxes, congress had approved a 1980 budget with expenditures 70 percent greater than those for the preceding year.[15] Admittedly, the 1979 budget submitted by the military was artificially low, a last-ditch effort to demonstrate fiscal responsibility. But the major part of the increase was attributable to the spending spree undertaken by the Bucaram-led congress. As always, regional interests also played a role. Financing for strictly local projects, such as a university hospital for Guayaquil, already vetoed by Roldós but overridden by the congress, contributed to a budget more than 8 billion sucres in excess of the president's request.[16] The unforeseen increase in international interest rates compounded an already serious budget problem. Interest payments on Ecuador's public external debt—driven up, first, by the large accumulation of debt between 1975 and 1980, and, second, by sharply rising international interest rates in the 1980s—increased from $17.6 million in 1975 to $286.5 million by 1980.[17] Not surprisingly, the government was obliged to resort to additional foreign borrowing to finance the large budget deficit.

By January 1981 the economy had deteriorated to the point where the administration was forced to consider implementing austerity measures, even though these would have been certain to contribute to further erosion of popular support for the government. The border conflict with Peru at the end of the month, though potentially serious and an added strain on the government's scarce financial resources, did mobilize public opinion temporarily in support of the administration. Taking advantage of the opportunity, the president announced the implementation of the series of limited austerity policies he had previously threatened might be necessary. Principal among these was a long overdue increase in the domestic price of regular gasoline, formerly one of the lowest in the world, from 4.7 to 15 sucres per gallon.[18] Some restrictions on imports were introduced. To partially offset the negative effects of these measures on lower-income groups, the government also froze the prices of some basic consumer goods and introduced a variety of limited subsidies, such as that for student bus fares. Notably, no significant steps were taken to reduce the level of government expenditures.[19] Nevertheless, popular protest erupted, threatening to further weaken the government. On May 13, 1981, the national labor federation, FUT, successfully called its first general strike against the administration's policies. With the government under siege from broad sectors of the population, rumors of a military coup began to circulate. Then, on May 24, 1981, Jaime Roldós was killed in an airplane crash.

DEMOCRATIC POLITICS, PART II: OSVALDO HURTADO

The circumstances under which Osvaldo Hurtado assumed the presidency were highly unpropitious as well as disturbingly similar to those that had led to the overthrow of many of his predecessors, both civilian and military. Keenly aware of his own precarious position, the new president in his inaugural address simultaneously called for austerity by both public and private sectors and made a plea for support from all sectors of the population. Although Hurtado pledged to fulfill the reformist goals of the national development plan, including the proposed structural reforms, it was clear that most of his efforts would of necessity be dedicated to combating a severe economic crisis while struggling to preserve the country's fragile new democracy. The balancing act he was called on to perform between competing economic and political demands was a particularly difficult one, inasmuch as the austerity policies required to deal with economic problems such as the large public-sector deficit and the deteriorating balance of trade would be certain to cost him scarce political resources. His support from the congress was always uncertain, opposition from the economic elites intensified, and organized labor turned increasingly to mass protest.

One positive note was that Hurtado's relations with congress gave signs of becoming somewhat less tempestuous than those experienced by his immediate predecessor, Jaime Roldós. Like Roldós, he faced the problem of having to try to assemble a governing center-left coalition out of the constantly shifting constellation of splinter parties making up congress. By August 1981, for example, no single party controlled more than 12 seats out of a total of 69. But there were some favorable signs. Asaad Bucaram's death in November 1981 removed a major source of opposition, and the formation of an alliance of center-left parties under the title "Convergencia Democrática" (Democratic Convergence) promised, in the words of congressional leader Raúl Baca Carbo, to go beyond "the formal standard of traditional alliances to become a true point of programmatic agreement."[20] In spite of its promise, however, the alliance did not last more than a month before succumbing to the opportunism of traditional congressional alignments, thus setting the pattern for the remainder of Hurtado's term. As political scientist Howard Handelman has commented:

Ultimately, most parties' opposition to or support for the government had little to do with issues but was based instead on internal power struggles within the party, on whether or not the party desired Cabinet posts, on whether or not it wished to associate itself with a struggling administration and unpopular economic measures, on how it wished to position itself for the 1984 election, and on whether or not it wanted to encourage a military coup.[21]

Nevertheless, in contrast with Roldós's experience, Hurtado faced his heaviest opposition not from the congress but from organized pressure groups such as the chambers of production and labor. Indicative of his somewhat improved relations with the congress was his ability to muster enough support to implement most of his austerity policies and to secure passage of petroleum legislation designed to reverse the downward trend in production. The deadlock between the executive and the legislature during the first twenty months of the democratic administration had paralyzed efforts to pass new petroleum legislation. But in August 1982, Osvaldo Hurtado took advantage of the more favorable legislative climate to secure passage of Law 101, which amended the Hydrocarbons Act of 1978. Designed to attract additional foreign investment, the new legislation vested ownership of energy resources in the state but allowed CEPE to contract out exploration and production to private companies on terms that the industry cited as attractive, particularly in light of increased competition from Colombia and Peru for petroleum investment.[22] Texaco and CEPE raised their production through some new discoveries and higher liftings from existing fields. The 12 percent increase in petroleum production in 1983 was the largest such increase since 1973.

Private-sector opposition toward President Hurtado was immediate and vehement. Even during the campaign it was Hurtado's candidacy that had evoked the greatest cries of alarm from the business community. His Christian Democratic background had drawn charges of his "foreign ideology." Rightist critics, citing his concern, widely known from his writings, for redressing some of the glaring inequities in Ecuadorian society and his desire to greatly expand political and economic participation, denounced him as a socialist or "quasi-Marxist." To be sure, some injudicious comments Hurtado had made following his and Roldós's first-round victory provided fuel for his critics' remarks, but even then the moderate reformist character of his proposals was apparent to most careful observers. As vice-president, Hurtado had emerged as a leading spokesman for fiscal restraint. The proposals he made upon assuming the presidency in 1981 offered little explanation for the eruption of criticism from business leaders, orchestrated primarily through the chambers of production.

In considerable measure the hostility expressed by the private sector was the combined result of its continued lack of access to policy formulation and a declining economy. As Hurtado emphasized in a television address to the nation in December 1981, "Large economic interests [that] perhaps for the first time in history encounter a government to which they cannot give orders, in which they do not have employees to represent their interests, combat it solely for this reason."[23] Certainly the lack of access was nothing new; it had been an issue of private-sector resentment of varying degrees since the Rodríguez Lara government. In general, the petroleum-induced socioeconomic changes were contributing to the development of a less elitist, more inclusionary political system, as evidence by the growing strength of center-left parties. But the elimination of functional representation in the legislature with the adoption of the 1978 constitution had further narrowed traditional channels of elite influence. And the exhaustion of the petroleum boom and the diminishing recourse to international sources of credit meant that, in contrast to periods of rapid economic expansion, few decisions could be undertaken without imposing significant costs on different groups in society. In this context, private business elites were all the more anxious to regain their traditional privileged access to public policy formation.

During the petroleum boom the state had also acquired a degree of autonomy relative to the private sector that was unprecedented in Ecuadorian experience. The shift in revenue dependence from taxation of the private sector, primarily foreign trade, to the direct receipt of petroleum revenues greatly reduced the ability of Ecuador's economic elites to veto unpopular policies through their manipulation of public revenues. In 1965, for example, a shutdown of commercial activity organized by the Quito and Guayaquil Chambers of Commerce contributed to the overthrow of the military junta; in March 1983 a similar shutdown of commercial activity had little effect on the government. As one of the leaders of the 1965 commercial strike lamented, "We were able to bring down the government then. . . . Today when we organize such a stoppage, the government can laugh at us."[24] With traditional avenues of influence weakened, direct control of the state became an issue of increasing concern to the economic elites—a concern undoubtedly reinforced by Hurtado's sincere commitment to radically expanding the political participation of formerly excluded groups in Ecuadorian society.

The growth of the public sector also contributed to private-sector antagonism. Business elites excoriated the growing "statism"

TABLE 7.2
Aggregate public-sector growth, 1968-1983
(in millions of current sucres)

Year	Gross Domestic Product (GDP)	Percent Increase	Public Sector (G)	Percent Increase	G/GDP	Percent Increase
1968	27412		5476		19.98	
1969	30144	9.97	6716	22.64	22.28	11.53
1970	35019	16.17	7996	19.06	22.83	2.48
1971	40048	14.36	9059	13.29	22.62	-0.93
1972	46859	17.01	10663	17.71	22.76	0.60
1973	62229	32.80	13702	28.50	22.02	-3.24
1974	92763	49.07	25442	85.68	27.43	24.56
1975	107740	16.15	30023	18.01	27.87	1.60
1976	132913	23.36	36704	22.25	27.62	-0.90
1977	166376	25.18	50325	37.11	30.25	9.53
1978	191345	15.01	54433	8.16	28.45	-5.95
1979	233963	22.27	67023	23.13	28.65	0.70
1980	293337	25.38	90560	35.12	30.87	7.77
1981	348662	18.86	110334	21.84	31.64	2.50
1982	416959	19.59	135990	23.25	32.61	3.06
1983	565802	35.70	148841	9.45	26.31	-19.34
Annual Growth Rate 1968-1983		20.83		21.52		0.95

SOURCE: Calculated from Banco Central del Ecuador, *Cuentas Nacionales*, Nos. 1-6, and from unpublished data supplied by the Ecuadorian Central Bank. In this table the public-sector figures refer to total expenditures by the public administration plus capital expenditures by public enterprises.

of the Hurtado administration, citing what they believed to be evidence of its attacks on the private sector. Simply by virtue of the state's much greater involvement in the economy, public-sector decisions assumed far greater importance than they had held before 1972. As shown in Table 7.2, the public administration, a measure of the public sector that includes neither public enterprises nor public financial institutions, grew from 22 percent of GDP in 1969 to a high of almost 33 percent in 1982. The concomitant expansion of public enterprises and financial institutions also contributed to charges that the state was usurping private property rights. In considerable part, however, the private sector's criticism reflected its continuing frustration over the petroleum-induced shift in the locus of economic power from private elites to the public sector, a shift particularly galling to Guayaquil economic elites who also saw the regional balance of power tilt toward Quito.

Certainly there were grounds for some private sector complaints over the size of the public sector. The expanding bureaucracy placed a growing burden on private economic transactions. Guayaquil businesses, in particular, were irritated by what they perceived as increasingly obstructionist policies emanating from the Quito government. In February 1973, the Rodríguez Lara government had established the Superintendencia de Precios to regulate prices on a broader scale than had been undertaken previously. The following year a new public enterprise, the Empresa Nacional de Almacenamiento y Comercialización de Productos Agropecuarios (ENAC), whose function was to store and distribute basic foods, was added to a system of public food stores, the Empresa Nacional de Productos Vitales (ENPROVIT), established in 1971 by Velasco Ibarra. The rationale for both price regulation and the two public enterprises was to control the prices of basic commodities produced or distributed by a highly concentrated and protected Ecuadorian industry. Price regulation attacked the problem directly; the public enterprises introduced an element of competition into what was otherwise perceived as a highly monopolistic sector. Direct price regulation certainly did become increasingly cumbersome, contributing to shortages of some products such as wheat. Both ENAC and ENPROVIT competed with private business, providing fuel for charges of statism. Although in this case the argument for their creation on grounds of social efficiency was fairly compelling, there were other public enterprises whose creation was less easily defended.

But in their attacks on the Hurtado administration, the economic elites tended to forget that many of the problems they pointed to had originated long before 1981, and that many of the same elites had also benefited from the expansion of the public sector (see Table 7.3). Most of the expansion of the public sector after 1972 occurred under the military governments. Nor was the size of government small prior to that date. World Bank estimates for 1960 show that Ecuador ranked second in a group of nine Latin American countries with similar per capita GDPs.[25] Even the spending spree during the first year of the democratic government, which had been touched off by the release of populist demands under Bucaram and which left the public budget in a state of hemorrhage, was by no means unprecedented. Nor was it entirely attributable to the democratic administration. Both Roldós and Hurtado, but particularly the latter, had endeavored to impose some fiscal restraint. The problem was that the Ecuadorian government was behaving much as it always had, but now with access to far greater resources and with a far greater effect on the national economy.

The most important change in the Ecuadorian state was the expansion of public enterprises and financial institutions. This new development was attacked on the grounds that it brought the state

TABLE 7.3
Average annual rates of growth of the Ecuadorian public sector by administration
(in percentages)

Administration	GDP	Public Sector (G)	G/GDP
		CURRENT SUCRES	
Velasco Ibarra: 1968-1971	13.47	18.27	4.23
Rodríguez Lara: 1971-1975	28.07	34.93	5.35
Triumvirate: 1975-1979	21.39	22.23	0.69
Roldós: 1979-1981	22.08	28.30	5.10
Hurtado: 1981-1983	27.39	16.15	-8.82
		1975 SUCRES	
Velasco Ibarra: 1968-1971	5.03	5.22	0.18
Rodríguez Lara: 1971-1975	12.67	15.41	2.44
Triumvirate: 1975-1979	6.90	11.00	3.83
Roldós: 1979-1981	4.44	5.98	1.48
Hurtado: 1981-1983	-0.83	-6.38	-5.59

SOURCE: Calculated on the basis of Table 7.2 and from Ecuadorian national accounts data.

into unfair competition with the private sector. As an early manifesto from the private sector proclaimed, "When the state, from its privileged position, becomes an entrepreneur, it becomes a competitor of private enterprise . . . [and] it assumes responsibilities which do not belong to it."[26] Yet in its continuing attacks on the Hurtado government, the private sector ignored the fact that nearly all of this expansion occurred prior to 1980. Similarly, the private sector's criticism overlooked the fact that many of the new public enterprises had resulted from the nationalization of bankrupt private industries whose owners were only too happy to sell to the state (as in the case of the takeover of Ecuatoriana Airlines).

Organized labor, in spite of initial support for the new democratic administration, had already begun to oppose the government before Roldós's death. After the hard line taken toward labor by the triumvirate, the return to democracy and the election of a government pledging social and economic reforms was openly welcomed by most labor groups. During the early months of the Roldós administration, minimum wages were increased, the antilabor laws issued by the triumvirate were rescinded, and new legislation was introduced that facilitated labor organizing. By the end of 1980, the new administration had been responsible for the approval of 22 percent of all active labor organizations established since 1966.[27] But the administration's lack of progress in implementing its reform program disillusioned its labor supporters, bringing charges that the Roldós government had betrayed its popular base of support.

Part of labor's frustration was its limited participation in formal politics. Of the political parties, only the mainstream communist Broad Leftist Front (FADI) and the Maoist Popular Democratic Movement (MPD) had well-developed linkages to labor, and these won only two seats between them in the 1979 congressional elections. Thus, with the abolition of functional representatives, organized labor had virtually no representation in the legislature. In addition, no labor leaders held important administrative posts. But in contrast to the breakdown of communication between the government and the economic elites, the striking characteristic of the period after 1979 was an almost constant dialogue between the minister of labor and the national labor federation, FUT. It was when this dialogue failed that labor took to the streets with mass demonstrations. At the same time, admittedly, the FUT leaders had some interest in a certain number of mass demonstrations as a means of strengthening their control over both the country's fragmented labor organizations and their rank-and-file members, who had demonstrated a tendency to vote for nonleftist candidates in national elections.

After mid-1981, the deteriorating economy brought increasing opposition both from the economic elites, who articulated their concerns primarily through the Chambers of Commerce and Industry, and from organized labor. World petroleum prices began their downward slide. Because the country's import bill could not be financed by export earnings, the government turned to additional debt financing. The rate of growth of the economy in real terms declined from 3.9 percent in 1981 to a meager 1.8 percent in 1982.[28] Growth in the manufacturing sector slowed sharply, and the number of bankruptcies among firms in the private sector escalated. Unemployment, around 5 percent in the years immediately preceding the 1980s, rose to approximately 9 percent of the labor force by 1983. The rate of underemployment, an estimate of those who are only marginally employed, increased from 24 percent in 1975 to between 40 and 60 percent by 1983.[29] Inflation began to accelerate, cutting into the purchasing power of lower-income groups. Between 1980 and 1983, the purchasing power of a minimum-wage worker had fallen by 20 percent.[30]

The austerity policies adopted by Hurtado, though tempered by measures expressly designed to reduce the burden on lower-class groups, exacerbated the economic decline; as highly visible targets they also evoked increased criticism. In May 1982, Hurtado announced a 32 percent devaluation of the sucre. In October, this was followed by a package of policies that (1) raised taxes on beer, cigarettes, and luxury vehicles; (2) doubled the domestic price of gasoline; and (3) eliminated the subsidy for wheat. In November, the minimum wage was increased by 15 percent, and an additional payment was mandated to compensate for the increased cost of transportation following the gasoline price increase. But the latter measures were insufficient to forestall opposition from labor, which angrily denounced the government as "anti-popular" and "pro-oligarchic." The Unitary Workers' Front (FUT) charged that the policies "sharpened the general and fiscal crisis, accelerated inflation—[already] aggravated by the last monetary devaluation—all this to the benefit of the country's oligarchy."[31] Large national strikes were held in September 1982 and barely a month later in October to protest the government's policies. The Chambers of Commerce and Industry condemned the devaluation that had pushed up costs for importers and import-dependent industries. Large private-sector borrowing (in U.S. dollars) from international banks during the late 1970s and early 1980s exacerbated the negative effects of a devaluation on Ecuadorian business. From the end of 1975 to the beginning of 1980, privately held external debt grew twelvefold; from 1980 to the end of 1982, it rose an additional 130 percent to a high of $1.6 billion.[32] Already weakened by the economic crisis, the private sector panicked as the devaluation not only increased the costs of imported inputs but also drove up the burden of the external debt in sucres. After the May 1982 devaluation, 32 percent more sucres had to be earned in order to repay the same dollar amount of debt.

The economic crisis deepened in 1983. Burdened by falling petroleum prices, natural disasters, and the government's austerity program, Ecuador's gross domestic product ceased to grow and, indeed, fell by 3.3 percent. Severe flooding caused by a shift in ocean currents along the coast devastated the economically critical coastal agriculture. Both export crops and food for domestic consumption were destroyed. A potato blight in the highlands cut sharply into harvests of this staple food. Inflation, already rising from the effects of import restrictions and currency devaluation, exploded as food prices jumped 80 percent.[33] The government's austerity policies also began to bite deeply into economic growth. Alarmed by Mexico's threatened default, international banks had virtually closed off credit to Latin America by 1982, forcing Ecuador to begin talks with the International Monetary Fund (IMF) for assistance in renegotiating its external debt. In 1983, bolstered by IMF insistence on a reduction in public-sector expenditures, Hurtado finally managed to implement his own previously expressed concerns over the need for austerity in the government sector.[34] Facing vehement opposition from public-sector employees over proposed cuts in current expenditures, Hurtado chose to make his largest cuts in public investments, and government spending as a share of GDP fell by 20 percent.[35] A second devaluation in March 1983 decreased the value of the sucre relative to the dollar by a further 21 percent, and a program of automatic "mini-devaluations" was set in place, triggering yet another round of protest from organized labor and business elites. Even exporters, generally the primary beneficiaries of a devaluation, were disgruntled by the simultaneous abolition of export subsidies. On March 23, 1983, the democratic government confronted its fourth national strike. At the same time, the Quito and Guayaquil Chambers of Commerce, composed largely of importers, organized simultaneous commercial shutdowns in the two cities. Rumors of a military coup again began to circulate as some of the more conservative business leaders openly called for removal of the president.

Ironically, however, by the middle of 1983, when economic conditions had grown progressively worse, political opposition to the government moderated. Organized labor—which, although it certainly opposed many of the government's policies, had never sought its overthrow—began to realize that continued opposition would likely provoke a military coup. Recognizing that any military government would probably take a much harder line against labor, moderate leaders of the FUT "allegedly reached a private agreement with the government to restrain labor unrest."[36] Organized labor protests diminished after the March 1983 national strike, which was the last called against the Hurtado government.

Opposition from the chambers of production also abated, though for quite different reasons. First, during the early part of 1983, the government began discussions with the private sector over its external dollar debt. The devaluations had progressively increased the debt burden on the private sector, which charged that the government's tight money policy had dried up domestic sources of funds, thus obliging businesses to borrow dollars from foreign lenders. The government, for its part, initially maintained that the private sector knew the risks of borrowing in dollars and that at least part of the liquidity problem was due to the movement of capital out of the country and into investments such as Miami real estate. But antagonism between government and business moderated in the face of increasing bankruptcies, rising unemployment, and the threatened failure of some of the country's largest banks. By the second half of 1983 the government had agreed to a program of "sucretización," under which the government absorbed some of the private debt, stretched out payment periods, and essentially assumed the risk of further exchange rate fluctuations. Criticized as a sellout to the country's economic elites, the program did serve to help restore private-sector confidence and to moderate attacks from the chambers of production.

Second, as the scheduled 1984 presidential elections approached, the private sector's attention turned increasingly toward the launching of León Febres Cordero's candidacy. As Febres Cordero was considered a leading candidate, his election would give the political right direct control of the presidency for the first time in many years. Given the weakness of the traditional rightist parties, business elites began to convert the chambers of production into the primary vehicles for organizing Febres Cordero's campaign.

On August 10, 1984, Osvaldo Hurtado realized what he had stated to be the most important goal of his administration—that of presiding over the transition of power to a second democratically elected government, the first such transition in a quarter of a century. Certainly it was his commitment to the democratic process that had guided the country through a minefield of adversity to the August installation of León Febres Cordero as the next president. At the same time, after many years of frustration, the country's economic elites also realized their goal of winning direct control of the state.

Indeed, it was the careful nurturing of democratic institutions and processes that constituted the principal legacy of the Roldós and Hurtado administrations. Their reformist accomplishments were modest, limited by a variety of factors: by deteriorating economic conditions; by intransigent opposition from the country's economic elites, particularly during the Hurtado presidency; and by their inability to mobilize a base of support outside the traditional power contenders, namely, the unions and the economic elites. By contrast to previous periods of military reform, that inability to mobilize support was certainly not for lack of effort. Both Roldós and Hurtado had sought to broaden political participation in what had traditionally been a highly exclusionary system. Labor unions were encouraged and strengthened. Popular organizations, such as cooperatives, were promoted. The national literacy program was reformed and strengthened, contributing importantly to lowered rates of illiteracy. But although these efforts may prove important for future governments interested in social and economic reforms, and although they may have contributed to strengthening democracy in general, they were both too little and too late to save Roldós and Hurtado's reformist project from the unpropitious circumstances it faced.

NOTES

1. *The National Development Plan of Ecuador, 1980–1984: The Major Objectives* (Quito, 1980), pp. 12, 19.

2. Rob Vos, "El modelo de desarrollo y el sector agrícola en Ecuador, 1965–1982," *El Trimestre Económico*, Vol. 52 (4), No. 208 (México, October–December 1985), Cuadro 3, p. 1110. Both the volume and the value of agricultural production declined.

3. World Bank, *Ecuador: An Agenda for Recovery and Sustained Growth* (Washington, D.C.: The International Bank for Reconstruction and Development, 1984), p. 38. Earmarked taxes are those whose revenue is designated for a specific purpose.

4. David W. Schodt, "The Ecuadorian Public Sector During the Petroleum Period: 1972–1983," Technical Paper Series, No. 52 (Austin: University of Texas, Office of Public-Sector Studies, Institute of Latin American Studies, 1986), Table 2, p. 18. In a democratic government whose budget is subject to approval by the legislature, earmarking and decentralization reduce executive control over the public sector. At the same time the practice does insulate some public funds from a legislature that may be largely indifferent to revenue constraints.

5. *Análisis Semanal*, 9, 35 (September 10, 1979):363–369.

6. World Bank, *Ecuador: Development Problems and Prospects* (Washington, D.C.: The International Bank for Reconstruction and Development, 1979), Table 4, p. 21.

7. *The National Development Plan*, pp. 40–44.

8. Ibid., p. 52.

9. Ibid., pp. 56–68.

10. Quoted in John D. Martz, "The Quest for Popular Democracy in Ecuador," *Current History*, 78, 154 (February 1980):84.

11. Howard Handelman, "The Dilemma of Ecuadorian Democracy, Part I: Jaime Roldós and the Politics of Deadlock" (Hanover: University Field Staff International, No. 34, 1984), p. 3.

12. Martz, "The Quest," p. 69.

13. Nick D. Mills, *Crisis, Conflicto y Consenso: Ecuador, 1979–1984* (Quito: Corporación Editora Nacional, 1984), p. 40.

14. Handelman, "The Dilemma," p. 4.

15. Although the 70 percent figure was widely reported in Ecuador, it is slightly deceptive given that the *budget* accounts for only about 40 percent of total public-sector expenditures. The public sector increased by only 35 percent from 1979 to 1980. See Schodt, "The Ecuadorian Public Sector," pp. 18, 19.

16. Mills, *Crisis*, pp. 43, 44.

17. World Bank, *An Agenda*, p. 20. As with the majority of borrowing countries in this period, most of Ecuador's external debt was at interest rates pegged to the U.S. prime rate or to the London interbank rate (LIBOR).

18. The equivalent prices in U.S. currency would be 16.4 to 52.5 cents to the gallon. In spite of this increase, the effects of both constant domestic gasoline prices between 1973 and 1981 and domestic inflation were such that in real (inflation-adjusted) terms, gasoline was still cheaper after the price increase than in 1973.

19. *Análisis Semanal*, Año XI, No. 7 (February 23, 1981):65.

20. Mills, *Crisis*, p. 65.

21. Howard Handelman, "The Dilemma of Ecuadorian Democracy, Part II: Hurtado and the Debt Trap" (Hanover: University Field Staff International, No. 34, 1984), p. 4.

22. Frank E. Neiring, Jr., "Progress in Oil Sector," *Petroleum Economist* (May 1983):175–176; and Michael Crabbe, "Foreign Oil Investment Encouraged," *Petroleum Economist* (July 1985):246.

23. See Osvaldo Hurtado's address given to the nation on network television on December 7, 1981, in *Democracia y Crisis*, Vol. 2 (Quito: SENDIP, 1984), p. 111.

24. Quoted in Howard Handelman, "Elite Interest Groups Under Military and Democratic Regimes: Ecuador, 1972–1984" (paper presented at the annual meeting of the Latin American Studies Association, Albuquerque, New Mexico, April 17–20, 1985), p. 9.

25. World Bank, *Development Problems*, p. 73a. The countries are Colombia, Dominican Republic, El Salvador, Guatemala, Guyana, Honduras, Nicaragua, and Paraguay.

26. *Weekly Analysis* (September 14, 1973); cited in Catherine Mary Conaghan, "Industrialists and the Reformist Interregnum: Dominant Class Behavior and Ideology in Ecuador, 1972–1979" (Ph.D. dissertation, Yale University, 1983), p. 137.

27. Gilda Farrell, *Mercado de trabajo urbano y movimiento sindical* (Quito: Instituto de Investigaciones Económicos/Pontífica Universidad Católica del Ecuador (IIE-PUCE/ILDIS), 1982, pp. 39, 38; cited in Mills, *Crisis*, p. 186.

28. Banco Central del Ecuador, *Cuentas Nacionales No. 6* (1984), Cuadro No. 8, p. 32.

29. Banco Central del Ecuador, *Memoria 1983*, p. 71; and *Boletín Anuario*, No. 7 (1984), p. 198.

30. Banco Central del Ecuador, *Memoria 1983*, p. 42.

31. *El Comercio* (September 18, 1982); cited in Mills, *Crisis*, p. 165.

32. Banco Central del Ecuador, *Memoria 1983*, p. 123.

33. Banco Central del Ecuador, *Boletín Anuario*, No. 7, p. 103. Inflation averaged about 14.6 percent from 1980 to 1982 but rose to 48 percent by 1983. Although even 48 percent is low by the standards of many Latin American countries, it was more than double the highest rate recorded in Ecuador during the preceding twenty years.

34. *Análisis Semanal*, Año X11, No. 40 (October 11, 1982).

35. David W. Schodt, "The Ecuadorian Public Sector," pp. 19–20.

36. Handelman, "Hurtado and the Debt Trap," p. 6.

8

Patterns of Continuity
Amidst Change:
Prospects for the Future

Declining petroleum prices and the rising burden of debt service payments in the 1980s weakened the state relative to the early years of the petroleum boom. Ecuadorian economic elites, whose access to the formulation of public policy was highly circumscribed during the boom years, were able to take advantage of the relative weakness of the state to elect their own candidate as president of the country in 1984. Promising to reduce the power of the state and to reorient the economy toward a model of economic liberalization, the new government quickly discovered that its ability to do so was not free of the traditional economic and political constraints that had so frustrated earlier governments. As the administration moved to implement its economic proposals, an important question was whether Ecuador's recently revitalized democratic institutions could withstand the strain of an economic downturn and policies that held the potential to impose heavy costs on precisely those groups, such as urban professionals, that had been among the primary beneficiaries of the petroleum boom.

THE 1984 ELECTIONS: A SWING TO THE RIGHT?

The 1984 elections appeared to set the stage for a showdown between the new center-left parties and a resurgent right. With the deaths of Velasco Ibarra and Assad Bucaram, traditional populist parties had lost much of their electoral appeal; no similarly charismatic leaders had yet emerged to capture the populist vote. The leftist parties, too, were highly fragmented and without significant support among voters. The presidential campaigns began in earnest in August

1983 with the first-round election scheduled for January 29, 1984. Although nine candidates presented themselves for election, the contest was widely perceived to be one between the two front runners, the Social Christian candidate León Febres Cordero and the Democratic Left candidate Rodrigo Borja Cevallos. Febres Cordero, a leading government critic during both the preceding military and civilian governments, ran as the candidate of a coalition of rightist parties, the National Reconstruction Front (Frente de Reconstrucción Nacional, or FRN). Clearly favored to win the first round, Febres Cordero ran on a platform of opposition to what he denounced as the economic mismanagement of the previous administrations, promising to reduce the level of government involvement in the economy and to run the country with the kind of hardheaded pragmatism he claimed to have demonstrated as a private businessman. He offered the electorate a clear choice, but one he was careful not to delineate on ideological grounds or to closely identify with any party. Indeed, his disdain for parties and professional politicians was a major campaign theme.

Much to the surprise of most Ecuadorians, including the two front-runners themselves, Rodrigo Borja won the first round with 28.7 percent of the valid vote, narrowly edging out second-place finisher León Febres Cordero, who collected 27.2 percent of the vote. Third place went to populist CFP candidate, Angel Duarte, a little-known former minister of agriculture who won a surprising 13.5 percent of the vote. Marxist candidate Jaime Hurtado (no relation to Osvaldo Hurtado), of the far-left Popular Democratic Movement (Movimiento Democrático Popular, or MPD), took an equally surprising fourth place with 7.3 percent of the vote. Congressional elections, held concurrently with the first-round presidential elections, seemed to confirm the unexpectedly strong support for center-left candidate Borja. Democratic Left (ID) candidates won 24 of the 71 seats; the combined total for center-left candidates was 33. Rightist candidates won only 16 seats, with the remainder going to the populists (16) and the leftists (6).

The major issue for the second-round run-off election, scheduled for May 6, was whether the electorate would vote along ideological or regional lines. All of the losing left and center-left presidential candidates, except for Jaime Hurtado of the MPD, endorsed Rodrigo Borja. The populist candidates were more equivocal. The CFP, for example, allowed party officials at the provincial level to decide which candidate they would support. The Pichincha (Quito) CFP endorsed Borja; both the Guayas (Guayaquil) and the Manabí branches remained officially neutral but put the coastal CFP organization to work for Febres Cordero, continuing their unofficial collaboration with the political right begun under Assad Bucaram. Certainly, as many Ecuadorian analysts had predicted, if Borja had picked up the rest of the center-left vote and some of the populist vote, he would have won easily.[1] Yet, if voters had made their decision on regional grounds, the victory would likely have gone to Febres Cordero. The CFP split was one indication of this possibility; even one of the center-left parties, Francisco Huerta's Partido Demócrata (Democratic party, or DP), had its base of support on the coast.

Rodrigo Borja, confident of victory if he could hold the center-left vote, chose to continue his first-round strategy, emphasizing the ideological differences between himself and his opponent. Febres Cordero, on the other hand, well aware of the pivotal importance of the populist vote, shifted his campaign to increase his appeal to this group. Basing his second-round strategy on a more personal appeal to voters, he adopted the populist slogan of "pan, techo, y empleo" (bread, housing, and jobs), borrowed from a recent successful Colombian presidential campaign. Portraying himself to voters as a man of the people, as a candidate above ideology and partisan political association, he nevertheless made it clear to his backers in the chambers that if elected he would chart a free-market course for the Ecuadorian economy. His closest economic advisers, all impassioned advocates of economic liberalization and certain to be tapped for major policy posts in a Febres Cordero administration, attested to his commitment.[2]

The run-off election results again confounded the experts, who had assumed that Borja would win easily if voters demonstrated even a moderate degree of ideological consistency. León Febres Cordero was elected president of Ecuador with a narrow 51.5 percent of the valid vote. With illiterates voting for the first time in a presidential election, the percentage of the population casting ballots reached 31 percent—the highest yet recorded and considerably greater than the 21 percent who voted five years earlier. Borja had won 15 out of 20 provinces, down from his first-round total of 19, in which only Guayas had gone to Febres Cordero. Although the latter picked up an additional four provinces in the run-off, it was his overwhelming win in Guayas, the most populous province, that assured Febres Cordero the presidency. Clearly, ideological considerations were of secondary importance to the voters' run-off election choice. Regionalism, particularly its populist manifestation, appears to have been the dominant consideration, although some of the increased vote for Febres Cordero undoubtedly reflected a protest against the deteriorating economic conditions experienced during the Hurtado administration. Particularly those Guayaquil voters who had supported CFP candidate Duarte in the first round switched overwhelmingly to Febres Cordero.

Ecuador's new president, León Febres Cordero, was the first representative of the Ecuadorian political right to hold that office since Camilo Ponce Enríquez's victory in 1956. Born in 1931 in Guayaquil, Febres Cordero received a degree in mechanical engineering from Stevens Institute of Technology in New Jersey. Returning to Ecuador in 1953, he embarked on a business career, rising to prominence as an executive of the Noboa group, Ecuador's largest banana exporter and a major agribusiness conglomerate. He served as president of the Association of Latin American Industries and of the Guayas Chamber of Industry. He launched his political career in the 1960s, serving briefly as a senator. In 1979 he was elected to congress as a delegate of the small Social Christian party (PSC), earning a reputation as the leading critic of the Roldós and Hurtado administrations and as an outspoken champion of coastal business interests. Both Febres Cordero's educational background and his ideological orientation—he has asserted publicly that "there is great affinity between my economic philosophy and President Reagan's"—give him the closest ties to the United States of any Ecuadorian president since Galo Plaza.[3]

RESTRUCTURING THE ECONOMY: A NEW MODEL FOR ECUADOR?

Once installed in office, Febres Cordero lost no time beginning to implement policies that would restructure the Ecuadorian economy along free-market lines. Condemning the Hurtado administration for economic policies he claimed had left the nation's economy in a state of near ruin, Febres Cordero and his advisers proposed that the economy be unshackled from the burdern of excessive government regulation and that the industrialization policy be reoriented from its current emphasis on import substitution toward the promotion of manufactured exports. These objectives were to be accomplished by removing government controls over prices and exchange rates, eliminating import tariffs, and actively soliciting the participation of foreign capital. Febres Cordero had committed himself during the campaign to a major program of public housing construction. Aside from this program, however, economic growth and the anticipated accompanying expansion of employment opportunities were the means by which the benefits of economic liberalization were expected to reach lower income groups. No public-sector redistributive policies, such as land reform, were part of these proposals.

Advocates of economic liberalization argued, first, that the basic problem with the Ecuadorian economy was that producers were subject to an economic environment in which government policies not only distorted market price signals but also increased the degree of uncertainty surrounding those prices because of erratic policy shifts. Thus, in simple terms the administration's strategy was to eliminate government controls—to "get prices right"—and, once this was accomplished, to minimize future policy changes. Currency devaluation occupied a prominent position in these arguments. The exchange rate was believed to be the most important price to get right in an economy such as Ecuador's, in which foreign trade plays such an important role. As Alberto Dahik, then president of the Monetary Board, emphasized, the exchange rate is "a fundamental variable which must never give the wrong signals to the economy."[4] The new administration believed, in particular, that Ecuador's exchange rate had become seriously overvalued during the 1970s, thus discouraging exports, stimulating imports, and contributing to the country's chronic balance-of-trade deficits.

The second part of the argument for economic liberalization involved opening the country to foreign capital. Consistent with a general ideological commitment to eliminating government regulation over all aspects of economic activity, the anticipated inflow of foreign capital was seen as critically important for solving the problem of low domestic investment and for alleviating the balance-of-payments deficit. In the short run, foreign capital was necessary to increase petroleum exports through its financing of new exploration and development. In the long run, given Ecuador's large external debt and the heavy outflows of capital this entailed, it was only with large inflows of foreign capital that economic growth could be rekindled and the economy reoriented from its current emphasis on import-substitution industries to those producing manufactured goods for export.

Febres Cordero's proposals for economic liberalization were not new; similar policies had been tried before in other Latin American countries during the 1960s and 1970s. What distinguished Febres Cordero's economic program was his intention to implement within a democratic political system the kinds of policies that previously had been attempted only by highly authoritarian governments. Without question, there was a need for some of the economic liberalization measures proposed by the Febres Cordero government. The heavy debt burden and the falling price of petroleum mandated some immediate changes. The rapid expansion of the public sector during the 1970s had unnecessarily burdened other sectors of the economy. Certainly Ecuador's history of boom-and-bust export cycles suggested that a diversification of exports was desirable. But, at least in the short run, the major reorientation of the Ecuadorian economy proposed by Febres Cordero and his advisers would almost certainly depress the economy. The combination of devaluations, which would raise the cost of imported goods in an economy heavily dependent on imports, and the removal of domestic price controls could be expected to accelerate the pace of inflation. With stagnant production and rising prices, real wages would be likely to fall. In the long run, the expected expansion of export industries might provide a new source of economic growth. But the benefits from export expansion would likely be weakly linked to the rest of the economy unless the new export industries were highly labor intensive.

Such changes necessarily imply a realignment of costs and benefits across social groups relative to the previous development model of import-substituting industrialization. Traditional exporters are the clearest and most immediate winners from a policy of economic liberalization; the losers would include industrialists producing for the domestic market, importers, organized labor, and civil servants. Particularly in a time of economic austerity, this realignment of economic costs and benefits, without offsetting public-sector redistributive policies, would carry with it the potential for heavy political costs, thus seriously threatening the legitimacy of any government. It is by no means coincidental that previous Latin American experiments with economic liberalization have been associated with authoritarian political regimes.

Well aware of the negative results of similar policies adopted some years earlier by military governments in Chile, Argentina, and Uruguay, the Febres Cordero administration argued that it would not repeat the mistakes of these prior experiments in economic liberalization.[5] Yet its view of these mistakes was a largely technocratic one. A belief firmly held by Febres Cordero and the business elites who supported him was that, along with "getting prices right," Ecuador needed a dose of sound management practices. Febres Cordero campaigned on this assertion, appealing to business people such as the Quito industrialist who is reported to have commented that "a country is not too different from a company. . . . If you run a company inefficiently it goes bust; otherwise it makes profits."[6] But as Chilean economist Alejandro Foxley has cautioned, the successful implementation of economic liberalization policies depends on more than just technical proficiency:

> A final lesson to be learned from neoconservative experiments in Latin America is that economic stabilization cannot be separated from long-term changes and policies. These are influenced by ideologies, coalitions

in power, and the nature of the political regime. . . . If the political system is going to be a democratic one, economic policies must necessarily be a reflection of a basic underlying consensus. For these policies to have a chance, they cannot persistently generate increasing inequalities, nor can they systematically exclude significant sectors of society, as neoconservative policies so often have done.[7]

Although Febres Cordero proposed sweeping economic changes, long desired by Ecuadorian business elites, his government's ability to implement these changes (ironically, like the ability of preceding governments that had struggled to institute reformist programs) appeared to be severely circumscribed by all the familiar economic and political constraints. To be sure, the economy had shown some signs of improvement in 1984, as Ecuadorian production recovered from the devastating effects of the El Niño floods in the preceding year, and improved economic growth in the industrialized nations increased demand for Ecuador's traditional exports. The rate of economic growth, for example, reached 4 percent in 1984, the highest since 1980. But without large inflows of foreign capital or dramatic increases in nonpetroleum export earnings, the incipient economic recovery would remain precariously balanced between Ecuador's obligations on its foreign debt and its earnings from the export of petroleum. At the time of Febres Cordero's inauguration, Ecuador's foreign debt stood at $6.85 billion. In 1984, interest payments alone consumed nearly one-third of all export earnings.[8] Petroleum export earnings, accounting for more than 70 percent of the value of all exports, stagnated as sharp increases in volume barely offset declining world market prices. Inflation, which had begun to moderate during the latter half of 1983, remained at a historically high level, acutely sensitive to the effects of devaluations, increases in import prices, and the degree to which domestic price controls were sustained. By the end of 1984, Ecuadorian living standards, as measured by gross domestic product per capita, had failed to recover to what they had been in 1978.[9]

A weak economy was not the only obstacle confronting Febres Cordero. Elected without a strong popular mandate for his economic policies, he faced an opposition congress and was able to count on only 16 of the 71 delegates for unquestioned support. His victory in the run-off election was scarcely overwhelming, with a significant proportion of his supporters voting not because of his economic proposals but for reasons based on regionalism or protest against economic conditions experienced during the Hurtado administration. Febres Cordero's cabinet appointments, drawn almost entirely from the Guayaquil business community, did nothing to strengthen his support from the parties constituting the National Reconstruction Front (FRN), which had anticipated some patronage opportunities. Even among the country's economic elites, his strongest supporters, there were some signs of discontent as it became clear that not all business groups would benefit from the administration's liberalization policies.

Less than a month after his inauguration, Febres Cordero announced the details of his policies for economic liberalization. Central among these was a decree allowing most of the country's exports and imports to be shifted from a fixed to a theoretically floating, or market, rate of exchange, thus effectively devaluing the Ecuadorian sucre. Simultaneously, all import quotas except for those on automobiles were lifted, and import tariffs on industrial raw materials were reduced by one-half. Some tariffs on a limited number of consumer goods imports were also reduced to retard the growing contraband trade. Price controls on most domestically produced goods were eliminated. Interest rate ceilings were raised and floating rates were established for some types of deposits. In late December, domestic gasoline prices were raised by 70 percent. Surprisingly, given Febres Cordero's commitment to reducing government regulation and his vitriolic attacks on the Hurtado administration's economic policies, these measures were not perceived as a significant departure from those begun by the preceding administration. As was noted in a newspaper generally critical of the administration, "The measures are moderate with respect to the economic policies that were being attributed to the government."[10]

Policies to open the country to foreign investment and to attract new sources of foreign capital also proceeded apace. Petroleum companies had expressed renewed interest in Ecuador following the Hurtado administration's adoption of new risk-contract legislation. Agreements with Occidental and Exxon/Hispaniol petroleum companies, initiated by the Hurtado government but suspended just prior to the elections, were signed by Febres Cordero during the early months of 1985 with the hope that known reserves could be doubled by 1987.[11] During the next year, five additional petroleum companies signed risk contracts. Seeking to encourage foreign investment in other areas of the economy as well, the administration announced its intention not to be bound by Decision 24 of the Andean Pact agreement, which had established common restrictive standards for the treatment of foreign investment by signatory nations.[12] Despite such incentives, however, foreign investors appeared reluctant to commit additional capital, thus threatening the success of a key component of the president's economic plan.[13]

In early 1985 Ecuador concluded a highly favorable agreement for refinancing its foreign debt that stretched out the repayment period to twelve years and allowed an initial three-year grace period during which the country would not have to make payments on principal.[14] In January of the following year, Febres Cordero capitalized on his close ties to the United States and his commitment to free-market principles by securing $319 million in new public loans. Proclaiming the Ecuadorian government "the best in Latin America," the U.S. administration appeared ready to make Ecuador a test case under Treasury Secretary James A. Baker's plan for assistance to the indebted developing countries.[15]

The economic consequences of these policies at the end of 1985 were mixed and, indeed, difficult to disentangle from other changes in the domestic and international economies. Real gross domestic product increased by 3.8 percent, down slightly from the 4.0 percent growth registered in 1984. The rate of inflation declined somewhat, from an annual rate of 30.4 percent in 1984 to 28.0 percent in 1985. These price figures, however, mask both a deceleration in the rate of inflation through October 1984 as domestic agricultural production recovered and a renewed acceleration after this date as the new government's price decontrols took effect.[16] Living standards, as measured by real gross domestic product per capita, rose by less than 1 percent, still failing to regain the 1978 level. The distribution of income showed signs of increasing concentration as the wage share of national income continued to fall.[17]

Exports performed well and imports increased only moderately, with the result that the current-account deficit fell from $248 million the preceding year to $84 million in 1985. Petroleum exports performed strongly, as increases in volume were able to offset a continued softening of world petroleum prices. The traditional exports—bananas and coffee and cacao—all showed gains in 1985, with both price and volume increases contributing to their performance. Yet some part of these gains, such as those for bananas, were attributable primarily to the recovery of domestic production following the 1983 floods. And, although the new administration's debt-refinancing agreement had won it temporary reductions in its debt-servicing obligations, Ecuador's total external debt had increased to $7.4 billion, thus raising the specter of future balance-of-payments difficulties.

In 1985, the government budget generated a surplus—at 1.5 percent of GDP, the largest since 1970. Yet this improvement was not due to decreases in expenditures, which rose markedly over the period; rather, it resulted from revenue increases, notably from petroleum.[18] As a consequence, the share of petroleum revenues in total public-sector revenues increased from 47.6 percent in 1983 to more than 50 percent in 1985, thus making government expenditures even more sensitive to fluctuations in the world price of petroleum. In addition, the pattern of government spending showed a marked shift from expenditures for economic and social development to those for general services and provincial projects.[19]

The implementation of Febres Cordero's economic policies did not occur without political opposition. From the first day of his administration, the president faced bitter opposition from congress. The center-left parties organized an opposition block in the congress, the Progressive Front (Frente Progresista, or FP), composed of the deputies of the Democratic Left (ID), Popular Democracy (DP), Democratic party (PD), and Roldosista party of Ecuador (PRE). The populist parties—the CFP and the Alfarista Radical Front (FRA)—did not join the center-left bloc, preferring instead to maintain a semblance of independence from the FP and the progovernment FRN, although the CFP in particular tended increasingly to collaborate with the government. Relations between the legislature and the executive grew more and more acrimonious, escalating into a constitutional conflict over the naming of Supreme Court justices. The intransigence of both the president and the opposition front, and a demonstrably questionable commitment to democratic procedure on the part of the former, raised fears for the survival of Ecuadorian democracy. Former president Hurtado broke a self-imposed 100-day public silence to charge that "since October 2 Ecuador has had a quasi-dictatorship rather than a constitutional government."[20] Given the president's apparent willingness to abrogate the constitution, the opposition's ability to oppose executive proposals was constrained by its concern for preventing Febres Cordero from openly assuming dictatorial powers. Because the opposition lacked the kind of mass support that could make the costs to the president of imposing a true dictatorship unacceptably high, its bargaining position was weak. Unable to veto the president's proposals, the opposition was forced to oversee an increasing movement of the Ecuadorian economy toward the neoliberal model. And by the end of 1985, Febres Cordero had at last managed to engineer an agreement with the CFP, the FRA, and several independent deputies, thus finally assembling a progovernment majority in the congress.

In early 1986, world petroleum prices fell below $20 per barrel, with predictable effects on the Ecuadorian economy. The current-account deficit widened as export earnings fell, and the government budget, increasingly dependent on petroleum earnings, could no longer be balanced. The administration responded with a package of emergency economic measures, including a 14 percent devaluation of the sucre and, in an apparent retreat from its neoliberal program, the introduction of a system of multiple, fixed exchange rates.

Deteriorating economic conditions brought the costs of the administration's economic policies into sharp relief, thus strengthening the political opposition. Opposition from the national labor organization (FUT), which had been relatively ineffective up to this point, began to toughen. The support from business elites began to show some cracks in early 1986, as the Quito Chamber of Commerce called for a "revision of 'multiple aspects' of the measures adopted to offset the falling price for oil," and the Pichincha Chamber of Industry criticized the government for policies it claimed could lead to widespread bankruptcy among industrialists.[21]

Military support for Febres Cordero was also thrown into question by an unsucessful revolt, led by Air Force Commander General Frank Vargas, in March 1986. Apparently inspired by internal disputes, the revolt nevertheless exposed divisions within the military's support for the president, revealing a growing repoliticization of the armed forces. Although there was little reason to believe that the Vargas revolt signaled an imminent return to power by the military, the incident did have the effect of focusing public opposition to the president; it also increased the strength of the democratic opposition by serving notice on the executive that an open abrogation of the constitution might not find support within the armed forces.[22]

In the face of mounting public opposition, Febres Cordero's strategy appears to involve a retreat to the long-established Ecuadorian populist political formula in which the country's economic elites have sought to sustain an uneasy alliance with lower-class groups, particularly the pivotal Guayaquil voters, through public works expenditures. Febres Cordero came into office as the candidate of Ecuador's traditional business elites. Although nominally affiliated with the Social Christian party (PSC), his campaign was run largely outside the party system by the chambers of production.[23]

Like other populist leaders before him, Febres Cordero has sought to reach over the party system directly to the voters. Eschewing the balcony favored by an earlier generation of political leaders, the new administration has appealed to the masses through its skillful manipulation of the new political medium of television. Ideologically opposed to using the state as a major actor for social change yet well aware that his economic policies—although they promised to favor lower-income groups through economic growth—guaranteed immediate benefits only to the economic elites, Febres Cordero turned to a vigorous program of public works expenditures. Although his public housing program has limped along, crippled by its dependence on foreign funding, there is highly visible evidence of road and bridge construction projects, each bearing large signs proclaiming it to be "Otra Obra de León" (Another Project of León). Guayaquil, the stronghold of the president's support, has benefited disproportionately, as construction projects there have grown at a much faster rate than those in Quito.[24]

In early 1986, uncertain over the cohesiveness of the new progovernment congressional majority (by March both the CFP and the FRA had withdrawn) and mindful of the general debility of the traditional rightist parties, Febres Cordero went ahead with plans to consolidate a base of political support outside of the party system. Ignoring the congressional opposition, the president scheduled a national plebiscite, to be held concurrently with the midterm congressional elections in June, on whether independent candidates should be allowed to stand for elective office.

Dealt a resounding defeat in this plebiscite, which the opposition had managed to turn into a referendum on the government's performance, and facing a newly elected opposition majority in the congress, the government was expected to adopt a more conciliatory position. Nevertheless, these events appear to have made the president more determined than ever to push through his economic policies. In August 1986, Febres Cordero announced another package of austerity policies, thus completing the implementation of much of the neoliberal model. With the exception of petroleum, all foreign-exchange transactions were transferred to the free market, in effect devaluing the sucre by 35 percent. Export taxes were eliminated. Most interest rate ceilings were removed and bank reserve requirements reduced. Notably, however, there were no announcements of measures to slow government spending or to prevent what, without major increases in foreign borrowing, were certain to be large government deficits.[25] Yet it is difficult to know how successful a political strategy relying on large increases in public spending for its legitimacy can be during a period of economic austerity. Certainly, as the experience of past Ecuadorian presidents from Eloy Alfaro to Velasco Ibarra would amply attest, the traditional political formula has never fared well when falling export earnings sharply curtailed the ability of the government to spend.

PROSPECTS FOR THE FUTURE

Once again, Ecuador appears to have fallen victim to the collapse of its export market. From the perspective of 1972, petroleum appeared to offer hope for breaking what was traditionally a relatively tight linkage between the performance of export markets and domestic political stability. Perceived to be a far more reliable source of income, petroleum exports, unlike cacao or bananas, also greatly increased the ability of the Ecuadorian state to act independent of the domestic economic elites. Few, if any, could have predicted the rapid collapse of petroleum prices that began in the early 1980s. Nevertheless, the petroleum boom did bring rapid and sweeping changes to Ecuador— changes exceeding those experienced by any other Latin American nation during the past fifteen years. Per capita incomes between 1960 and 1980 rose from approximately 60 to 70 percent of the Latin American average.[26] The pace of industrialization accelerated rapidly. Road construction and other infrastructural development helped knit together the disparate regions of the country, reducing—though by no means eliminating—the traditional problems of regionalism. The educational system was strengthened, particularly in rural areas, thus contributing to a marked decrease in the rate of illiteracy.

To be sure, serious problems remained—in considerable part as a function of the weak linkages between petroleum and other sectors of the economy and of the failure of the government to direct sufficient resources to the least-advantaged groups in society. The incidence of poverty continued to be high, and the distribution of income remained among the most unequal in South America. The agricultural sector stagnated, and rural inhabitants, in particular, by no means shared equally in the petroleum wealth. Nor has industrialization provided jobs at the rate required to prevent rising levels of unemployment and underemployment in urban areas.

Against the backdrop of the rapid economic change engendered by the petroleum boom, the endemic weaknesses of the country's political system have been sharply revealed. The modernization of the economy has not been reflected in Ecuador's political institutions. Although the emergence of responsible, issues-oriented, center-left parties during the 1970s (such as the Democratic Left [ID] and the Popular Democracy [PD] parties) was an encouraging development, even these parties have so far failed to establish linkages to broad groups in society. Largely as a function of a pattern of economic development that resulted in fragmented popular organizations and limited differentiation among economic elites, the lack of articulation between parties and society was manifested both in the frustrated reformist efforts of Presidents Roldós and Hurtado and in the inability of the opposition parties to force major compromise on Febres Cordero. The lack of party discipline, the bewildering shifts of party allegiance by congressional deputies, and the frequent stalemates between congress and the executive are all in some degree manifestations of the problem of weak and fragmented parties. Even the growing debility of the rightist parties, and their replacement in recent years by interest group associations such as the chambers of production, owes something to the absence of mass-based opposition parties. Both modernization of the Ecuadorian political system and the establishment of a firm base for effective democracy require the development of strong parties on both the left and the right.[27]

The economic crisis afflicting the country since 1982 has placed severe stress on Ecuador's democratic political institutions. For the foreseeable future, the growth of the Ecuadorian economy will be highly constrained. Ecuador's ability to shift to alternative exports in the short run is doubtful. Petroleum prices are not likely to recover for a number of years, and the large production increases undertaken in recent years to boost earnings threaten to deplete existing reserves rapidly unless new petroleum discoveries can be made. The large outflow of capital associated with repayment of Ecuador's debt has greatly reduced the domestic resources available for investment. Foreign capital holds out some hope both for increasing petroleum reserves and for developing new export industries, but it is unlikely that any new inflows will be sufficient to offset the loss of export revenue. As Ecuadorian history amply demonstrates, political conflict tends to intensify when export earnings fall sharply or stagnate for prolonged periods. The important question for the future is whether Ecuador's democratic institutions have matured sufficiently to withstand the inevitable stress of the coming years of limited economic growth.

NOTES

1. See, for example, Alberto Acosta et al., *El Ecuador en las Urnas* (Quito: Editorial El Conejo, 1984); and Howard Handelman, "The Dilemma of Ecuadorian Democracy, Part III: The 1983-84 Presidential Elections" (Hanover: University Field Staff International, No. 36, 1984).

2. See, for example, *Análisis Semanal*, No. 20 (May 18, 1984), and No. 21 (May 24, 1984).

3. *New York Post* (January 13, 1986), p. 75.

4. *Latin America Weekly Report*, WR-86-09 (February 28, 1986):7.

5. See, for example, *Latin America Weekly Report*, WR-86-09 (February 28, 1986):6-7.

6. *Latin America Regional Reports Andean*, RA-84-07 (August 31, 1984):7.

7. Alejandro Foxley, *Latin American Experiments in Neoconservative Economics* (Berkeley: University of California Press, 1983), pp. 205–206. Foxley uses the term "neoconservative economics" to refer to what I have called "economic liberalization."

8. This proportion was calculated on the basis of Banco Central del Ecuador, *Memoria 1985*, p. 276.

9. See Banco Central del Ecuador, *Cuentas Nacionales No. 7* (Quito, 1985), p. 29; and *Memoria 1985*, p. 186.

10. *Hoy* (September 7, 1984), quoted in *Análisis Semanal*, No. 36 (September 10, 1984):440.

11. Michael Crabbe, "Foreign Oil Investment Encouraged," *Petroleum Economist* (July 1985):246.

12. Ecuador signed an agreement to this effect with the United States in November 1984. Other member nations, also eager to attract additional foreign investment, were expected to follow. See *Latin America Regional Reports Andean*, RA-84-10 (December 14, 1984).

13. *Análisis Semanal*, No. 18 (May 12, 1986):9.

14. *Análisis Semanal*, No. 50 (December 26, 1985):615–616.

15. *Latinamerica Press*, 18, 6 (February 20, 1986):1–2. The Baker plan proposed a total of $29 billion in additional loans to Latin America.

16. Corporación de Estudios para el Desarrollo (CORDES), "Coyuntura Económica Ecuatoriana, 1985–1986, *Apunte Técnico No. 5* (Quito, May 1986), pp. 28–29.

17. See *Memoria 1985*, p. 186; and *Cuentas Nacionales, No. 8*.

18. See *Memoria 1985*, pp. 205–206. A devaluation increases the government's revenues in sucres.

19. CORDES, "Coyuntura," p. 21.

20. *El Comercio*, International Edition (November 22, 1984):1.

21. *Latin America Weekly Report*, WR-86-14 (April 11, 1986):2.

22. See, for example, Gonzalo Ortiz Crespo, *La Hora del General* (Quito: Editorial El Conejo 1986), for an account of the Vargas revolt.

23. The term "chambers of production" refers collectively to the Chambers of Agriculture, Industry, and Commerce.

24. *Latin America Weekly Report*, WR-86-14 (April 11, 1986):5.

25. CORDES, "Coyuntura," p. 13; and *Latin America Weekly Report*, WR-86-33 (August 28, 1986).

26. James W. Wilkie and Adam Perkal, eds., *Statistical Abstract of Latin America*, Vol. 23 (Los Angeles: University of California Latin American Center Publications, 1984), p. 16.

27. See Catherine M. Conaghan, "Between Classes and the State: Evolution and Crisis in the Party System of Ecuador" (paper presented at the Latin American Studies Association Meeting, Albuquerque, New Mexico, April 18–20, 1985), for an excellent discussion of these issues.

Glossary and Acronyms

Andes: Mountains running north and south through Ecuador
Arriba: Native variety of Ecuadorian cacao
Audiencia: Spanish court and governing body for designated area
Ayllu: Basic community unit of Inca social structure
Balance of payments: A summary account of a nation's financial transactions with the rest of the world
Balance of trade: The difference between the value of a country's exports and the value of its imports
Campesino: Peasant
Caudillo: Strong, usually military, leader
CEPE: Corporación Estatal Petrolera Ecuatoriana (Ecuadorian State Petroleum Company)
CFP: Concentración de Fuerzas Populares (Concentration of Popular Forces)
Chambers of production: Regional interest group associations such as the Guayaquil Chamber of Commerce, the Pichincha Chamber of Industry, and the Guayas Chamber of Agriculture
Concertaje: System of forced labor involving debt to bind the worker to the employer
Cordillera: Mountain range
Corregidor: Chief Spanish magistrate, or judge administrator of a district
Corregidor de indios: A corregidor in charge of a rural Indian district
Corregimiento: The district of jurisdiction of a corregidor
Criollo: Native-born person of Spanish descent
Current account: The net value of all external flows of goods and services, such as exports, imports, freight, and interest
Devaluation: Official reduction in the exchange value of a country's currency relative to another
DP: Democracia Popular (Popular Democracy)

Encomenderos: Spanish colonizers who received the right to collect tribute from Indians in a designated area, theoretically in return for their protection

Encomienda: The grant of Indian peoples held by an encomendero

Foreign exchange: A country's holdings of other countries' currencies; the ability to import

FADI: Frente Amplio de Izquierda (Broad Left Front)

FP: Frente Progresista (Progressive Front)

FRA: Frente Radical Alfarista (Radical Alfarista Front)

FRN: Frente de Reconstrucción Nacional (National Reconstruction Front)

FUT: Frente Unitario de Trabajadores (Unitary Workers Front)

GDP: The total value of final goods and services produced within a country's boundaries

GNP: The total value of final goods and services claimed by residents of a country; usually closely related to GDP

Hacienda: Large landed estate, usually with a resident Indian labor force

Hectare: Approximately 2.47 acres

Huasipungo: Plot of land received by a highland worker in exchange for labor services

IMF: International Monetary Fund

ID: Izquierda Democrática (Democratic Left)

Latifundia: Large estate

Marginados: Unemployed or underemployed workers, usually urban

Mestizo: Descendant of mixed Indian-white parentage

Minifundio: Small landholding

Mita: Colonial system of rotating forced labor

Monilia: Fungal disease that attacks the cacao tree

Montoneros: Irregular peasant militia important in the civil wars that took place around the turn of the century

Montuvio: Coastal peasant

MPD: Movimiento Democrático Popular (Popular Democratic Movement)

Obraje: Colonial period textile mill

Oriente: Literally "east," referring to the Amazon region of Ecuador

PD: Partido Demócrata (Democratic party)

Personalismo: Roughly refers to the importance of personality or charisma to political figures

Popular groups: Urban and rural lower class and lower-middle class

Populism: Political movement typically involving a charismatic leader, a multiclass coalition drawing on urban middle-class and lower-class groups, an interest in expanding the electorate, and a set of moderately reformist policies

PRE: Partido Roldosista del Ecuador (Ecuadorian Roldosista party)

Progresista: Political party of moderate conservatives and liberals important around the turn of the century

PSE: Partido Social Cristiano (Social Christian party)

Quechua: Common language of the Inca empire, a dialect of which is spoken by many contemporary Ecuadorian Indians

Quichua: Ecuadorian dialect of Quechua

Sucre: Unit of Ecuadorian currency

Tagua: Nut used as artificial ivory, particularly for the manufacture of buttons prior to the widespread use of plastics

Velasquismo: Political movement associated with José María Velasco Ibarra

Brief Bibliography of English–Language Books

Blanksten, George I. *Ecuador: Constitutions and Caudillos.* Berkeley: University of California Press, 1951.

Cueva, Agustín. *The Process of Political Domination in Ecuador.* New Brunswick: Transaction Books, 1982.

Cushner, Nicholas P. *Farm and Factory: The Jesuits and the Development of Agrarian Capitalism in Colonial Quito, 1600–1767.* Albany: State University of New York Press, 1982.

Fitch, John Samuel. *The Military Coup D'Etat as a Political Process: Ecuador, 1948–1966.* Baltimore: The Johns Hopkins University Press, 1977.

Gibson, Charles R. *Foreign Trade in the Economic Development of Small Nations.* New York: Praeger Publishers, 1971.

Handelman, Howard, and Thomas G. Sanders. *Military Government and the Movement Toward Democracy in South America.* Bloomington: Indiana University Press, 1981.

Hemming, John. *The Conquest of the Incas.* New York: Harcourt Brace Jovanovich, 1970.

Hickman, John. *The Enchanted Islands: The Galapagos Discovered.* Dover, New Hampshire: Tananger Books, 1985.

Hurtado, Osvaldo. *Political Power in Ecuador.* Boulder, Colo.: Westview Press, 1985.

Luzuriaga, Carlos, and Clarence Zuvekas, Jr. *Income Distribution and Poverty in Rural Ecuador, 1950–1979.* Tempe: University of Arizona, Center for Latin American Studies, 1980.

Martz, John D. *Ecuador: Conflicting Political Culture and the Quest for Progress.* Boston: Allyn and Bacon, 1972.

Miller, Tom. *The Panama Hat Trail: A Journey from South America.* New York: William Morrow and Company, 1986.

Phelan, John Leddy. *The Kingdom of Quito in the Seventeenth Century.* Madison: University of Wisconsin Press, 1967.

Philip, George. *Oil and Politics in Latin America: Nationalist Movements and State Companies.* Cambridge, England: Cambridge University Press, 1982.

Pike, Frederick B. *The United States and the Andean Republics: Peru, Bolivia, and Ecuador.* Cambridge, Mass.: Harvard University Press, 1977.

Plaza, Galo. *Problems of Democracy in Latin America.* Chapel Hill: University of North Carolina Press, 1957.

Redclift, M. R. *Agrarian Reform and Peasant Organization on the Ecuadorian Coast.* London: The Athlone Press, 1978.

Rodríguez, Linda Alexander. *The Search for Public Policy: Regional Politics and Government Finances in Ecuador, 1830–1940.* Berkeley: University of California Press, 1985.

Thomsen, Moritz. *Living Poor.* Seattle: University of Washington Press, 1969.

Thomsen, Moritz. *The Farm on the River of Emeralds.* Boston: Houghton Mifflin, 1978.

Watkins, Ralph J. *Expanding Ecuador's Exports.* New York: Praeger Publishers, 1967.

Weil, Thomas E., et al. *Area Handbook for Ecuador.* Washington, D.C.: Government Printing Office, 1973.

World Bank. *The Current Economic Position and Prospects for Ecuador.* Washington, D.C.: The International Bank for Reconstruction and Development, 1973.

World Bank. *Ecuador: Development Problems and Prospects.* Washington, D.C.: The International Bank for Reconstruction and Development, 1979.

World Bank. *Ecuador: An Agenda for Recovery and Sustained Growth.* Washington, D.C.: The International Bank for Reconstruction and Development, 1984.

Index